PRAKṚTI

The Integral Vision

General Editor

KAPILA VATSYAYAN

VOLUME 5

Man in Nature

Edited by
Baidyanath Saraswati

Indira Gandhi National Centre for the Arts
New Delhi

D. K. Printworld (P) Ltd.
New Delhi

Cataloging in Publication Data — DK

Prakṛti : the integral vision / general editor,
Kapila Vatsyayan.
Includes bibliographical references.
Includes index.

1. Nature. 2. Cosmology. I. Vatsyayan, Kapila, 1928-

ISBN 81-246-0036-8 (set)
ISBN 81-246-0041-4 (vol. 5)

First Published in India in 1995

Publishers
Indira Gandhi National Centre for the Arts
Central Vista Mess, Janpath, New Delhi - 110001

D.K. Printworld (P) Ltd.
Regd. office : H-12, Bali Nagar, New Delhi-110015

Printed at : D. K. Fine Art Press (P) Ltd., New Delhi

Foreword

In 1986 when the first of the Multidisciplinary and Cross-cultural Seminars was held under the aegis of the Indira Gandhi National Centre for the Arts, there was a trepidation. In my Introduction to the Volume on ***Concepts of Space : Ancient & Modern*** I have shared with the readers the sense of challenge as also of gratification. Then, it was not easy, nor has it been easy in the subsequent years to bring together people from different parts of the world of diverse disciplines and levels of society to speak through a multiplicity of languages to reflect and converse, and have a meaningful dialogue on the fundamental concerns of humanity in the past or present, in science or religion, philosophy and the arts, in civilizations as far apart as Egyptian, Chinese, Greek and Indian, permeating expressions through the written or the oral word, generating a language of myth and symbol which communicates across cultures.

The gathering, the dialogue and the discussion on a single concept of **Space** (*Akasa*) made it evident that the more fundamental and universal the concept, the greater the probability and possibility of diverse interpretations at multiple levels. The single concept of **Space** had taken us through the journey of the concepts of cavity, cave, aperture, fountainhead, body, air, sky, vacuity, cipher, point and much else. The scientist and the technologist explored the concept through their method of empirical investigation, the philosopher and the metaphysician, artists and the sociologist through perennial questioning and speculation. The two approaches and methods we learnt were complementary and not in conflict. The arts, architecture, sculpture, painting, music and dance enclose, embody and evoke space. Poetry creates vast edifices of space as spatial situations, and evoke the experience of outer and inner space.

The concern with **Space** (***Akasa***) could not be dissociated from the concern — the concept of **Time** (***Kala***). Two years later, a similar gathering with many familiar faces (who communicated with one another with greater ease) gathered to deliberate upon the many dimensions of **Time** (***Kala***). Once again, the discussions at that Seminar revolved round the micro and the macro levels of the single concept, from molecular time to the cosmic time, from the time of biologists to the time of astronomer, from the time of the seer and meditator to the time of the architect, sculptor, musician, dancer and the poet. Besides the familiar faces, there were others who had joined the family of the IGNCA. The enlarged family gave this Seminar a depth and richness, unique and unparalleled. The experiences His Holiness The Dalai Lama articulated in words lucid and resonant, were juxtaposed with the precision and meditation of a scientist – the late Professor D.S. Kothari. The depth of the experience of **Time** in religious traditions, Islamic, Christian, Hindu, Buddhist, Jain and Hebrew, and the embodiment of inner and outer **Time** in poetic language was shared through rapt silence through the voice of the Poet Kathleen Raine.

Logically and naturally, from these two fundamental and universal concepts the next step in our quest for exploration of a single universal theme through diverse paths recalling the Rgvedic Verse, **Truth is one; man knows it by different names**, was to explore the concept of the primal elements (five or four) in different civilizations which have governed and determined the evolution of civilization and culture. Perhaps, the first conscious awareness of Man was the fact that his life depended on water, Earth, air, fire and, above all, space. Understandably, in all civilizations, at the most sophisticated level as also at the simplest level, the recognition that the primal elements were primary and indispensable for Man, is universal. Myths of the origin of the universe, creation, cosmology and cosmogony, have been developed on the concept of the elements which are four or five. There is a vast body of primary sources and equally extensive and complex a history of critical discourse on the nature of primal elements and their indispensability, not only for Man but for all life on Earth.

The subject was too vast and too monumental to be taken up in a single Seminar. Organizationally, therefore, this time it was decided to hold five successive but interlocked Seminars, one leading to the others, so that they could all culminate in a final international cross-cultural multidisciplinary Seminar. Since cultures, disciplines, and levels of society are not completely autonomous and insulated, there was a planned and understandable overlapping between one Seminar or Workshop and another.

The five Seminars were divided more for facility than the autonomous nature of each area or field. The discussions, therefore, at one Seminar were taken up and did interpenetrate into the next.

Logically, the first of these Seminars focused attention on the articulations of cohesive communities in the world who have lived in harmony with nature and who have communicated with the five elements in a continuous unceasing dialogue. To them the nature of the five elements — water, earth, air, fire and space — is not a matter of intellection or breaking down into separation and divisions of totality or a whole; instead, it is a question of life here and now. This is manifested in ritual practices which sacrilize nature so that man can live as an integral part of the universe, the rhythmic movement of the changing seasons, and the symmetrical punctuation and cycle of seed sprouting, growing, flowering, fruiting, decaying and renewing. In modern discourse this is understood as the need for man to live in harmony with the environment for an evolution of socio-cultural systems and methodologies for ensuring the maintenance of ecological balances. The lives and lifestyles of these cohesive groups have begun to acquire renewed validity on account of what man has done to pollute, contaminate, desacrilize and desecrate the very fundamentals that sustain him and make it possible for him to live on earth. The first Volume is based on the papers submitted at this Seminar.

The second Seminar moved the emphasis to the textual traditions. There is a vast body of literature in Greek, Chinese and Indian sources where philosophic discourses have been held on the nature of the universe, the nature of matter, the elements and the possibility of transmutation of the gross to the subtle. In India all branches of the philosophic streams have discussed the nature of the *Bhutas* and the *Mahabhutas*. The discussion ranges from the earliest articulation on the subject in the *Rgveda* to the philosophic schools of Vaisesikas, Vedantins, Saiva and the *Agamas*. The old system of *Ayurveda* in India, as much of medicine in Greece in a very different way, is based on the concept of the *Mahabhutas* in the constitution of the body itself. The very conception of the five elements constitutes the body. Texts for Indian astronomy, chemistry, metallurgy are replete with discussions on the elements. This discussion cannot be dissociated from a speculation, and discourse of, the nature of the universe, cosmology, cosmogony. The second Seminar delved deep into each of these aspects specially in the Indian tradition – Vedic, Brahmanical, Upanisadic and Tantric. In addition, there was a consideration of the concept of the *Mahabhutas* in Buddhism and Jainism. This Seminar unfolded the very complex and subtle aspects of the discourse on the nature of the matter, the fivefold organic matter and the five external objects. It also brought forth the many convergences as also divergences of viewpoint between and amongst these different streams of Indian thought as exemplified in the textual tradition. The Seminar was hosted by the Department of Sanskrit, University of Poona, Pune. The second Volume of this series is based on the papers and the discussions held at this Seminar.

Logically, the third Seminar had to and did explore the discussions as also the manifestations of the five elements in the Indian arts, along with their Agamic background. As is wellrecognized, while the *Upanisads* provide the basis for speculative thinking, the *Brahmanas* give the methodology of ritual practice (*Yajna* and *Prayoga*). Parallel is the development in early and later medieval India where the texts on *Vastu* and *Silpa* provide the frame-work of the abstract principles of creating concrete structures through different media and in different forms. The *Agama* is the twin which provide the methodology of enlivening, giving life and breath to the concrete structures and forms of art. If monumental architecture, sculpture, painting, music or dance, poetry or theatre, is created on the comprehension of space and time, they are even more built on the system of correspondences first for embodying and then evoking the five elements. The fascinating and unceasing cycle of the movement from the inner experience to the creation of form, which would incorporate the five elements and the employment of a methodology of ritual, is outlined in the Agamic texts only to achieve the end experience of the transformation of the gross to the subtle. This was the subject of this Seminar. From different vantage points of the architect, sculptor, painter, musician and dancer, the field was re-opened to examine the structure of the Indian arts at its primal level.

Naturally, theories of aesthetics which have emerged from such a viewpoint had to be discussed and many questions asked. The third Volume incorporates the span of the papers presented and the discussions held at this Seminar.

If the arts deal with the process of transmutation and mutation of the subtle to the gross, and the evocation of the subtle from the gross, in other words, the process of the abstract and the concrete suggesting, stimulating and evoking the abstract, then the astrophysicist deals with the nature of primal matter itself. No discourse on the elements could have been completed by excluding the discussion on modern physics of elementary particles and the most recent developments in microbiology. The fourth Seminar took up the question of the nature and function of matter itself and discussed the theories of the creation of the universe and emergent cosmologies in the modern physics. This was juxtaposed with the consideration on the nature of matter and consciousness. It was obvious that the new developments in science were, perhaps, not all that far remote from the earlier insights in the context of consciousness. The debate between the nineteenth Century mechanistic science and the modern physics was re-opened. This was juxtaposed with speculations and the philosophic discourses in the Indian philosophic schools. If the second Seminar dealt with the textual traditions and the philosophic schools of *Samkhya*, *Mimamsa* and the *Vaisesikas*, this Seminar looked at these traditions as structuralistic traditions from a scientific point of view. The dialogue created between the method of science and the method of speculation was invigorating. The fourth Volume comprises papers and discussions at this Seminar.

The fifth and the last Seminar was a coming together of cultures as also disciplines. Coordinators of the earlier Seminars presented brief Reports on each of the Seminars which provided the background and the landscape. The international community, comprising scientists, biologists, philosophers, anthropologists, ecologists and artists shared not only the myth and cosmology of their particular societies but also there was a most meaningful dialogue between those who lived in the awareness of the primordial myths of the elements and those who had employed the tools of science to explore the nature of the phenomenon of matter.

The putting together of the deliberations of the five major Seminars, as a single or a multiple-volume, is a daunting task. Through the combined efforts of the Coordinators of each of these Seminars and, particularly, the Chief Coordinator – Professor B.N. Saraswati and his associates – it has been possible to prepare the five Volumes based on the deliberations of these Seminars as also a companion exhibition which was called "**PRAKṚTI: The Integral Vision**".

It is my hope that these Volumes will provide material for further discussion and dialogue. The perennial nature of the theme and its urgent and contemporary validity will, I hope, make these Volumes significant. As I have said earlier in my Introduction, Man stands today at a moment where he is threatened by the pollution, inner and outer, of his own making. The primal elements and the urgent need for purification through austerity and discipline are not the matters of intellectual discourse alone. Their maintenance and sustenance, and the purity of these that are primary and primal, are the objectives of our life, lest death overtakes us.

9th June, 1994 **Kapila Vatsyayan**

Contents

Foreword vii
— Kapila Vatsyayan

Introduction 1
— Baidyanath Saraswati

1. MAN, NATURE AND THE UNIVERSE 9
— Jayant V. Narlikar

2. COSMOGONY AND THE ELEMENTS : THE INTUITION OF COSMOS IN SCIENCE AND MYTH 17
— John McKim Malville

3. TRANSMUTATION FROM ONE FORM TO ANOTHER : THE INTERACTION OF COLOUR AND THE ELEMENTS – SOME SCIENTIFIC AND AESTHETIC CONSIDERATION 37
— A. Ranganathan

4. HOLISTIC SCIENCE AND CONSCIOUSNESS 53
— S. C. Malik

5. NATURE AND LIFE : OLD IDEAS, NEW QUESTIONING 79
— Ananda Wood

6. NATURE AS FEMININE : ANCIENT VISION OF GEOPIETY AND GODDESS ECOLOGY 103
— Madhu Khanna

7. ON SOME ASPECTS OF BHUTAS DURING BIRTH-DEATH PASSAGES 117
— Gian Giuseppe Filippi

8. AKASA, FROM SPACE TO SPACELESSNESS : MEDIEVAL INDIAN MYSTICS' CONCEPT OF AKASA 123
— S. G. Tulpule

9. AMRTAMANTHANA : THE VEDIC SOURCES OF HINDU CREATION MYTH 131
— Natalia R. Lidova

10. ELEMENTS OF NATURE AND THE ORDER OF CULTURE 141
— Baidyanath Saraswati

11. THE ZUNI VIEW OF NATURE 157
— Triloki Nath Pandey

12 FIRE AND SUN, THE POSITIVE ENERGY OF THE COSMOS IN MESO-AMERICAN COSMOVISION 169
— Yólotl González Torres

13. PRE-CHRISTIAN EASTERN SLAVIC REFLECTIONS ON NATURE 179
— Molly Kaushal

14. THE COSMIC NATURE OF BUSHMAN LAW 187
— A. J. G. M. Sanders

15. NATURE AND HUMAN DEVELOPMENT AMONG THE BAKA PYGMIES : CONCEPTS AND PERCEPTIONS 195
— John Mope Simo
— Paul Nkwi Nchoji

16. PANCATATTVA IN ARTISTIC MANIFESTATIONS : A CASE STUDY OF TRIBAL GUJARAT 203
— Haku Shah

17. NATURE, MAN AND ART : AN IRANO-ISLAMIC PERSPECTIVE 207
— Amir H. Zekrgoo

18. FIVE ELEMENTS OF ECOLOGY 219
— Satish Kumar

19. COMMON ROOTS OR TRANSFER OF CULTURE 225
— M. Vannucci

20. MODERNIZATION AS A FORM OF CULTURAL ADAPTATION TO THE ENVIRONMENT 245
— Napoleon Wolanski

List of Contributors 259

Index 263

Introduction

What does a fish know of water in which it swims all its life? What does a man know of nature of which he is an integral part? The ancient answer is: he knows and he knows not.

Men through the ages, through popular wisdom, philosophies, religions, and sciences have tried to understand their place in nature, their linkage with the universe. The twenty papers here collected, which are based on the IGNCA seminar on '**Prakrti**', held at New Delhi, on 5-12 January 1993, offer some thoughts on this profound concern. Being the fifth and the final of the series of seminars concerning the *mahabhutas* or the five-elements, this volume culminates in a cross-cultural and multi-disciplinary expedient thinking about 'Man in Nature'. It can be read independently of the four preceding volumes which deal with the 'Oral Tradition', the 'Vedic, Buddhist and Jain Traditions', the 'Agamic tradition and the Arts', and 'The Nature of Matter'. IGNCA's main concern in this project (see Foreword) is : (i) to explore the fundamental and universal concepts capable of rejuvenating man's perception of his primary foundation, and (ii) to create a harmonic understanding and communication through a developed multi-disciplinary vision.

The sole aim in these introductory pages is to present a conceptual overview of technical matters raised at the seminar.

The Views of Modern Science

Modern era, from the beginning of the seventeenth century, has been dominated by a scientific-technical worldview where man is regarded as the central player. With the publication of Isaac Newton's masterpiece, *Philosophiae Naturalis Principia Mathematica*, in 1687, the old idea of the universe faded. The Newtonian view of matter as inert substance struck roots in Western thought and culture. Industrial Revolution was its logical and direct consequence. Experimental technological development created a new confidence in man, and Europe eventually became the light and leaven of a new world. The shadow side of this turning was the disintegration of a coherent cosmology and the danger of a catastrophe. With the new machine age the forces of nature were harnessed, the face of the Earth was drastically altered, and the 'new man' began to look at himself as the master of nature, the maker of history and the measure of all. By tragic irony science itself came to be controlled by technology. Much faster than expected, the pursuit of science and technology became the most significant of all human affairs, effecting and affecting politics, economics, religion and social life. The machine-mindedness, accompanied by the erosion of a unified vision, resulted in complete demoralization and depersonalization. In this overthrow some men of science see the 'inadequacies of the human mind' (see Narlikar) and the mistake of materialism.

Today scientists describe man's place in the universe in terms of the perfect cosmological principle and the anthropic principle (see Narlikar, also Malik). In essence these principles present a picture of steadily expanding universe in which man the observer has attained a certain level of intelligence in the course of the evolution of life. One important contribution of the cosmological principle is that it has dethroned man from the 'centre' of the universe. According to current ideas, all galaxies in the universe have the same status and man in his galaxy is just one of them. Some scientists, such as Stephen Hawking, propose two versions of the anthropic principle, the weak and the strong. The weak anthropic principle states that it is only in certain regions of the universe that necessary condition for the development of intelligent life, a typical human, exists. According to strong anthropic principle there are other regions of the universe or universes, each with its own initial configuration and its own set of laws, where the conditions would not be right for the development of intelligent beings. However, as Narlikar maintains with characteristic clarity, "It is not sharp enough for believers in the principle who would like to demonstrate that physical parameters are finely tuned to human existence, nor it is convincing enough to persuade sceptics who might attack its speculative nature, because we still know too little about the formation of planets, about the origin and adapatability of life, about the evolution of intelligence, and so on."

The search for extraterrestrial intelligent life can advance only if there is a clarity about what exactly life is. There is no difficulty in recognizing the various forms of life on Earth. But until today the ontological difference between the living and the nonliving has remained unsettled. Since Darwin it is conjectured that origin of life on Earth was simply another step in general evolutionary sequence. Malville, with a spirited wit and sophistication, examines the origin of chemical elements which have biological significance. Giving extraordinary importance to supernova explosions in the formation of Elements that build planets or life, he reconstructs the origin: "The iron which reddens the soil of Earth and Mars and which courses through the veins and arteries of reptiles, fish and mammals originated in an ancient supernova. Slowly but steadily most galaxies acquired the ingredients necessary for life. Our galaxy planets were formed with the stars; other planets also contain mud, fire and perhaps even alien versions of blood." To corroborate his findings in astrophysics, Malville presents the cosmogonies of the America's intertwined blood, bones and earth which find reference throughout the ruins of Mesoamerica.

The notion of Elements as building blocks of life is widely accepted in science. The transmutation of one form of Element to another is a subject which has illuminated the imagination of a large number of scholars in various fields. Ranganathan provides several examples of illustrious scientists, artists and philosophers who have contributed to the fascinating field of interaction of colour with the Elements. C. V. Raman, for instance, was able to relate the perception of colour in some areas of physics and astronomy to a holistic perception which included the application of the quantum theory of light to physiology and human consciousness in its sweep: "Raman's holistic perception of colour has an epic grandeur which is similar to Niels Bohr's holistic theory of complementarity and Roger Penrose's new theory of physics with the phenomenon of consciousness in the new areas of psychology and neurophysiology".

Appropriately, Malik traces the development of this holistic theory from the discipline of science, but goes beyond it to show that holistic perception is a phenomenon of universal consciousness: "The universal principle of organization immanent in all things manifests itself in a cosmic pattern, in which it is particularized in successive wholes, constituting various scales as self-enfoldment. In this way the world comes to consciousness of itself and explicitly realizes its essential nature, in its reflective awareness and interpretive conceptualization by intelligent human beings."

What overtakes scientific thinking today is the problem of life. Although it seems clear that there exists other planets with chemical elements having biological significance, the possibility of intelligent life existing elsewhere in the universe is still remote. However, the notions of 'cosmic self-organization', 'Earth as one living organism', 'universal consciousness', and 'holistic theory of complementarity' have gained considerable prominence in contemporary thought.

The Vision of Ancient Sages

Advances in the new physics have affirmed that on matters concerning the universe there is no fundamental difference between the experimental scientists and the mystical sages. Of the post-mechanistic paradigms, for instance, the concept of 'expanding universe' agrees with the Upanisadic notion of 'expanding *Brahman*', and the cosmologists claim that the universe has been borrowed from the 'vacuum' echoes in the philosophy of '*sunya* (zero) *Brahman*'. The other theories built around the scientists' conception of the world such as 'liberation of matter', 'cosmic strings', 'galactic seeds', and the 'living universe' can be traced back to the Vedic sages.

Adopting this view of the nature of scientific truth, Narlikar has pointed out that "information regarding the origin of the living systems and the universe may find echoes in ancient wisdom". Malville has produced striking evidence of how "overriding insight is the same from astrophysics and the origin myths of cosmogonies".

Taking the thought a little further one may find that in explaining nature and the universe the traditional vision offers a richer and more encompassing worldview. The *Sankhya* and *Vedanta* philosphies of *purusa-prakrti,* for instance, provide a very clear formulation of the natural phenomena of the universe. Wood attempts to interpret nature (*prakrti*) and consciousness (*purusa*) in a new way as a philosophical division of experience into objective and subjective parts: "The objective principle of nature is represented by conceptions of divine immanence in the changing manifestations of creation; and the subjective principle of consciousness is represented by conceptions of a transcendent spirit, both as a transcending God in the macrocosm of the external universe, and as an inner or spiritual essence of soul in the microcosm of individual experience".

Given the spiritual context, one might argue that such intellectual division of experience is neither right nor wrong. Mind is inseparable from the matter-dominated body, and nature does not exist independently of the universe. Moreover, an experience identified with the ultimate reality is nothing but that reality where the object and the subject remain undifferentiated. At the level of intellectual awareness of experience (which is **not** the experience) there is, of course, a distance between the subject and the object. It is this integral vision and experience of *prakrti* which Khanna tries to present in her paper. To express man's critical awareness of cosmological kinship there could be no better imagery than of the Earth Mother as supporter, as womb, as sacred totality, and so on.

The physical biology of the universe has been described in the *Upanisads* in terms of life (*jiva*) and the self (*atman*). As Wood puts it, "Traditionally life is considered as the vital breath that animates the activities of nature. In modern terms, life as 'vital breath' or 'breathing spirit' or 'aspiration' or 'inspiration' are metaphors for the expression of consciousness in living behavaiour. This expressive activity of life is described by *prana* which is derived from the word *ana*, meaning 'breath', and the prefix *pra* meaning 'prior to' or 'continuing on' or 'going forth'. The essential principle of life is consciousness, which is the supporting basis and the unchanging cause of the living activities of the body."

To better understand the integral biology, the subtle distinction between *jiva* and *prana* has to be made explicit. Filippi does it quite clearly through a meaningful interpretation of the *pancabhuta*, the five-elements that constitute the body, and the *pancakosa*, the five-envelops worn by the self. The combination of these two assumes a fundamental significance that are not apparent when considered separately. The basic assumptions are as follows: Life (*jiva*) is complete in its own components. The body (*sthula sarira*) , made up of the organic compound of the five-elements, enables the early stage of life (*prana*) to develop human and other forms of life, and the real being (*atman*) uses the body as an instrument to modify its own condition or destiny. After death the constitutive elements of the body (corpse) return to the gross level of nature. The five-envelops of cosmic construction are schematically presented: The first, or the highest, in the hierarchy of *kosas* is *anandamayakosa*, the beatific envelop, followed by *vijnanmayakosa*, the intellectual envelop, *manomayakosa*, the mental envelop, *pranamayakosa*, the vital envelop, and finally, *annamayakosa*, the vegetative envelop. This order is reversed at the death and dissolution of a living being . What remains at disintegration is the *anandamayakosa* of the cosmic person (*purusa*). This residuum is space (*akasa*) from which, as the Upanisadic sages have said, all beings emerge and in which all are finally absorbed.

Tulpule brings in medieval Indian mystics concept of 'spacelessness' for consideration to describe the ultimate reality. "Spacelessness", he says, "is a void, but not of the nature of an abyss or a bottomless pit, but of the nature of the vast and expansive space itself. The concept of the ultimate as a state of void, unbound and eternal is submerged in the mortal's desire for immortality."

Lidova's paper on the Vedic cosomogonic myth of *amrtamanthan* is significantly linked with this primeval idea of immortality.

One of the central intuitions of the traditional vision consists in seeing the cosmos in its fullness: man as a part of nature, and nature as a substratum of the universe. Within this worldview, the universe (*Brahman*) has no other structure than its own *kosas* (matter, mind, intellect, vital breath, and consciousness) which envelop the entire natural world. Clearly, then, the perfect cosmological principle and the anthropic principle in modern science are the negative theories.

The Voice of Popular Wisdom

The views of modern science are the views of man the 'observer', the views of ancient sages are the views of man the 'visionary', and the views of popular wisdom are the collective views of man the 'natural being'. But man as species is one single configuration of the cosmic Elements, which is rooted in the unknown and yet knowable in terms of its physical, metaphysical, biological, psychological, material, and spiritual dimensions.

The popular wisdom, to be evolved through the oral and the textual modes of transmission of Cosmic Intelligence, affirms that there is a transcendent order of nature which is inviolable and interlinked with the natural order of culture. Saraswati suggests a speculative model: "Nature is a set of self-originating, self-organizing and self-sustaining forms. Life renders matter the binding abilities, interlocking powers, overlapping characters and a transcendent state. The transcendent order is that (*prakrti*) which natures nature. The Elements of nature are set into a technical order that causes biosocial types. Like natural forms, the forms of culture are also subject to the fivefold order of origination, binding, interlocking, etc. The ecological man of matter is culturally processed and transformed into a moral person through a transcendental superpsychic process of intellectual cultivation and ritual purification".

There are in this volume a series of simple but profound illustrations from the 'ecological republic' where man looks upon nature as a self-existing reality of which he is an inseparable part at all levels. Pandey, who lived for five years among the Zuni, the Hopi and the Navajo of the American Southwest, reflects on the perspective of one such man. He points out the most simple basics of their worldview: "The Zuni fuse man and nature into one more or less harmonious medium. It also shows that stability in human life is derived from the continuity of natural rhythms. Rhythm is implicit in nature, made explicit by the regular performance of rituals and the annual production of crops. It is symbolized by the Zuni calander, determined and maintained by the Sun priest and his associates."

Torress examines the ancient Mesoamerican cosmic vision which considers Fire and Sun as the positive energy of the cosmos. She describes with lucidity how "the personal energy of all the human beings had to be in a constant feeding back to this cosmic energy, which the Mesoamericans translated into a need of the human heart and blood to keep the world going."

Reporting on the Eastern Slavs, particularly the pre-Christian Russians, Kaushal mentions: "Fire, Water and Earth are the fundamental axes of their pantheon. The relationship between the three can never be hierarchical, as life can be generated only when the three come together. The male Fire, or the male dry Seed/Sun/Fire, soaked in the female Waters enters the womb of the Mother Earth and keeps the eternal rhythm of life going."

Sanders' study of Bushman of Southern Africa shows: "In the worldview of these hunter-gatherers, man constitutes the beginning and end, or rather the cycle of life. Man is the immediate carrier of life but over and above man stand the planets, and then there are rain clouds, water wells, trees, plants and animals, all of which are considered to be predeceased and transformed Bushman."

In their description of the Baka Pygmy in the equatorial Africa, Simo and Nchoji have drawn attention to the fact that "there is no dividing line in Baka life between the physical and the spiritual. They adore Kamba, their supreme god, who is the creator of all things and who exists as an explanation for the Baka's presence in the forest and for the order of the world arround them".

The voice of popular wisdom is 'heard' and 'seen' in the artistic manifestations. Shah, himself an artist of repute, presents a case study of tribal Gujarat in western India, making several significant statements: "The theme of the tribal creative expression mostly deals with 'life', known and unknown forces. Form evolves automatically through intuition. Almost all their creative manifestations evolve out of their own environment. Their respect for *prakrti* is like a part of their own selves. Thus art form becomes a living identity, a part of their tribal self, family, village, and that way, the universe-cosmos."

Zekrgoo emphasizes the opposition between the Islamic and the modern views of art: "Central to the Islamic and traditional view is a belief in the oneness of nature and man. Nature and man are of the same origin, and like man, nature is alive and intelligent. One of the many names of Allah is 'Musawwer' or the 'Artist'. Man is considered the greatest work of art created by Allah. Art, in the Islamic tradition, extends beyond nature into the wisdom contained in its depths, depths which can only be reached by the pure in mind and spirit."

What characterizes the popular wisdom is the originality, that is, the faithfulness of the first order. Nature is divinized, even humanized (as in the case of Bushman). The distinction between man and nature is superficial at the behavioural level. At the ideational level a symbolic structure of the universe emerges in terms of male/female polarities (as in the case of Mesoamerica). The transcendent order (implicit in the rhythm of nature) is expressed in the ultimate externalization of life (seen as cosmic energy of the Sun and Fire) and internalization of nature in culture (art and ritual).

The Value of Nature

While the 'modern' man may find the traditional vision quaint or amusing on the one hand and smelling superstitious on the other, it is taken seriously by those who have cared to realize the catastrophic implications of technology and the mistake of materialism. The quest for a coherent meaning in natural philosophy, a new paradigm of the universe, and a re-appraisal of traditional thoughts (in which 'spirit' is central to the nature of physical reality and matter relegated to mind) has become a greater imperative.

Kumar, explores the new paradigms of the universe to spot that these are not new as they may appear: "The traditional Indian concept of *vasudhaivakutumbakam* (the whole Earth is one family) came first and then the Gaia hypothesis of the Earth as one interconnected entity. The ideas of Permaculture echo in the American Indian belief that whatever one does is going to affect the seventh generation. The concept of Bioregionalism as decentralized, logically-based economy is what Mahatma Gandhi called *swadesi*. Creation spirituality (in the sense of the sacred as an essential part of an ecological worldview) has been present in ancient beliefs and practices of the people of India holding all rivers and mountains sacred."

To develop her idea of the sacred as common roots in traditional cultures, Vannucci turns to the relevant concepts of the Vedic ecology: "*Rta* as the law and order of nature that varies in the space-time continuum; *Hiranyagarbha* as the golden embryo that makes the auspicious beginning of all; the Vedic hymns dedicated to the frogs revealing a mature concept of the five basic environmental Elements, their mutual interrelationships and their interaction with other Elements, and so on." She brings comparative views of several other traditions to broaden the spectrum of Indian examples.

Man's second environment is his culture. Wolanski thinks in new ways to explain the interface between nature and culture: "Culture, which sustains the 'animal' nature of the humans, is subjected to evolution. Paradoxically it inhibits the biological evolution of the human beings. Many scientists argue that biological evolution of the humans is finished. Adjustment of society to environment is problematic. Over five billion brains of the contemporary humans conceive ideas and transform the world, whereas their bodies require food, clothes, apartments, and still need new products of civilization for a comfortable life. Modernization is a new kind of adaptation. But its values change from positive to negative, and the real values of the same changes can be different, depending on the situation, e.g. environmental conditions and habits."

The ultimate issue in the value of nature is this: Is nature 'useful' to man the observer? Scientific theories of Gaia, Permaculture, Biosphere, etc. seem to have originated in fear, caused by such events as ecological disaster, holocaust, depression, and so on. Traditional theories of *rta*, *purusa-prakrti*, *pancabhuta*, and *pancakosa* have originated in faith, firmed by the claiming and celebration of man's kinship with nature the vessel of divine power, the ordering principle of culture. For modern man, of course, nature is important in survival and hence the human adaptability to nature has been given a positive value and a practical necessity.

This picture of *Prakrti* leaves unresolved one sobering difference that concerns human attitude. Modernity is based on the *logos* of experimental empirical science; tradition, on the contrary, takes a position of faith not for a strategy but as fruit of divine descent. Yet so long as both are abstractions of the ever-inexhaustible mystery, the difference in the appearance and the reality would hardly matter in the pursuit of the ultimate.

Baidyanath Saraswati

1

Man, Nature and the Universe

Jayant V. Narlikar

Whenever we probe into the writings or sayings of the wise and the thinkers of the past and compare them with their present scientific counterparts, we encounter a commonality in the following respect. The discussions centre on a triangle whose vertices are:

1. Man.
2. Nature.
3. Universe.

There are interrelations of any of the three vertices with the other two. Moreover, an attempt is made to make all three fit into a self-consistent picture.

Experience has warned us time and again that a self-consistent picture may not necessarily mean the correct or factual picture. Rather, it may well happen that a basically sound description appears full of contradictions because all facts are not yet at hand. Didn't Arjuna complain to Krsna in the *Gita* about his apparently contradictory words?

vyamisrene'va vakyena,
buddhim mohayasi'va me
tad ekam vada niscitya
yena sreyo'ham apnuyam
[Chapter III, Verse 2]

With an apparently confused utterance thou seemest to bewilder my intelligence. Tell (me) then decisively the one thing by which I can attain the highest good.

In modern times man occasionally perceives in nature an apparently contradictory behaviour. The advent of quantum theory brought in a culture shock to theoreticians accustomed to the Newtonian expectations of definitiveness in the behaviour of nature. Special relativity gave a jolt to the ingrained perception of time as an absolute, uniformly flowing entity. But the overall self-consistency of the scheme began to make itself manifest gradually. Today we understand the micro-behaviour of nature better than at the beginning of this century, but several foundational issues remain.

How are laws of nature related to the large scale structure of the universe? Does the universe determine the laws or is it *vice-versa*? Are both unique? Or could there be many possible universes in which nature follows the same laws? Or does the universe as a unique system permit many alternative laws?

The relationship of man and the universe has many facets too. Granted that the human being is an observer making and noting measurements of the universe: how does its consciousness relate to this observing process? or the irreversible flow of time that we all experience, does it relate to the large scale dynamics of the universe? Does our own *bhautik* composition tell us about the large scale structure of the universe?

There are several issues that come up in the man-nature-universe triangle. I will briefly highlight a few points in this presentation. My viewpoint is necessarily that of a physicist and astronomer: I lay no claim to scholarship of our ancient heritage. But the scholars may perceive some parallels between what I describe and what has been discussed in ancient times.

The Perfect Cosmological Principle

Let us take the problem of observing and interpreting the universe. As a man at the present epoch observes the distant parts of the universe he sees them not as they are today but as they were a long time in the past. This is because all his observed information has travelled with the speed of light. (at least that is the assumption all scientists start with!). So a galaxy a billion light years ago is seen by him today as it was a billion years ago. How, therefore, does he interpret his observations of such a galaxy?

To make any interpretation he needs a yardstick, viz., the laws of science available to him today. Using these he can estimate how bright the galaxy was, how massive it was and so on. But to what extent is he sure that his yardstick of present times also applied to the remote galaxy a billion years ago? In other words, is he not implicitly assuming that the yardstick of natural laws has remained unchanged over such a long period? This was the question asked by two British physicists — Hermann Bondi and Thomas Gold, two of the three creators of the so-called steady state cosmology in 1948.

The motivation which led Bondi and Gold to the steady state concept sprang from the speculative nature of physics and cosmology in the early post-big-bang era. Theoretical physicists in the 1940s were not willing to speculate about the very early universe. The reason, as Bondi and Gold perceived, was that the physical conditions and the laws governing them in those early epochs would be markedly different from those being studied 'here and now'. Rather than get caught up in untestable speculations, they proposed an alternative scenario which could readily be tested, a scenario which rested on the premise that the overall physical conditions in the universe and the laws governing them do not change at all.

In a sense the Bondi-Gold notion of an unchanging universe is a logical extension of the cosmological principle used by most cosmologists. The cosmological principle states that the state of the universe and the laws of physics influencing it are identical here and elsewhere **at the same cosmic time**. Astronomical observations, on the other hand, tell us about far-away regions in the universe not at the **present** cosmic time, but at **earlier epochs** when the light arriving now left them. So to guarantee a meaningful comparison of observations with theory, we require the universe and its physical laws to be unchanging **with time** as well as space. This is the essence of the 'perfect cosmological principle' (PCP) which led Bondi and Gold to the steady state theory.

An unchanging universe does not necessarily mean a static universe. In fact, in a static, infinitely old universe, physical systems would reach a thermodynamic equilibrium, when the distinction between sources of radiation and their receivers disappears. Every point radiates and absorbs heat in equal quantities. This certainly is not the case with the present universe where we have such powerful radiators of energy as the Sun and the stars and such cool places as the polar caps on the Earth. The alternatives provided by the PCP are either a steadily contracting universe or a steadily expanding universe, of which the former is again ruled out by similar thermodynamical arguments. So we are left with the alternative that the universe has been expanding steadily. Notice that this deduction was arrived at without any dynamical theory like general relativity.

I will not go into technical details but simply state that the deductive power of the PCP also tells us what the space-time geometry of the steady state model should be like. It was emphasized by Bondi and Gold that the PCP combined with local observations of the universe tells us **everything observable** about the universe. Their main stress was on the testability of the PCP, which made unequivocal claims about the large-scale structure of the universe, and was therefore much more vulnerable to observational constraints than the rival big-bang models, which ascribed the bulk of the present observable state of the universe to speculative, very early epochs.

In the end, the strongest observational challenge to the PCP and the steady state universe came from the discovery of the microwave radiation background. This background must be unchanging, according to the PCP, and it must be continually regenerated as the universe expands. Its origin must therefore be entirely astrophysical in nature. But how can this be? A related problem arose *vis-a-vis* the abundance of light nuclei, especially helium and deuterium. Since there was no hot epoch in the past in the steady state universe (because there is none now), these elements must also be produced continually now. But how? These questions swung the balance of opinion heavily towards the big-bang model in the 1960s.

I will not go into details of how a revival of the steady state concept today is based on the answers to these questions. I present this as an example of man-nature-universe interaction: how the consistency argument requires the universe to conform to what man observes and his interpretation of physical laws.

The Arrow of Time

All living systems 'grow old' in an irreversible way! The biological clock cannot be turned back in real life. Even in our day-to-day perceptions we encounter other phenomena that seems to go only one way. Given two photographs of a china cup, one showing it intact, the other broken to pieces, we can tell which photo was taken **earlier** and which one **later**. A battery driving a wireless transmitter eventually stops working because all its energy has been radiated away. The energy store of the battery steadily diminishes with time.

Why don't we get younger day by day? Why don't broken cups become whole? Why doesn't the transmitter receive energy and charge the battery? These are one-way phenomena which impress upon us the unidirectional nature of the flow of time. The three examples given by me here correspond to three 'arrows' of time: biological, thermodynamic and electrodynamic.

The astronomer can point to a **fourth** arrow of time from his observations of the large scale structure of the universe: the universe is apparently expanding! This discovery was made during the 1920s by E.P. Hubble and M. Humason who found that the spectra of light from galaxies are most invariably 'shifted' towards the red end. This shift is noticed by doing spectroscopy of galaxies, by measuring the wavelengths of certain dark lines in the galactic spectra. These lines seem to appear with wavelengths **longer** than expected. A naive interpretation of this result is that the source of light or the galaxy is moving away from us.

If all galaxies are moving away from one another, it is more appropriate to use the notion of the universe expanding itself! If we took a number of photographs of galaxies at different epochs, we can arrange them chronologically by looking at their separation. At earlier epochs the galaxies will be closer to one another than at later epochs. Thus we have the **cosmological arrow of time**.

The basic question 'why an arrow?' may be eventually answered. A first step is to understand why all four arrows point the way they do. For example, why don't we grow young in an expanding universe? Why do we see a transmitter lose energy as we grow old and not the other way round?

Again, I shall not go into technical details except to say that some progress has been made in understanding the alignment of the electrodynamic and the cosmological arrows of time. Using certain theoretical formulations one can say why in an expanding universe of a certain kind (like the steady state model just described) an electric transmitter must radiate and not receive energy. This is another example of the man-nature-universe interaction.

The Anthropic Principle

The Copernican revolution was the first step in man's dethronement from the 'centre' of the universe. The steady erosion of man's privileged status reached its ultimate stage in the cosmological principle (or the PCP if the steady state model had turned out to be right). In the homogeneous isotropic universe all galaxies have the same status. Man in his Galaxy is just one of them. Since the trend towards democratization of the universe started with Copernicus, we may call this ultimate concept of cosmic equality the 'Copernican principle'.

A reaction to the Copernican principle, however, was initiated by Robert Dicke in 1961, with the so-called **anthropic principle**. In general terms this principle amounts to the statement that the universe is in the way it is because we are here to observe it. By 'we' is implied the typical human observer who has attained a certain level of intelligence in the course of the evolution of life in the universe. Had the universe been different in its structure and evolution, it would not have been possible for such human observers to evolve to their present stage. This is what the anthropic principle is all about. It is a deductive principle which, one hopes, might narrow the ranges of the parameters in the physical theories and the initial conditions, and lead to a unique model of the universe.

Consider the following application of this principle proposed by Brandon Carter to show how the magnitude of the gravitational constant, G, turns out to be strongly related to our existence. To follow Carter's argument, let us consider the stars which derive their luminosity from nuclear fusion of hydrogen into helium. This process goes on steadily for a considerable period, which constitutes the bulk of the life span of a star. Now in such a state there is a definite relation between the luminosity, L, and surface temperature, T, of a star. In a logarithmic plot of L against $1/T$, such stars lie on a narrow band called the 'main sequence', which extends from high values of L and T, at the so-called 'blue end', to low values of L and T, at the 'red end' of the sequence, the names corresponding to the dominant colour in the star's radiation.

Now, the crucial parameter which determines where a star is on the main sequence is its gravitational mass. Stars of large mass are at the blue end and are called 'blue giants', whereas those of low mass, 'red dwarfs', are at the red end. So long as the star derives the bulk of its radiated energy from the fusion of hydrogen to helium, it stays on the main sequence. Our Sun is in this state and is located about midway between the red and blue ends. It is also the case that the hydrogen fusion reaction goes fast in high-mass stars and slow in low-mass stars. Red dwarfs therefore take longer to finish off their hydrogen fuel and consequently remain on the main sequence considerably longer than blue giants.

Now consider the origin of life and its evolution to an intellectually advanced state. Suppose that this event occurs on a planet going round a star, and that the energy for sustaining life comes from the star. This evolutionary process requires a certain amount of time as well as sufficient radiation. Blue giants have the radiation but not the time, whereas red dwarfs have the time but not the radiation. The conclusion? That life originates and evolves only around stars which are somewhere in between these two extremities. The sun, lying in this middle region, satisfies these two conditions.

If we now imagine a universe with a considerably larger gravitational constant than the one we actually have, the gravitational masses of all stars in it would be effectively higher. Thus the stars in that universe would tend to be like the blue giants in our universe. Similarly, in a universe with a weaker gravitational constant the stars would be like our red dwarfs. In neither case would life as we know it be possible. Therefore G must take values in a moderately narrow range around its observed value.

The argument as presented about illustrates how the anthropic principle operates. As given here, it is not sharp enough for believers in the principle who would like to demonstrate that values of physical parameters are finely tuned to human existence. Nor is it convincing enough to persuade skeptics who might attack its speculative nature. After all, we still know too little about the formation of planets, about the origin and adaptability of life, about the evolution of intelligence, and so on to be able to conclude definitively 'what would have happened, if . . .'

As for sharpening the Carter-type argument, some progress has been made in bringing other physical constants into the discussion of the anthropic principle — for example, the fine structure constant and constants related to nuclear binding. Of course, the ultimate success or failure of this line of reasoning must await a deeper understanding of biology.

Biology and Cosmology

The biological considerations peeping out of the anthropic principle may turn out to be the thin end of a wedge. The question 'how probable is the origin of life in the universe?' has cosmological connotations regardless of whether life exists anywhere beyond the Earth because of the possibility of emergence of certain life supporting organic molecules under a favourable environment. What is the chance of such an event occurring by accident? The following argument by Hoyle suggests that the chance may indeed be extremely small.

Enzymes play key roles in the interactions of biological systems with their environment. For example, there are enzymes which are responsible for repairing the damage caused by X-rays and ultraviolet light; there are others responsible for absorption of sugars, for breaking linkages in polysaccharides, and so on. The enzyme, which is made up of a chain of amino-acids, has to be specifically constructed to serve as a catalyst in a particular chemical reaction. In other words, an enzyme is not an arbitrarily chosen chain, like a code word chosen at random from a jumble to convey a significant message.

Even estimated conservatively, each chosen arrangement for a particular enzyme is one among many. For example, as estimated by F.B. Salisbury in 1969, at least fifteen amino-acids must be correctly ordered in a typical enzyme. With twenty alternatives available at each link of the chain, the number of such randomly made chains is 20^{15}, or nearly 10^{20}. The chance of a particular enzyme being made out of such random links is therefore 1 in 10^{20}. Since there are at least 2,000 such enzymes which play key roles in the behaviour of living systems, the chance of arriving at them by a spontaneous accidental process is $10^{-20} \times 10^{-20} \times \ldots$ (2,000 times) = $10^{-40{,}000}$. This absurdly small number according to Hoyle, highlights the improbability of living systems arising purely by accident.

Francis Crick, in his book *Life Itself*, has indulged in a similar game of probability computation. Looking at proteins as vast chains of randomly assembled amino-acids, Crick computes the chance of a 'correct' chain of 200 links emerging this way to be 1 in 20^{200} – that is, about 10^{-260}. Again, the probability of spontaneous emergence of life by chance is far too small, and one wonders if the big-bang universe has had time enough at its disposal to allow such a rare event to take place. The analogies which spring to mind are typified by questions like these: How long will a monkey randomly hitting a typewriter keyboard produce a Shakespearean sonnet by chance? Or how long will be a spontaneous random assembly of component parts, nuts and bolts and so on, take to produce a jumbo jet?

It could be argued that the computation of the probability of an event after it has occurred can be misleading. It is also arguable that events that seem entirely unconnected and whose probability of occurrence in a given sequence therefore appears to be too small to be realistic may in fact be connected in a way which we do not yet know. There might seem to be a very small probability that the regular arrangements of electrons in atoms came about by chance. Yet the quantum theory of atomic structure fully accounts for those arrangements as natural ones. Likewise, could these low probabilities in biology be unrealistic because we lack an underlying theory?

However one chooses to look upon these low probabilities of spontaneous generation of life, one is driven to the conclusion that biology contains as yet unravelled information which cosmologists may one day find highly relevant to their subject and in future we may find information regarding the origin of living systems to have a bearing on what model we choose to describe the universe. Until such information is forthcoming, our view of the universe, of its present composition and its past history, will necessarily remain incomplete.

Conclusion

In a composition volume devoted to *Prakrti* such issues may find echoes in ancient wisdom. I will be interested to discover how issues of this kind had bothered the truth seekers of the past. As J.B.S. Haldane put it: "The universe is not only queerer than we suppose, it is queerer than we can suppose", implying the inadequacy of the human mind to understand the universe in its entirety. Nevertheless the statement has to be looked at as a challenge to human ingenuity in pushing back the frontiers of the unknown. In that sense my triangle is also expanding!

2

Cosmogony and the Elements

The Intuition of Cosmos in Science and Myth

John McKim Malville

Our origins are clear: we come from the stars. This planet and the life which its supports resulted from 10-20 billion years of slow cooking in the interiors of stars or explosive fusion in the violence of supernovae. In that expanse of time between the present and our sidereal past lie chemistry and myth, matter and spirit, described variously in images of protons, chemical bonds, bones, blood, and mud.

The overriding insight is the same from astrophysics and the origin myths of cosmogony: because of our heritage we are thoroughly interwoven into the fabric of life on our planet, and ultimately into that ordered and harmonious system which we call **cosmos**. In same manner as the discovery of common ancestors can establish a feeling of family, the discovery of our common astronomical origins can lead to a recognition of an interconnected and interrelated cosmos.

In the words of Teilhard de Chardin (1959), "It is impossible to cut into this network, to isolate a portion of it without it becoming frayed and unraveled at all of its edges. All around us, as far as the eye can see, the universe holds together, and only one way of considering it is really possible, that is, to take it as a whole, in one piece".

In this paper I begin by sketching our current understanding from astrophysics of the origin of the chemical elements, an extraordinary story which identifies our parents as ancient stars that destroyed themselves as supernovae. As Heraclitus has put it, "The upward path and the downward path is one and the same", and since our origins lie equally in the earth as in the skies, I present a number of earth-diver myths that attest to such an intuition. Finally, turning to ancient architecture I explore those material objects contained in the archaeological record that give some of the earliest expressions of our elemental constituents and of a harmonious, interconnected cosmos.

Nucleogenesis in the Stars

We live in a universe of galaxies, the seamless whole with no center which started expanding some 15 billion years ago. The elemental building blocks of life and the forces which glue them together are found everywhere in today's universe. But most of those chemical elements that form earth, air, fire, and water were absent when the universe was very young. Carbon, silicon, and oxygen can later. Those processes of nuclear energy generation that give light to the stars have slowly turned primordial matter into the 92 stable chemical elements.

Our universe started with the simplest of elements: hydrogen and a little helium. Even the first stars were formed exclusively of hydrogen and helium. But in order for a star to be self-luminous it also must necessarily be a factory for the manufacture of new elements. All the chemical elements heavier than helium and hydrogen, were synthesized in the hot centers of stars at advanced stages of their evolution and/or during explosive events such as supernovae.

Stars such as our sun in whose outer layers heavy elements are observed are second (or higher) generation objects. They are the progeny of earlier stars that blew apart and scattered their debris in places where new stars were being born. Likewise planets and all forms of life on our planet are the brood of self-sacrificing stars.

Our sun has been converting hydrogen to helium during the 4.5 billions years since its birth. In some 5 billion more years it will have depleted so much of the original hydrogen that in its death throes the sun will expand into a red giant. In that bloated condition, the outer layer of the sun will reach to the orbit of the planet Mars. Caught inside the sun the inner planets including Earth will gradually vaporize. Sometime later the sun will shrink into a white dwarf, a small, cooling, and dying stellar ember.

For all its effort during all its years of struggle from conception to death, our sun is incapable of creating an element more complex than helium. Only stars that are more massive than the sun can carry synthesis of elements beyond that of helium. Once hydrogen has been exhausted in their cores these stars generate energy by synthesizing helium into carbon and oxygen. Only the most massive of stars, more than perhaps 12 times that of the sun, can carry the process of synthesis of elements all the way to completion and can disperse those elements in a supernova explosion.

Were there no explosive release of matter, new elements would remain locked up in the stars, hoarded like the gold of dragons, to be carried with them to their graves. The massive stars generate element after element, building onion-like shells of elements with iron in the core (*Fig.* 2.1). The iron core is unstable and splits by fission back down into hydrogen and helium. The star collapses violently, falling in upon itself with speeds as high as 1/4 the speed of light. The infall is reversed in a spectacular bounce off of the hot, dense matter in the center, and part of the star is blown off as the supernova remnant.

The blazing supernova is the singular event that signals the scattering of new elements in a galaxy. If no supernovae ever occurred in a galaxy, there would be no elements from which to build planets or life. The iron which reddens the soil of Earth and Mars and which courses through the veins and arteries of reptiles, fish, and mammals originated in an ancient supernova.

During the past 2000 years eight supernovae have probably been seen in our galaxy. They brighten by a factor of 10 billion and briefly become as luminous as an entire galaxy. The Chinese reported seeing 'guest stars' as early as 532 BC and supernovae were reported in AD 185, 386, 393, 1006, 1054, and 1181. Those of AD 1572 and 1603 significantly influenced the lives of Tycho Brahe and Johannes Kepler. The most brilliant supernova was that of AD 1006 which was nearly as bright as the quarter moon. The most famous of all first appeared in July AD 1054. Carefully monitored by the Chinese, it produced the Crab Nebula now visible in the sky near the star, Tien Kuan (Gate of Heaven). So bright that it could be seen in the daytime sky for several weeks, the remnant of the supernova remained visible at night until April AD 1056.

Slowly but steadily, portions of most galaxies such as ours acquired the ingredients necessary for life. We astronomers believe that in our galaxy planets were formed with the stars, that planets may be as abundant and ubiquitous as stars, and that many of those other planets also contain mud, fire, and perhaps even alien versions of blood.

Elements of Earth

We come from below as well as above, from the earth as well as the stars, and powerful images of earth and water juxtapose with those of the sidereal realms in our creation mythologies.

The cosmogonies of the Americas intertwined blood, bones, and earth, and we find references to these elements throughout the ruins of Mesoamerica. The Aztec sun stone, carved in commemoration of the fourteenth-century Aztec king Axayacatl, displays the roles of fundamental elements in the creation and destruction of the world (*Fig.* 2.2). At the center is Tonatiuh, the sun. From his mouth hangs, instead of a tongue, the sacrificial flint knife, ready for blood sacrifices. The four panels around Tonatiuh recall the four previous ages or 'suns'.

The Mesoamerican cosmos is characterized by a rhythm of disasters which destroy one age after another. The ages are identified not by the creative forces that formed them but by the destructive forces and elements that eliminated them. The first age was that of Jaguar, inhabited by giants, dwelling in caves, who did not farm the earth as the gods had expected and hence were destroyed by Jaguars, **earth** monsters. In the second age, that of **wind**, another imperfect human race was destroyed by that element; the creatures were transformed into monkeys, that they might better cling to the world. In the third world, that of fire-rain, some creatures survived the rain of **fire** by being transformed into birds. And finally in the fourth world, just preceding ours, the world was destroyed by **water** and creatures were transformed into frogs and fish.

In another creation story from Mesoamerica, the responsibility for the formation of our current fifth world is given to Quetzalcoatl, the feathered serpent, a classic image of the conjoining of earth and air, reminiscent of the *makaram* of India. Quetzalcoatl dives into the earth, to request from the lord of the dead, Mictlantecuhtli, the bones of the ancestors to make a new race of humans. Quetzalcoatl is given the impossible task of blowing on a shell trumpet that is not hollow and has no holes. He calls upon worms to drill out the shell and bees to make it sing. He escapes with the bones. But they are broken as a result of a fall and places them in a jadestone bowl. When they are ground up, Quetzalcoatl adds blood and from this mixture a male child and a female child are born.

Throughout Mesoamerica, blood is the fundamental element of life. Blood feeds the Hummingbird God, Huitzilopochtli, which is the sun in the morning, preparing him for his nightly battle with the forces of darkness. Human blood was needed to sustain the sun, a feat which was accomplished through human sacrifices, many of which occurred on the summit of the Templo Mayor of Tenochtitlan where were located the twin shrines of the gods of sun and water.

Earth Diver

The set of myths known as **earth diver**, ancient and world-wide in scope, is one of our preeminent cosmogonic allegories. The basic elements of the universe are extracted from the depths of primeval waters.

Earth Diver myths have been identified as the most widely distributed of all North American Indian myths. In the Americas these myths describe the descent into the waters by a creature who returns into the light of the sun with a few grains of mud under its finger nails or paws.

> In North America Indian myths of the origin of the world, the culture hero has a succession of animals dive into the primeval waters, or flood of waters, to secure bits of mud or sand from which the earth is to be formed. Various animals, birds, and aquatic creatures are sent down into the waters that cover the earth. One after another animal fails; the last one succeeds, however, and floats to the surface, half-dead,

> with a little sand or dirt in his claws. Sometimes it is Muskrat, sometimes Beaver, Hell-diver, Crawfish, Mink who succeeds, after various other animals have failed. The tiny bit of mud which is then put on the surface of the water and magically expands to become the world of the present time. (Wheeler-Voegelin 1949)

The predominant symbols of earth diver myths include **water** as the unformed, pure element out of which the universe develops, **descent** into the dark waters, which parallels descent into the underworld or return to the womb as an experience of renewal, and **return** to light with the germs of creation as well as knowledge to change the world.

There are variants to this myth which place the creatures on the central mountain of the earth or on the world tree, both symbols of the *axis mundi*:

> The whole earth was once covered with water, and there were no living creatures, save an eagle and a crow. There was a stump of a tree that projected above the surface of the watery expanse, and upon this the two birds were wont to stand and hold converse. Finally they became weary of the solitude and between them they managed to create a duck, which swam about the stump. One day the duck dove to the bottom and brought up some earth on his bill. This struck the eagle and crow as worth looking into since they had never seen anything like it. They were very tired of having nothing but the stump to roost on, and as the mud brought up seemed promising, they entered into an agreement to keep the duck constantly diving for it. They could not agree, however as to where the mud should be deposited. So they divided the world into two portions. (Count 1935)

The myth in its various forms always begins with the element water. The creatures are located on four types of places: a central mountain, a tree, raft, or on the surface of the water itself. Even though the animal may die while diving or after surfacing, a handful of earth is taken from its feet or a few grains from its fingernails. The earth is placed on a raft and expands to become the world. Some versions describe that a ball is made from the mud by the creator; after he blows on it (thereby adding air to the elements earth and water) the ball grows; in other stories the mud is kneaded to form an island which floats on the ocean surface to become eventually the earth.

Hindu myth provides a memorable version of the earth diver myth. Measured just in terms of body weight Varaha, the boar *avatar* of Visnu, must be the greatest earth diver of all time. Mother Earth had been taken prisoner to the dark floor of the cosmic ocean by the demon of darkness and chaos. The proper flow of time was imperilled. The great boar plunged into the dark waters, vanquished chaos, raised the earth from beneath the waters, and placed her in the sunlight on the surface of the ocean. The earth floats because she had been kneaded: flattened and spread out. "The earth stayed like a great ship on the top of the flood of water and did not sink, because her body was so spread out."

Early Intuitions of Cosmos

How far back in time can we discover material evidence of the intuition of a universe which is an ordered and harmonious system, integrating humans, earth, and heavens? The brightest objects in the heavens, sun and moon, are the most natural candidates for identification as elemental forces, together with earth. Emerging as embryos when the dark waters of time were released from the coils of Vrtra, the sun and moon are our first elements. The sun is the sole provider of energy for our world while the moon brings light to the night and rhythm to the year. The moon also played a primary role in the origin of life in the oceans of our planet, keeping the waters alive and well-stirred through the constant action of the tides.

THE SUN AT NEWGRANGE

One of the earliest manifestations in the archaeological record of a belief in the parallelism of cycles of the sun and life may be found at Newgrange, perhaps dating to about 3200 BC (O'Kelly 1982). Death, winter solstice, and the sun are all represented in the tomb on a ridge above the River Boyne. At winter solstice, light of the rising sun penetrates a darkened passage and, reaching eighty feet to its end, illuminates a triform chamber. With intertwined spirals, evocative symbols of the intertwining of the realms of the cosmos, carved on its walls the space may have once held cremated remains of several individuals (*Fig*. 2.3). It may have been the intent of its builders that the dead buried there would be magically enfolded into the rhythm of the cosmos, the solstice to solstice cadence of the sun. There may have been hope that somehow the cycle of life and death of a monarch would resonate with the cycle of the sun and the dead would be brought to life. At winter solstice the cold sun, low on the horizon dies, but is soon born again.

Newgrange may evidence the belief in a form of sympathetic magic that couples the rhythm of human life and death with the life and death of the sun. But it may also contain symbolism about those elements that lie at the foundation of our world. Thus, the annual illumination of the ground at the base of the deep passageway could have been symbolic of the conjoining of the elements of earth and sun to create life.

THE MOON AT STONEHENGE

Stonehenge is more complex and vastly more controversial than Newgrange (Hawkins 1965; Newham 1972). Including alignments to the moon as well as the sun, the earliest structures at Stonehenge, built at approximately 3100 BC, display a remarkably complete set of lunar and solar cycles (*Fig.* 2.4). Besides lines to the sun at winter and summer solstice there are also lines to the major and minor standstills of the moon. While these lines do not have the accuracy to function as observational devices for a calendar (much less a 'computer'), they may have honored, commemorated, and/or celebrated the repeating cycles of the sun and moon. Since it is likely that human burials were placed within or in the neighborhood of Stonehenge, these standing stones may be mute acknowledgment, similar to Newgrange, that the cycle of human life is intertwined with the complex cycles of moon and sun.

The moon is more than simply a convenient time keeping device. In its waxing to maturity as a full moon and waning to invisibility as a new moon, it is a body whose life appears to be subject to the same universal law of birth and death as that of human life. For three nights every month the sky is without a moon. But the death of the moon is never final, and the waning slender crescent preceding death is always followed by the rebirth of a waxing slender crescent in the west just after the setting sun.

This perpetual return to its beginnings every 29.5 days makes the moon the unique heavenly body associated with time and the rhythms of life. No other heavenly body provides so tangible a set of cycles, so accessible a cosmic rhythm, or so visible a statement that death is not final. The cycles of the moon give explicit demonstration of the "intimate parallelism" (Wheatley 1971) of heaven and earth. These are the cycles that encouraged imitation of celestial archetypes by ancient peoples (Eliade 1959) and became religious symbols expressive of the order of nature (Geertz 1973).

Hunting cultures often ascribe success of the hunt to the moon and give the moon greater status and power than the sun. The reverse is generally true for agricultural societies for whom the powerful role of the sun in evoking life from the earth is undeniable. For example, in the mythologies of the Bushmen of southern Africa and the Australian aborigines the moon is more important than the sun. Hunters pray to the moon for success partly because hunting is a nighttime activity when the moon provides illumination, especially during the bright half of the lunar month preceding full moon.

Besides the lunar month of 29.5 days there is the human biological (menstrual) month also of approximately 29.5 days. In his provocative proposal for a lunar origin of culture, Knight (1989) argues that the monthly organization of hunting expeditions would have influenced the menstrual periods of the women who were periodically abandoned. The return of the hunters with raw meat near the time of full moon would have intertwined moon, fertility, blood, fire, and food.

YIN AND YANG AT BEIJING

Established as his capital by the emperor Yong le in the third Ming dynasty, Beijing was the "place where sky and earth met" (Wheatley 1971), and astronomy was the official business of the city (Krupp 1989). The emperor was the pivot of the world, and ruling from the Forbidden City with the mandate of heaven, he harmonized the world and maintained order by maintaining the calendar.

Dominating the planning of the city was the ancient *yin-yang* world-view of Chinese philosophy. The beginning of the world was understood to be the 'limitless', *wuji*, an ultimate reality which transcends all words and concepts (Meyer 1991). When considered positively it is known as the "supreme ultimate", *taiji,* also as Dao. Initially passive and undifferentiated, the Dao appears in our world when its divides into the two cosmic principles *Yin* and *Yang*, which in turn generate the dualities of the world: light/dark, male/female, east/west, birth/death, etc. Through the interaction of the *Yin* and *Yang* change takes place as season follows season, day and night, heat and cold, follow each other in an orderly sequence. The interactions of *yin* and *yang* give birth to the five 'phases' of water, fire, wood, metal, and earth, the *wuxing*. These have most frequently been translated as the five 'elements', but Meyer (1991) argues that 'phases' better conveys the dynamic, transformative nature of the concept.

> The *Wuji* gives birth to the *Taiji*
> [The *Taiji*] moves and gives birth to *Yang*
> Rests, and gives birth to *Yin*
> *Yang* shifts, *Yin*, unites,
> Then is born water, fire, wood, metal, and earth.
> The *Five Breaths* make things flourish in their proper order;
> The four seasons progress according to them.
>
> (Meyer 1991)

The Axial Way of Beijing provides a dominating north-south axis with balanced structures placed symmetrically on each side. Starting in the south at the Eternal Foundation Gate, the path terminates in the north with the Drum Tower. With nearly perfect symmetry, on opposite sides of the axis, are the Altar of the Moon, *Yuetan* (west) and the Altar of the Sun, *Ritan,* (east).

The symmetry about the axis is clearly evident in maps of the Forbidden City (*Fig.* 2.5). The circumpolar regions of the sky lie north of Beijing, and the emperor of heaven, Shangdi, ruled the cosmos from the immovable pole, facing south to Beijing. The north-south axis from the emperor of heaven to emperor of earth was thus a line of dominion as well as an axis of *yin-yang* symmetry.

The city was built to imitate the heavens and achieve a mirror image of the celestial capital of Shangdi. The palace was designed to be the earthly counterpart of the circumpolar zone of the heavens, that region of stars revolving so closely to the immobile center of the heavens that they never set. The polar region in the sky was

Plate 2.1 Polar Stars

Plate 2.2 Kitt-Peak Observatory, Arizona

the *lingam*, the central pole of a tent used for dance, and the tree of life are other examples of sacred or ritual pillars (Vatsyayan 1983). The stalk of the lotus bearing Brahma, the four-faced creator of the universe, is another cosmogonic pillar from which creation emanates.

In the Indian gnomon we encounter the remarkable union of a technical and a ritual device (*Ajitagama:* Dagens 1984). It is placed in a square area, which had to be "as smooth as a mirror", checked with a water level. Around the gnomon is traced a circle with a radius equal to the height of the gnomon. In the simplest of approaches two points are marked on the circle where the shadow of the gnomon touches it at midmorning and midafternoon. These two points are joined by a straight line which is close to true east-west.

This method, often referred to as the Indian Circle method, produces an alignment to the true cardinal directions which is only approximately accurate during most of the year. Swinging between its winter and southern extremes at the solstices, the sun moves most rapidly at the equinoxes. At the time of vernal equinox, for example, since the sun moves northward between midmorning and midafternoon, the Eastern point, produced by the afternoon shadow is shifted slightly southward of the Western point. The line connecting the two points would thus be tilted south of east in the spring and north of east in the fall.

Brahmagupta (born AD 598) is credited with the first recorded recognition of this defect of the method (Yano 1986), although he did not give a formula for correction. Sripati (AD 1039) was the first who successfully versified the formula in Sanskrit, and after him the formula apparently became common knowledge among Indian architects and astronomers (Yano 1986):

$$s = h\,[\sin(\mathrm{dec}_1) - \sin(\mathrm{dec}_2)]/\cos(\mathrm{latitude})$$

where s is the distance of the tip of the shadow from the east-west line, h is the hypotenuse of the shadow, and dec_1 and dec_2 are the respective declinations of the sun at the time in the morning and afternoon when the shadows touch the circle. Similar to latitude of the earth which measures the angular distance from the earth's equator, declination measures the angular distance from the celestial equator. Thus at equinox the declination of the sun is 0° and at summer solstice its declination is 23.5°.

Even on the days of equinox, the effects of the movement of the sun in declination are slight compared to the best measurement that could have been achieved before the invention of the telescope. During 6 hours from midmorning to midafternoon, the declination of the sun varies at most by 6' (1/10 of a degree), only 1/5 the angular diameter of the sun.

The amount by which the sun changes its declination during the day decreases as the sun moves away from equinox, and on the days of solstice the change is zero.

For the two month period around solstice, the maximum error is only 3' and within 10 days of solstice, the maximum error has fallen to 1'.

A fascinating and impressive array of other methods were also available to achieve the same corrections (Yano 1986; Staal 1983). I have described this method in some detail to demonstrate the robust role of measurement within the Indian tradition. The resolution of the human eye is at best 1.5-2 minutes of arc, and the corrections achievable by these methods and computations exceed the highest precision that could have been achieved in pre-telescopic times.

Not just temples, but cities in India have been built mindful of the importance of precise measurement. The greatest of medieval cities of India, Vijayanagara, echoes the symbolic seriousness of careful measurement. In a manner remarkably similar to the north-south axiality of Beijing, a north-south line extends from the summit of Matanga hill into the middle of the royal center passing through a major ceremonial gateway (*Fig*. 2.6). In the case of Beijing the north-south axis is a line of dominion extending from the Emperor of Heaven to his terrestrial counterpart. In Vijayanagara there are multiple levels of meaning contained in the axis, some of which may be related to our theme of cosmogony and the elements: (1) The north-south line crosses and is tangent to the Tungabhadra river just where it turn north, reminiscent of the northward flowing of the Ganga at Kashi. North is the direction of birth and the north-south axis of the City thus acquires a cosmic symbolism paralleling that of Kashi itself. (2) The axis crosses the remains of an artificial lake that was constructed just south of Matanga hill. This lake, which does not seem to have served any practical needs of the city, may have been a metonym for the Ocean of Milk, one of the great symbols of fertility and cosmogony in Hindu texts. The lake may have been involved in ritual processions between the summit of Matanga hill and the royal center. (3) The axis may be symbolic protection of the city by the sage Matanga (Malville and Fritz 1993), which figures prominently in the creation mythology of the city. (4) The axis establishes a well-defined symmetry by dividing the royal center into public/private, male/female dualities.

Standing at night in that ceremonial gateway of the royal center, looking north, one sees the North Star, fixed and unmoving, lying directly above the *sikhara* of the Virabhadra temple on the summit of Matanga hill. As viewed from that spot, the north pole of the celestial sphere is displaced from the *sikhara* by only 0.8'. The visual symbolism of that nighttime vista is forceful and commanding, and the cosmological symbolism actually works! The north celestial pole lies on the cosmic axis that passes through Matanga hill. Who could doubt that Matanga hill lies at the center of the universe or that Vijayanagara is a magical and powerful city?

To the south of the gateway is another remarkable example of precise measurement within the royal center. In this case measurement appears to legitimize with cosmic authority the two (public/private) realms of kingship. The largest palace in the Western area balances the 100 column audience hall in the east. The midpoint between their two centers, **a fulcrum of kingship** lies only a few meters from the north-south axis of the royal center which passes through the celestial north pole and Matanga hill (*Fig*. 2.7). The respective roles of the king and queen appear thus to be symmetrical and balanced. A symmetry is found in Beijing involving the temples of the sun and moon (Krupp 1989). But here it appears to speak to the fundamental role of the queen as developed in the *Ramayana*. It also symbolizes a refusal within Hindu mythology to grant precedence of the elemental Male over the Female Energy: the queen as *Pakrti* or *Sakti* energizes the 'inert' lump of matter that is the male, *Purusa*, and is just vital for the well-being of the empire as is the king.

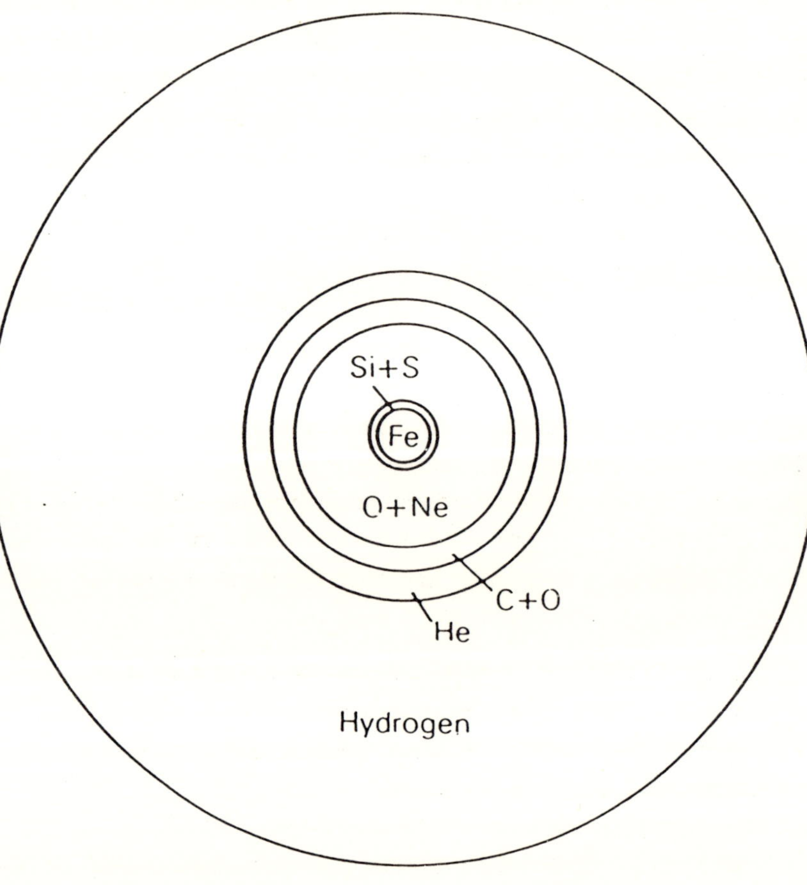

Fig. 2.1: The interior of a massive star just before the collapse which triggers the supernova explosion showing the layers containing different elements.

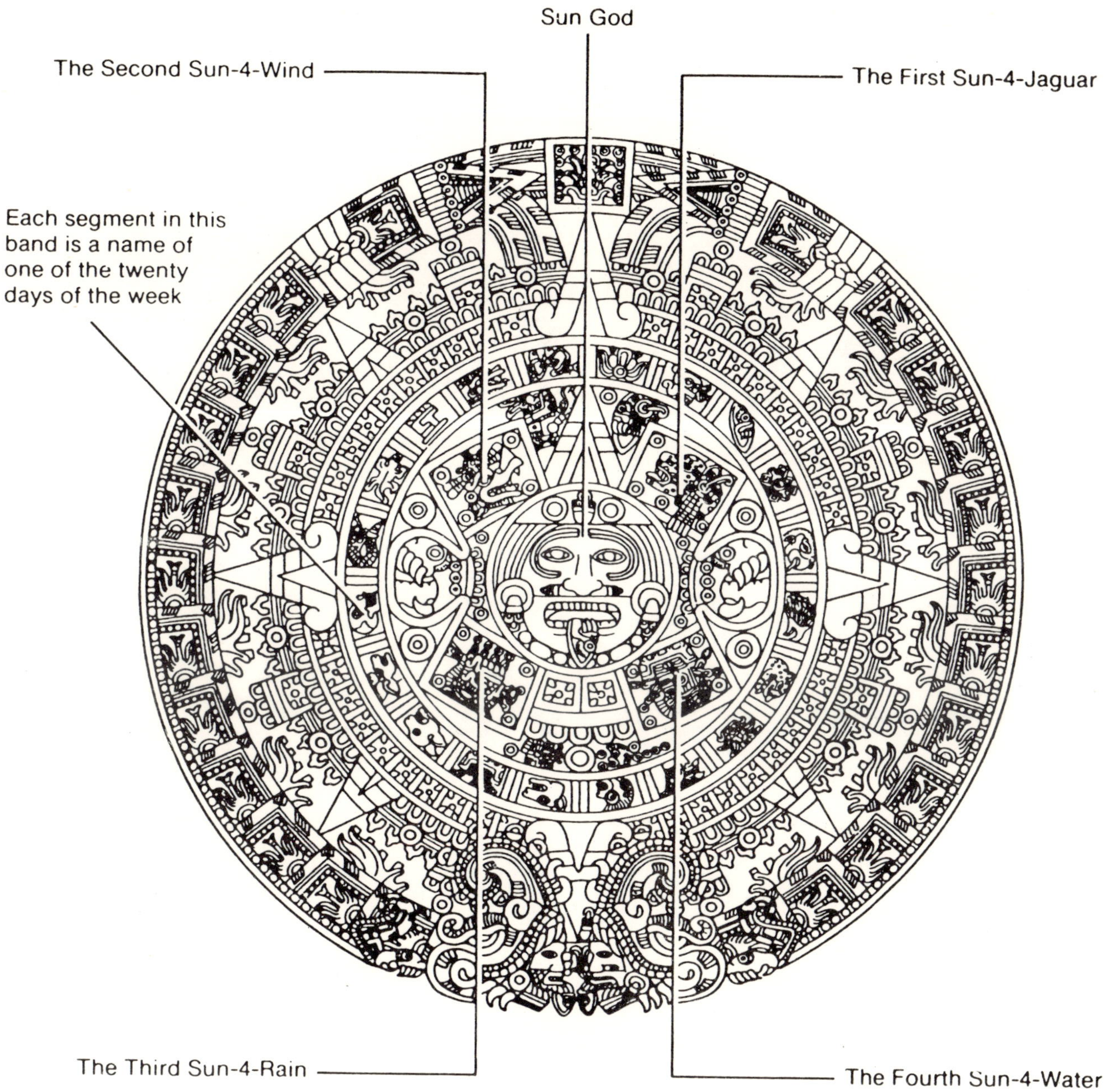

Fig. 2.2: The Aztec sun stone. The sun god, Tonatiuh, is in the center. The next ring contains depictions of the four great ages of the world, destroyed successively by Jaguars, wind, rain of fire, and water. The next ring contains the twenty days of the week which comprise the 260 day sacred calendar. Cimi (*Maya*) or Miquiztli (*Aztec*) representing death is indicated (after Coe).

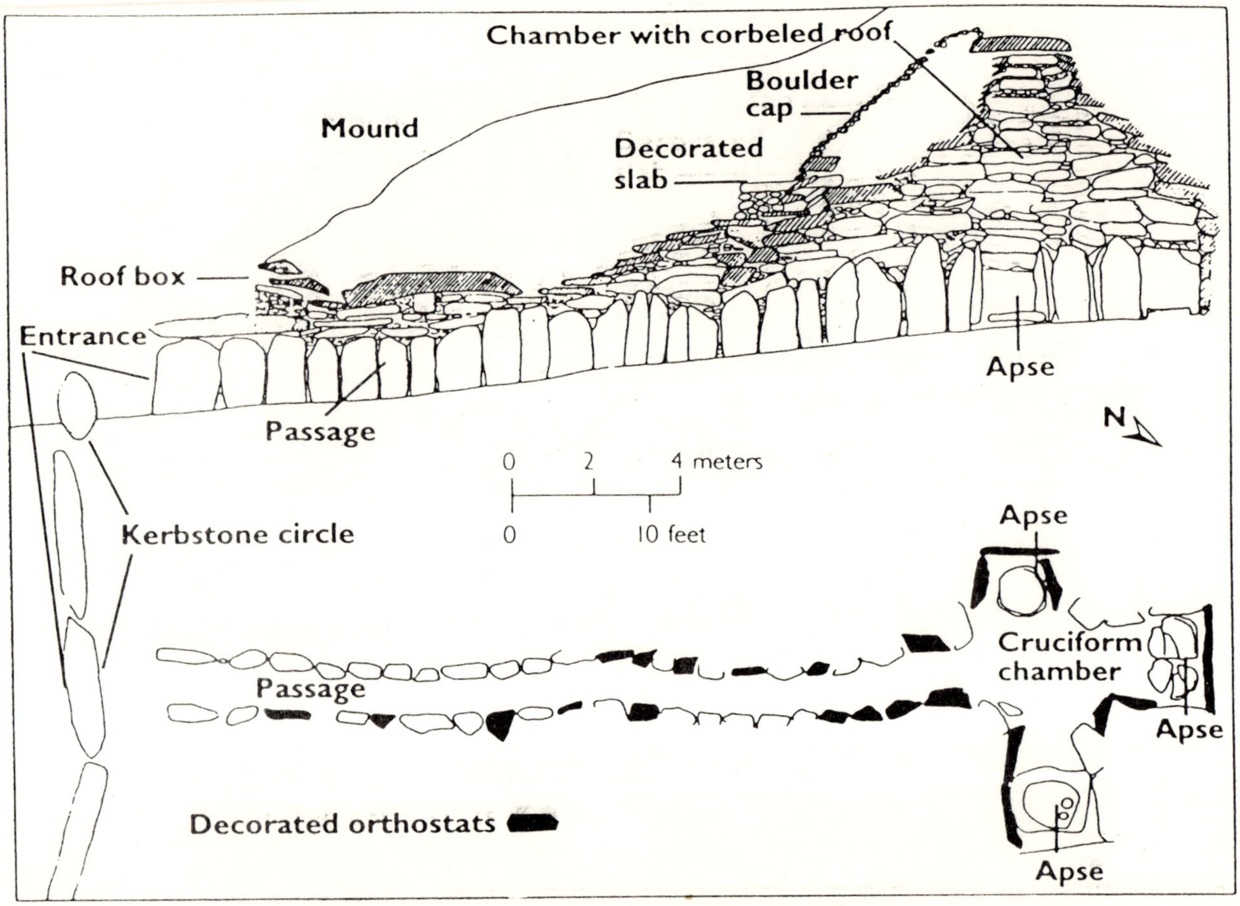

Fig. 2.3: Newgrange. The cross-section of the mound and a view from above showing the orientation of the passage to the rising sun at winter solstice (after O'Brien).

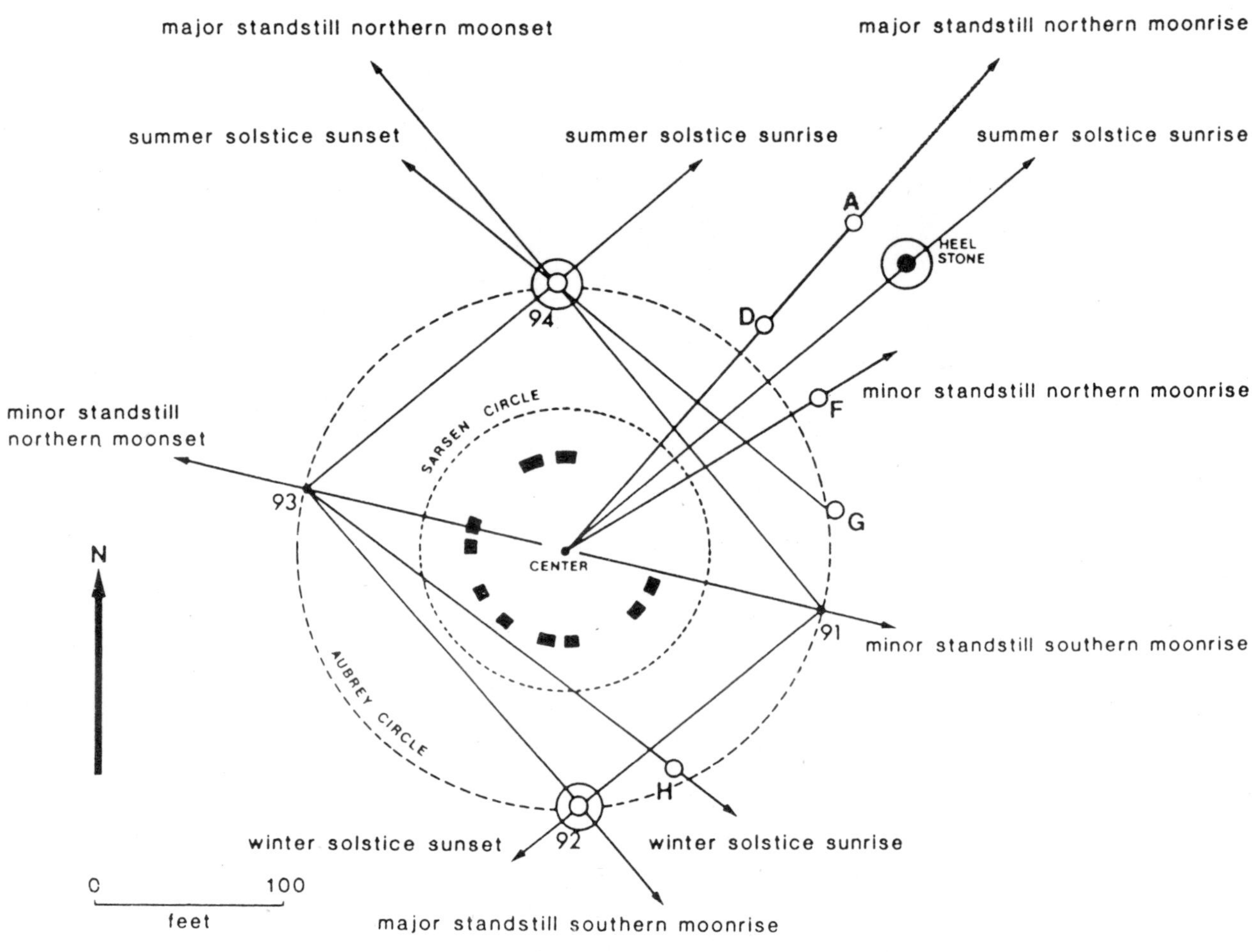

Fig. 2.4: Stonehenge, showing alignments to the major cyclic positions of the sun and moon (Griffith Observatory).

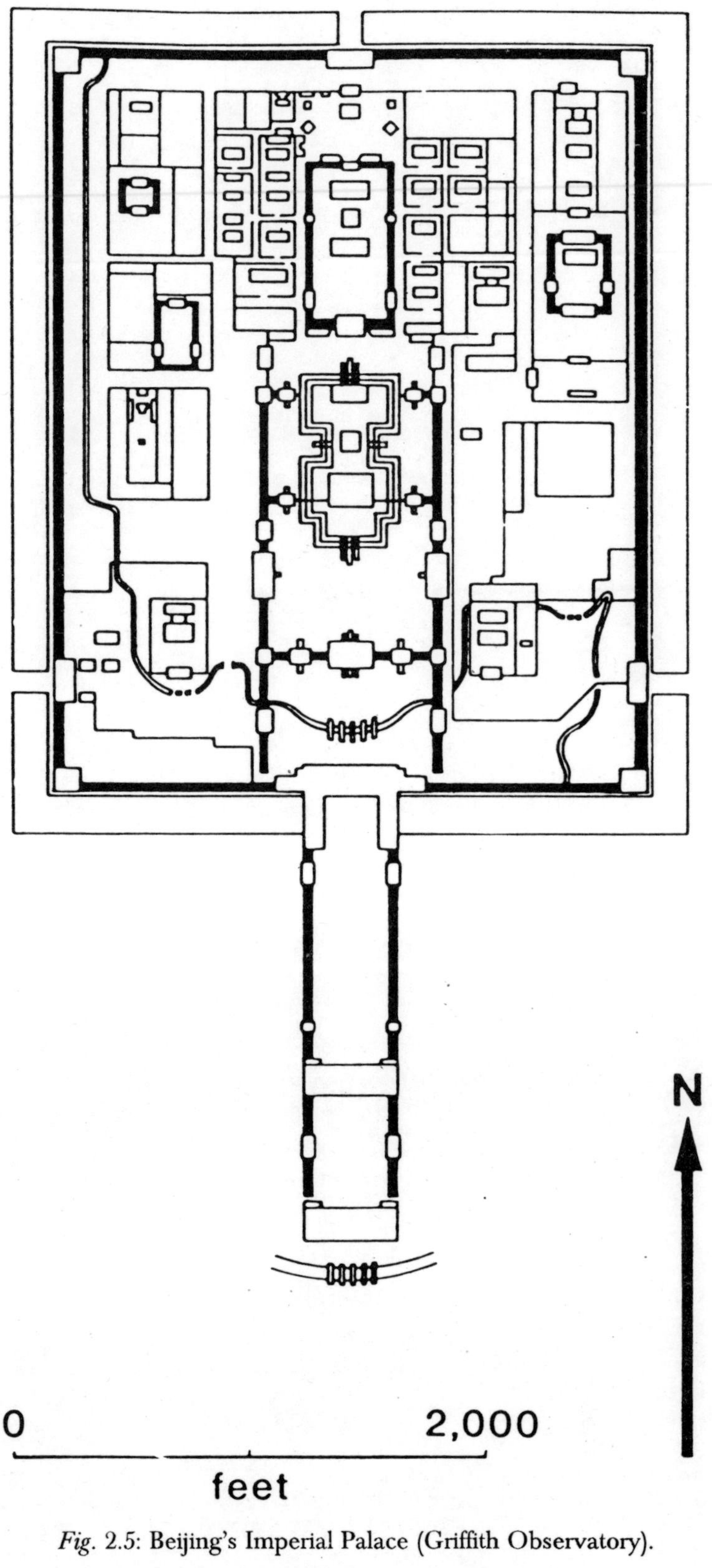

Fig. 2.5: Beijing's Imperial Palace (Griffith Observatory).

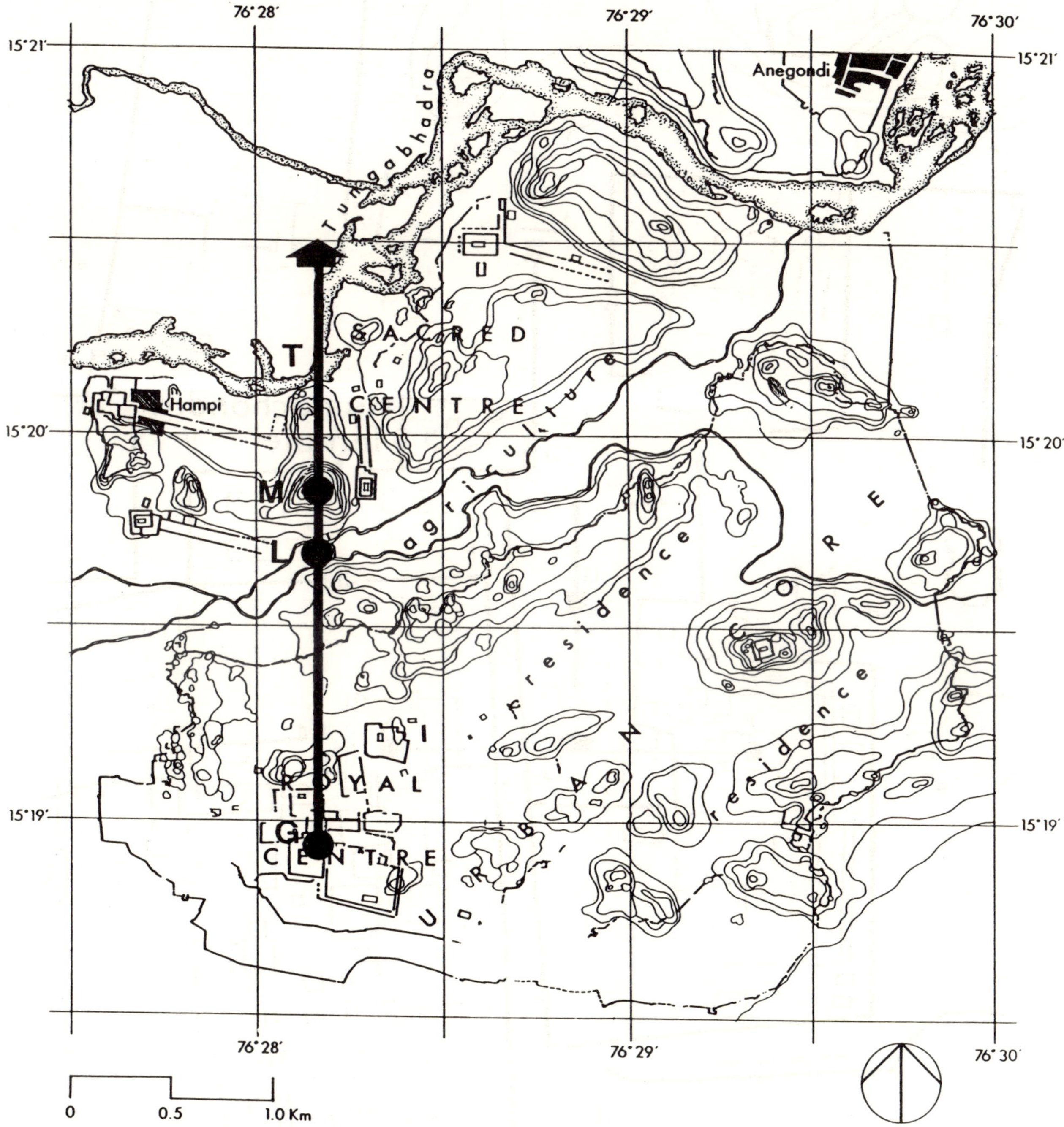

Fig. 2.6: The north-south axis of Vijayanagara, crossing the Tungabhadra River (T) where it turn north, the summit of Matanga hill (M), the artificial lake (L) which may symbolize the Ocean of Milk, and the ceremonial gateway (G) in the royal center.

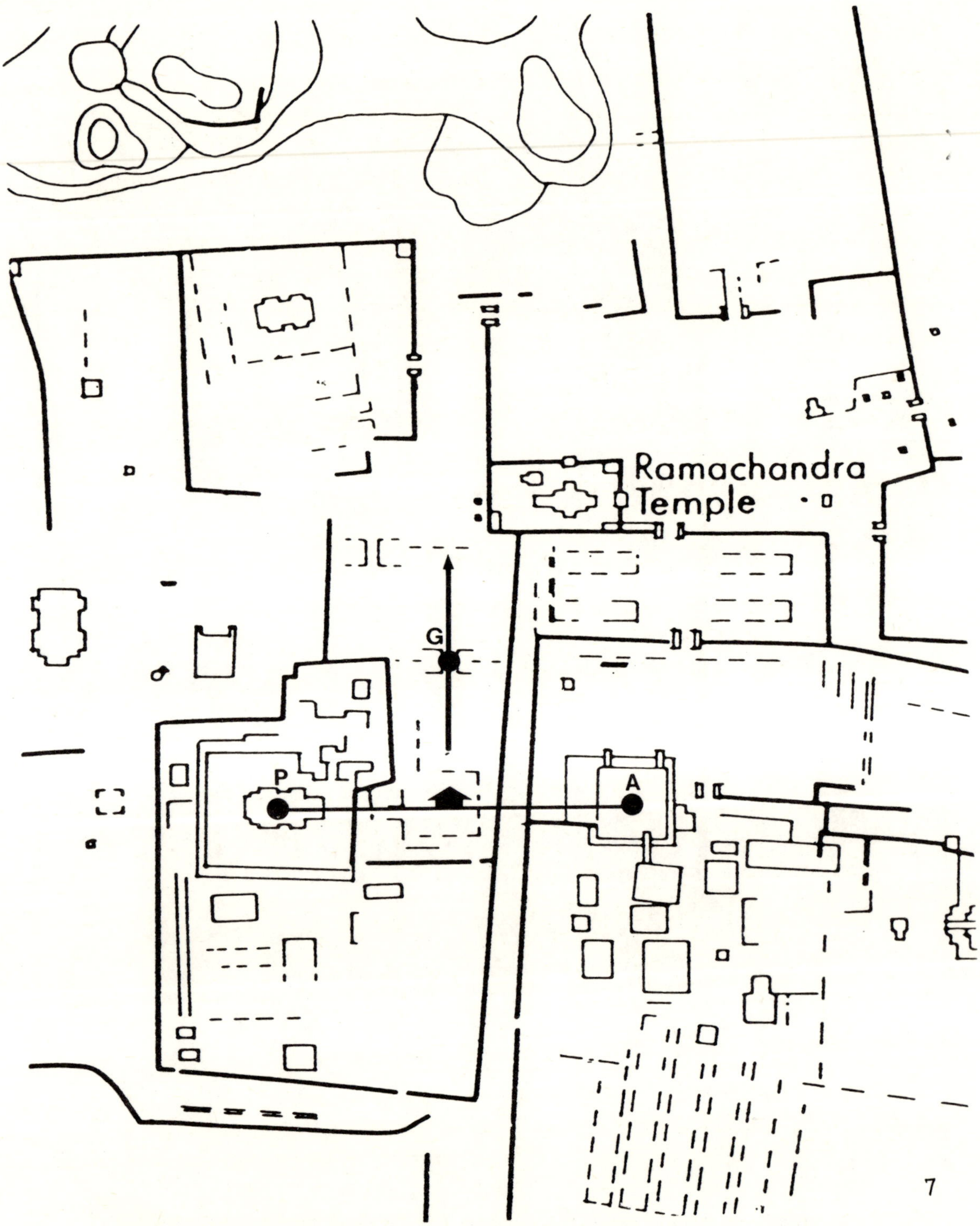

Fig. 2.7: The north-south axis where it crosses the royal center through the ceremonial gateway (G). The symmetrical placement of the queen's palace (P) and the king's 100 column hall audience hall (A) are shown.

Conclusion

I started this discussion with astrophysics and, coming nearly full circle, I conclude with physics. There is an almost uncanny similarity between the role of Vedic measurement in evoking elements from primordial chaos and that of quantum mechanical measurement in 'actualizing' the objects of the world. According to the Copenhagen interpretation of quantum mechanics championed by Niels Bohr (1963), "discrete objects such as electrons do not come into existence until they are measured". Prior to the act of measurement, electrons exist only as probabilities. The Many Worlds Hypothesis, collapsing wave functions, and, even, the death of Schroedinger's cat are various features of this insight of modern physics that the material world is created by the human act of measurement (Wigner 1961).

Both myth and science are human creations, and it should come as no surprise that they often converge with common insights (Malville 1975). The actors in our cosmogonic drama have had many roles and many costumes ranging from creation mythologies to quantum mechanics. Elements have come to us from all directions of space and time: falling from the sky, emerging out of earth and water, born of the union of *Yin* and *Yang*, and evoked in that mysterious yet simple act of making a measurement in this extraordinarily interconnected cosmos which we call home.

References

Bohr, Niels, 1963. "Quantum Mechanics and Philosophy — Causality and Complementarity", In *Essays 1958-1962 on Atomic Physics and Human Knowledge,* Richard Clay and Company, Bungay, Suffolk.

Count, Earl W, 1935. *The Earth-diver: An Attempt at an Asiatic-American Correlation*, Ph.D. dissertation, University of California at Berkeley.

Dagens, Bruno, 1984. *Architecture in the Ajitagama and the Rauravagama.* New Delhi, Sitaram Bhartiya Institute.

Eliade, Mircea, 1959. *Cosmos and History: The Myth of the Eternal Return,* Harper Torchbooks, New York.

Geerth, Clifford, 1973. *The Interpretation of Cultures*, Basic Books, New York.

Hawkins, Gerald S., 1965. *Stonehenge Decoded,* Doubleday & Co, Garden City, NY.

Knight, Chris, 1989. "The Lunar Analogue and the Origins of Culture", In *Analogy*, edited by E. Lyle, University of Edinburgh, Edinburgh.

Kramrisch, Stella, 1981. *The Presence of Shiva.* Princeton University Press, Princeton.

——, 1991. "Space in Indian Cosmogony and in Architecture", In *Concepts of Space,* ed. by Kapila Vatsyayan, pp. 101-04.

Krupp, E. C., 1989. "The cosmic temples of old Beijing", In *World Archaeoastronomy,* edited by A. F. Aveni, Cambridge University Press, Cambridge.

Malville, J. McKim, 1975. *A Feather for Daedalus: Explorations in Science and Myth,* Cummings

Publishing, Menlo Park.

——, 1992. "Cosmogonic Motifs in Indian Temples, in *Sacred Architecture in the Traditions of India, China, Judaism and Islam,* edited by Emily Lyle, Edinburgh University Press, Edinburgh.

Malville, J. McKim and John M. Fritz. "Mapping the Sacred Geometry of Vijayanagara", In *Mapping Invisible Worlds,* ed. by Gavin Flood and Emily Lyle, Edinburgh University Press, (in press).

Meyer, Jeffrey, 1991. *The Dragons of Tianamen,* University of South Carolina Press, Columbia.

Newham, C. A., 1972. *The Astronomical Significance of Stonehenge,* Moon Publications, Gwent Wales.

O'Kelly, M. J., 1982. *Newgrange: Archaeology, Art and Legend.* Thames and Hudson, London.

Staal, Fritz, 1983. *Agni: The Vedic Ritual of the Fire Altar,* Berkeley.

Teilhard de Chardin, Pierre, 1959. *The Phenomenon of Man,* (originally published as *Le Phenomene Humain,* Editions de Seuil, Paris, 1955) Harper and Row, New York.

Vatsyayan, Kapila, 1983. *The Square and the Circle of the Indian Arts,* Atlantic City.

Wheatley, Paul, 1971. *The Pivot of the Four Quarters,* Aldine Chicago.

Wheeler-Voegelin, Erminie, 1949. "Earth Diver", In *Standard Dictionary of Folklore, Mythology, and Legend,* edited by Maria Leach, vol 1, New York.

Wigner, Eugene, "Remarks on the mind-body question", In *The Scientist Speculates,* ed. I.J. Good, Heinemann, London.

Yano, M., 1986. "Knowledge of Astronomy in Sanskrit Texts of Architecture", In *Indo-Iranian Journal* 29, pp. 17-29.

3

Transmutation from One Form to Another

The Interaction of Colour and the Elements Some Scientific and Aesthetic Considerations

A. Ranganathan

Since time immemorial, man has been fascinated by the blue sky,[1] the blue of the sea, the beauties of the sunrise and sunset, the halo around the moon, the reflections in placid lakes, the loveliness of the rainbows and the exquisitely beautiful colour schemes in great works of art. Naturally great poets have immortalized the skies and seas. For example, one is reminded of the beautiful lines of Shelley in his *Adonais:*

> As long as skies are blue, and fields are green
> Evening must usher night, night urge the morrow.

To cite another example, Byron wrote in his *Childe Harold's Pilgrimage:*

> Roll on, thou deep and dark blue ocean, roll!

Again, the neon lights and the laser technologies which flash through the modern cities, constitute a new addition to a series of visual impressions and manifestations. Moreover, it is worthnoting that the interaction of light with matter results in several phenomena – reflection, refraction, scattering or absorption of light by the objects, which reveal the presence of the objects as well as their colours.

It is interesting to reflect on the fact that the eye which perceives these colours is sensitive to a small range of the electromagnetic spectrum which is the 400 to 700 nanometer (billionth of a meter) wavelength region or the violet to red radiation of the visible spectrum. Also the interaction of colour with the elements is based on the physical theory that the electrons in atoms and molecules occupy various discrete energy levels. Again the incident light directs energy to these electrons and raises them in an excited state to higher, unstable energy states. Naturally these electrons fall from an excited state to the lower lying ones by emitting photons. And the perception of colour arises when these photons carry energies ranging between 1.77 and 3.1 electron volts, corresponding to the wavelengths of the red and violet colour light.

The interaction of colour and the five elements – earth, water, fire, air and the sky (*akasa*) – illuminates not only several disciplines such as Indian philosophy, Western philosophy, comparative aesthetics, modern physics and photochemistry, but also highlights the physics of elementary particles which had inspired Werner Heisenberg's essay on 'The Representation of Nature in Contemporary Physics'.[2] Again, in actuality, colour (except at the microscopic level of particle physics) is a strikingly visible manifestation of some of the subtle effects that constitute the structure of matter. Not surprisingly, the interaction of light waves with electrons is a major preoccupation of twentieth century physics. For the duality between wave and particle aspects concerning light is now adopted to describe the properties of matter. And Prof. N. Bloembergen argued in his lecture 'Reflections on Light'[3] that "in the beginning of the twentieth century, the concept of light particles was revived by the theoretical studies of Planck and Einstein regarding the nature of Black-body radiations".

This paper is confined to a discussion of such concepts as Ananda Coomaraswamy's explanation of the Indian theory of painting, the scientific basis of Leonardo da Vinci's *Treatise on Painting*, the mathematical inadequacy of Goethe's *Theory of Colour* in contrast with the abstract reasoning of Newton's *Opticks*, the Rayleigh explanation of the blue sky, C.V. Raman's explanation of the blue colour of the Mediterranean Sea, Professor Penrose's Holistic theory of Physics, Psychology and Neurophysiology, Professor Chandrasekhar's bifocal view[4] of the patterns of creativity that constitute the landscapes of General Relativity and the Series Paintings of Claude Monet and the rediscovery of the Pythagorean idea of a "pre-established harmony" in Gell-Mann's world of quantum numbers. Furthermore, an attempt will be made to underscore the relevance of Leonardo da Vinci's holistic view of colour – which embraced the earliest scientific explanation of the blue sky as well as the theory underlying the colour schemes in Renaissance paintings – to the modern world of Rayleigh Scattering (derived from the theory that the scattering of sunlight by particles in the atmosphere is proportional to the inverse fourth power of the wavelength and thereby contributes to the blue colour of the sky) and the contemporary marvels of colour photography and the television industry based on colour technology.

Viewed historically, it is a tribute to the versatility of the Leonardesque mind, that some of Leonardo's reflections on the nature of Renaissance Paintings contribute to a deeper understanding of Ananda Coomaraswamy's Indian view of Aesthetics. Indeed, in his major works of scholarship entitled *History of Indian and Indonesian Art*, *The Transformation of Nature in Art*, *Christian and Oriental Philosophy of Art*, *What is Civilization and other Essays* and *Essays in Early Indian Architecture* and in his technical essays such as *The Technique and Theory of Indian Painting* Coomaraswamy dealt with the meaning of Indian art, the philosophical symbolism which is its distinguishing characteristic and the Indian aesthetic view derived from the thesis that "the eyes are extended to meet the ears no less in colour than in word-painting". Here, it is worthnoting that the representation of the human form is not an end in itself, even in the European artistic context. As Leonardo da Vinci emphasized in his *Treatise on Painting*: "That figure is most laudable which by itself action expresses the passion which animates it". For he noted that a sophisticated painter ought to know anatomy.

The memorable quality of the mural of the *Last Supper* in Santa Maria Delle Grazie relies no less upon Leonardo's religious passion than upon his use of the anatomical form, subtle chiaroscuro and aerial perspective. However, the canons and conventions of Indian art are different. Indeed Coomaraswamy argued[5] in his essay on *The Technique and Theory of Indian Painting* that: "The Indian artist sees indeed ideally, but he does not idealize, he imitates. He does not draw according to his taste but from the intellectual image; not 'knowing what he likes' but liking what he knows . . . The Indian artist painted in the express likeness of what he saw 'as if in a mirror', and yet not such a 'looking-glass image' as we see in the mirror . . . That art is essentially an intellectual act is a conception remote indeed from the contemporary view of art as a sensational experience which view is also presupposed in the unsatisfactory word 'aesthetic', for which there is no Sanskrit equivalent; but it cannot be distinguished from the view of art that prevailed in Europe throughout the middle ages and of which full account must be taken by every serious student of Byzantine or Romanesque".

In one of his great scientific essays, Leonardo da Vinci referred to his discovery (made at a time when modern physics was not even in its infancy) that the sky became much darker while scaling the Alpine Peak of Mount Rosa. For da Vinci had intuitively realized that the blue sky was simply the blue light of the sun which is visually rerouted to us through dust and air molecules. Interestingly, commenting on Rayleigh's explanation of the blue colour of the sky which was formulated several centuries later, Prof. C.V. Raman remarked[6] in his work on *The Physiology of Vision* that it was "a consequence of the masking or suppression of all the other colours in the spectrum by its blue section". However, it is seldom realized that Leonardo da Vinci's explanation had anticipated the mathematically sophisticated theory of Lord Rayleigh relating to the colour of the sky by several centuries.

Just as Plato is said to have inscribed "Let no man ignorant of geometry enter here" above the entrance to his Academy, so did Leonardo da Vinci proclaim "Let no one read me who is not a mathematician". Indeed, according to Leonardo, his work *Treatise on Painting* was an extension of the theory that "Painting is a Science". For Leonardo's great paintings were based on geometric principles. Actually, his *Treatise on Painting* is a fascinating example of the dialogue of scientific and aesthetic cultures. Not surprisingly, Leonardo da Vinci had discussed the effect of air as well as of light on what he termed the "obscuring medium" intervening between the eye and the object. And this line of enquiry enabled him to study the impact of distance on objects and the manner in which their colour is partially changed by the environment.

Leonardo da Vinci wrote in one of his Notebooks,[7] "There is no certainty where one can neither apply any of the mathematical sciences nor any of those which are based on the mathematical sciences". What Leonardo wished to emphasize was the inadequacy of an observation of a natural phenomenon in qualitative terms. This thesis naturally reinforced the relevance of accurate measurements and quantitative relations to a study of natural phenomena. Travelling back in time, one notes the historic role of Pythagoras – in realizing that qualitative differences in sense perception are based on mathematical reasoning. Significantly Professor S. Chandrasekhar adverts to just the relationship derived from scientific exactitude and aesthetic meaning in his Lecture, "Shakespeare, Newton and Beethoven or Patterns of Creativity": "The discovery by Pythagoras that vibrating strings, under equal tension sound together harmoniously, if their lengths are in simple numerical ratios, established for the first time a profound connection between the intelligible and the beautiful. I think we may agree with Heisenberg that this 'is one of the truly momentous discoveries of mankind'." Here one can make a similar jump in time to the ancient Indian era, to realize how an equally ancient stream of aesthetics – for instance, that based on the acoustical perfection of the ancient Indian drum – bears what Professor Raman noted as the "remarkable testimony to the inventiveness and musical taste of its progenitors".

Leonardo da Vinci had stated in his *Treatise on Painting* that "there are three parts of Perspective as used in Painting: of them, the first includes the diminution in the size of opaque objects, the second treats of the diminution and loss of outline of opaque objects, and the third treats of the diminution and loss of colour at large distance." He characterized them *Linear Perspective*, *Perspective of Disappearance* and *Perspective of Colour* respectively. Commenting on the *Perspective of Disappearance*, Leonardo wrote: "Every object as it becomes more remote loses first those parts which are slenderest. Thus of a horse, one would lose the legs before the head, because the legs are thinner than the head; and the neck before the body for the same reason. Hence it follows that the last part of the horse which could be discernible by the eye would be the mass of the body in an oval, or rather in a cylindrical form, and of this one would lose its thickness before its length." Naturally he advises the painter: "You must diminish the definiteness of outline of objects in proportion to their increasing distance from the eye of the spectator." This argument led on to the conclusion that objects become bluer as a result of the distance due to the colour of the intervening air. And this change of colour towards the blue becomes more pronounced in the shadow or with the darker colours than with the lighter ones. As he put it, "you know that in an atmosphere of equal density the remotest objects seen through it, as mountains, in consequences of the great quantity of atmosphere between your eye and then appear blue . . . . . Hence you must make the nearest building of its true colour, but make the more distant ones less defined and bluer. Those who wish to look farther away you must make them proportionately bluer."

Here is Leonardo's advice to the painter: "Take care that the Perspective of Colour does not disagree with the size of objects, that is, that the colours diminish as much from their natural strength in proportion as the objects at various distances diminish from their natural size". Elsewhere Leonardo wrote in the same strain: "White, is no colour of itself, it changes and adopts part of the colours around it . . . That side of a woman which is illuminated by the light from the sky will have a bluish hue. Should she stand near a meadow between the sunlit grass and the sun itself, the folds of the gown of which the light of the meadow will show the reflected light on the green meadow." In other words, Leonardo had visualized some of the ideas of the Impressionists.

Leonardo da Vinci was familiar with the techniques of the masters of early Renaissance Painting, who knew the effect of light and shade in highlighting the form of objects. In fact, Masaccio had experimented with light and shade in modelling his forms. However, Leonardo was the first painter to introduce the concept of space around his figures in order to work out the compositional unity of his paintings resulting movement which had inspired the artistic imagination of Rembrandt. And significantly enough, Leonardo observed "that a Painter is not Admirable unless He is Universal."

Seen in the historical perspective, the eminent scientist-artist Leonardo da Vinci who preceded Goethe by several centuries had visualized the Rayleigh theory of the blue sky. It is interesting to note that the word Chiaroscuro is derived from the Italian terms *Chiaro* ('Light' or 'Bright') and *Oscuro* ('Dark' or 'Shade') and reveals the modelling of forms through the use of light and shadow. Furthermore it is well to remember that though the technique of Chiaroscuro had been discovered by the Greek painters in the Hellenistic age and was also used by the Roman painters, it was forgotten during the dark middle ages. Indeed there is an historical appropriateness in the fact that the technique of Chiaroscuro was rediscovered during the Renaissance. And just as Leonardo had anticipated the wave-nature of Sound in his Notebooks, his studied emphasis on the technique of Chiaroscuro inspired Rembrandt's Night

Watch. Incidentally, it is not generally realized that Rembrandt had actually intended to highlight a scene in the late afternoon. In fact, when the painting was cleaned in the mid-forties, it became clear that its nocturnal effect was due to the darkening of the layers of varnish that had been applied over the paint. It is certainly a tribute to Rembrandt's expertise in the application of the technique of Chiaroscuro that the painting had darkened to such an extent that it is difficult to determine whether the scene had taken place during the day or night! For this great painting, which can be described as a Chiaroscuro in a Chiaroscuro, is a tribute to Leonardo da Vinci and Caravaggio. Small wonder that the great mathematician-philosopher Prof. A.N. Whitehead argued in his *Science and the Modern World*[8] that Leonardo da Vinci's emphasis on "the patient observational habits of the naturalistic artists" as well as the Leonardo contribution to "the practice of physics" had contributed to the scientific imagination of the modern world.

Leonardo's *Treatise on Painting* is relevant to the contemporary artistic scene even today. For Leonardo flourished in an era which was not familiar with the well-known scientific fact that red, green and blue are the primary colours which can additively produce any shade between red and violet in the visible spectrum. Furthermore this idea is imaginatively used in modern colour technology. Yet it is truly remarkable that Leonardo had an intuitive understanding of this scientific fact. Actually Leonardo da Vinci argued that "Green and blue are invariably accentuated in the half-shadows, yellow and red and white in the highlights." And the argument relating to the primary colours in Leonardo's *Treatise on Painting* to the modern theory – derived from 'The Three Colour Principle' – which forms the basis of the commercial exploitation of the physics of colours in the areas of colour photography as well as colour television of the modern colour television industry.

Johann Wolfgang von Goethe, the great German poet and author of the classic *Faust* is also known for his scientific studies ranging across *The Theory of Colour Comparative Anatomy and Plant Morphology*. Actually he is renowned for his pioneering contribution as the earliest historian of science. However, his work on *The Theory of Colour* is not only controversial but also unconvincing on three counts. First, Goethe proceeded on the assumption that the mathematical principles underlying Newton's experiment with the prism had clashed with his belief that the human organism is the best instrument for studying nature. Naturally Goethe tried to argue that Newton was wrong in demonstrating that coloured lights could be combined to form white light. Again, arguing in this strain, Goethe rejected Newton's scientifically acceptable theory that light rays themselves are not coloured but that the sensation of colour is registered in the brain. For Goethe rejected not only the well-known Newtonian principle that coloured lights could be combined to form white light but also suggested (without adducing any evidence) that all coloured lights were mixtures of light and darkness.

Second, Goethe maintained that *The Theory of Colour* as he viewed it,[9] "has been hurt and greatly hindered in its progress by being lumped with the area of optics dependent on geometry. It may, in fact, be considered entirely separate from geometry". In fact, Goethe also argued[10] that "another problem arose because a fine mathematician [the reference is to Newton] had adopted a completely false concept of the physical origin of colour; his great accomplishments as a geometrician long served to sanction his scientific error in a world ruled by constant prejudice." For, according to Goethe, "light is one and indivisible"— a phenomenon which cannot be interpreted by any theory of particles! And Goethe observed: "No group with aristocratic pretentions has ever looked down on outsiders with such insufferable arrogance as the Newtonian school has shown from the beginning in dismissing everything accomplished before its founding and beyond its confines". Surely this Goethe observation is not convincing. And, as Bertrand Russell wrote wittily in *An Outline of Philosophy*: "Physics is mathematical not because we know so much about the physical world, but because we know so little: it is only its mathematical properties that we can discover!"

Finally, Goethe commented that Newton's *Opticks* could be "compared to an old castle originally laid out by the builder with youthful impetuosity and later expanded and furnished as required by time and circumstance. It was then gradually fortified and secured against strife and enemy attack." Indeed, Sir Isaac Newton cannot be disposed of that easily. Here are two Queries from Newton's work on *Opticks* which had been published in 1704: "Do not Bodies act upon Light at a distance, and by their action bend its Rays?" and "Are not gross Bodies and Light convertible into one another?" These Queries clearly reveal that Newton was conjecturing the gravitational bending of light and the equivalence of mass and energy – which are the main consequences of the General and Special Theories of Relativity – and which were formulated by Einstein two centuries or so after the death of Newton. And in the ultimate analysis, Goethe's *Theory of Colour* – based on his reflections on colours and colour perception, more subjective than scientifically convincing – can at best be viewed as a spectrum of individualistic responses to Newton's *Theory of Light* in the history of ideas.

In the "History of Science", observed Professor C.V. Raman in his 1930 Nobel Lecture,[11] "we often find that the study of some natural phenomenon has been the starting point in the development of a new branch of knowledge". Indeed Lord Rayleigh's observations concerning the colour of the sky and their experimental verification by Cabannes, as well as Raman's experiments and theoretical formulations on the colour of the sea are not only two major essays in the borderland between Optics and Aesthetics, but also reinforce the Raman thesis that the study of natural phenomena constitute the starting points in the development of new branches of knowledge.

Lord Rayleigh had calculated the number of molecules in a unit of volume in air, while enjoying the scenery of Mount Everest from the terrace of his hotel, in 1899. Again, while viewing the dimness of this towering Himalayan mountain's outline, Rayleigh concluded that an appreciable part of its light was scattered away. He found that the scattered light was conspicuously blue as a result of the radiation which varied with the fourth power of the frequency. For he noted that the higher frequencies were re-emitted even more powerfully than the lower ones. This piece of mathematical reasoning enabled Rayleigh to determine the scattering power of each molecule from the refractive index of air. Furthermore, it led to the result that the number of air molecules per cubic centimeter at sea level were 3×10^{19} – a result which was experimentally confirmed by Cabannes. In fact the work of Rayleigh and Cabannes had provided not only the theoretical and experimental framework for the blue colour of the sky but also established the fact the air molecules were non-spherical in the wake of a depolarization effect. At the other end of the spectrum, it is well to remember that Raman had climbed the Dodabetta in the Nilgiris to measure the depolarization of the light scattered by the sky. And Raman attributed[12] the residual depolarization to the anisotropic (possessing different physical properties in different directions) nature of the air molecules.

The validity of the subsequent Rayleigh theory that "the much-admired dark blue of the deep sea is simply the blue of the sky seen by reflection"[13] was questioned by Raman while voyaging through the Mediterranean and Red Seas in 1921. In fact, even on board the ship Raman felt that the Einstein-Smoluchowski concept of thermodynamic fluctuations – which was developed to explain special optical phenomena near the critical point – could be extended to explain molecular diffraction in liquids. It was this characteristic intuitive flash that explains the memorability of the Raman paper on the colour of the Mediterranean Sea. Actually, in the wake of quenching the surface reflection of the sky in the sea through a polarising Nicol Prism at the Brewesterian angle, Raman observed that the colour of the sea was not only impoverished but actually spectacularly improved. It was clear therefore that the blue Opalescence of the Mediterranean Sea was due to the scattering of the sunlight by the molecules of the water.

The visual impact of the blue of the Mediterranean Sea on Professor Raman's scientific imagination led on to the 1922 Royal Society Paper 'On the Molecular Scattering of Light in Water and the Colour of the Sea'.[14] Actually, the theory underlying this discovery is based on the fact that the variations of density owing to molecular vibrations or fluctuations alter the refractive index of the fluid and thus result in the scattering of Light. Raman demonstrated that water at thirty degrees centigrade ought to scatter light 160 times as intensely as dust-free air under normal conditions. He arrived at the result that 50-metre deep water appeared as blue as the

Zenith Sky if the absorption of water is not considered. At this point Raman applied a correction for absorption by working out a satisfying agreement between theory and observation. And in his concluding remarks, he wrote that "a sufficiently deep layer of pure water exhibits by molecular scattering a deep blue colour more saturated than skylight and of comparable intensity. The colour is primarily due to diffraction, the absorption only making it of a fuller hue."

This celebrated paper on the colour of the Mediterranean Sea resulted in the discovery named after him – which is known as the Raman Effect. Indeed, commenting on the Raman Effect which was discovered in 1928, Albert Einstein observed that "C.V. Raman was the first to recognize and demonstrate that the energy of the photon can undergo a partial transformation within matter." Again, the paper on the Mediterranean Sea is also as much a fundamental contribution to Optics as it is to Visual Aesthetics. For the Raman paper recalls an aesthetic sensibility that one can still experience while reading Galileo Galilei's *Starry Messenger* which recorded the first Galilean sight of the night sky through a telescope. And viewed in retrospect, it is interesting to note that Raman had transformed the sky at Dodabetta in the Nilgiris and the Sea (while voyaging through the Mediterranean Sea) into laboratories!

It is well-known that Professor Raman devoted an important phase of his career to an understanding of colour phenomena. In fact, he was concerned with the fundamental importance of colour in several scientific disciplines. Here it is interesting to recall Raman's 'sight-seeing' at Mount Wilson Observatory in 1924. And commenting on the account relating to Professor Raman's 'sight-seeing' at Mount Wilson Observatory, Professor S. Ramaseshan observed:[15] "During a visit to California (in 1924) Raman viewed the nebulae through the 60-inch and 100-inch telescopes of Mount Wilson Observatory near Pasadena. He recounted vividly that the Right nebula Lyra exhibited flaming colours changing progressively from the external edge of its ring to its inner margin while the great nebula in Orion was a blazing area of variegated colour determined by the line emission of gases of which it is composed." Obviously Raman's 'sight-seeing' was rewarding during the two nights at Mount Wilson Observatory. For he was able to view the Orion and Ring Nebulae closely despite the fact that the two nebulae are more than 180 degrees apart on the sky. And in his essay on "A Celebration of Colour in Astronomy" Dr. David Malin of the Anglo-Australian Observatory in Sydney, Australia remarks[16] that the Raman 'sight-seeing'[17] at Mount Wilson Observatory "is the only account I know of where the colours of astronomical objects are so vividly described."

Just as Professor Niels Bohr formulated his principle of complementarity in the wider perspectives of physics and philosophy, Professor C.V. Raman related the perception of colour in some areas of physics and astronomy to a holistic perception which included the application of the Quantum Theory of Light to Physiology and human consciousness in its sweep. For Raman's intellectual heroes were Leonardo da Vinci and Herman von Helmholtz. Indeed, the similarities are truly striking. In fact, Niels Bohr worked out a philosophical framework for the theory of Complementarity in order to discover the "great inter-relationships between all areas of knowledge." Actually Bohr had propounded the philosophy of *The Unity of Human Knowledge,*[18] with special reference to the basic areas of Classical Physics, Quantum Physics, Physiology, Philosophy and Schroedinger's work on the substance of life (1960). In fact, his aim was to "promote mutual understanding between nations with very different cultural backgrounds." Actually, Bohr had already presented to different audiences his holistic perceptions, such as "Causality and Complementarity" at the Second International Congress for the Unity of Science, Copenhagen, 1936, "Biology and Atomic Physics" at the International Congress for Physics and Biology, Copenhagen, 1937, and "Natural Philosophy and Human Culture" at the International Congress for Anthropology and Ethnology, Copenhagen, 1938. And interestingly enough, Professor C.V. Raman had cut across the differences between the classical description and the quantum description of physical phenomena in a philosophical sense in an essay, "The Molecular Diffraction of Light",[19] which was published as early as 1922.

Raman's holistic perception of colour has an epic grandeur which is similar to Bohr's philosophy of Complementarity. In the words of Professor Raman, the inter-disciplinary questions derived from the perception of colour "touch the two great fields of exact knowledge and a third field of which at present we have only glimpses. The first field is physics and what it has to tell us about the nature of light, its properties and behaviour. The second is physiology, which concerns itself with the structure and functioning of the sense-organs, such as our eyes, and their connections with the cerebral centres. The third field of knowledge lies where mind and matter meet and we seek to penetrate the mystery of human consciousness and its awareness of the external world. And it is by bringing the physical and physiological aspects of our problem simultaneously into focus that one can hope to find satisfactory answers on the material plane to the questions which interest us."

It is well to remember that Raman had arrived at his holistic perception of colour during the pre-computer era of modern science. In a sense, Raman's argument was continued by Roger Penrose in his recent publication *The Emperor's New Mind: Concerning Computers, Minds and the Laws of Physics.*[20] In fact, Professor Penrose's work is a piece of writing woven together through an entertaining and extensive commentary which affords a visionary glimpse of the possible connections between the mathematical universe of twentieth century physics and the world of consciousness. Indeed, Professor Penrose links his vision of a new theory of physics with the phenomenon of consciousness in the new areas of psychology and neurophysiology.

Actually, his assertion that Quantum Gravity must be time-asymmetric is startling. For it may be difficult for the physicists, who believe that Quantum Physics and Relativity are time-symmetrical in a setting where their equations work equally well whether they run forward or in reverse, to accept the Penrose viewpoint that time will flow from the past toward the future and not in reverse. And the distinction of this work lies in Professor Penrose's ability — despite some disagreements on certain issues — to arrive at a new holistic perception derived from a variety of disciplines such as Cosmology, Relativistic Dynamics, Neurophysiology and Mathematical Logic.

At this point, it is necessary to refer to Query 28 of his historic publication *Opticks* in which Sir Isaac Newton rejected the wave theory of light. Here the controversy centering round the Wave and Corpuscular Theories of Light is not important. What is important, however, is Newton's inspired use of the metaphor in physics. Indeed, in his 1672 paper on light and colour, which was published in the *Philosophical Transactions of the Royal Society*, Newton described his famous experiment with a prism. In fact, Newton darkened his chamber and allowed a ray of sunlight to enter a prism, enabling it to spread out into the the colours on the opposite wall. Actually, this experiment with a prism formed the basis of Newton's explanation of this phenomenon in terms of a theory of Light. Similarly Maxwell's mechanical model for a mathematical conceptualization of electricity and magnetism, including the ether, was obviously a piece of fiction. However, it helped Maxwell to work out the correct equations. And Professor Chandrasekhar's visualization of the phenomenon of Alice crossing the 'event horizon' in Lewis Carroll's *Through the Looking Glass* — as illustrated in the well-known Chandrasekhar paper "How One May Explore the Physical Content of the General Theory of Relativity" — is yet another inspired use of the metaphor in physics. Professor Chandrasekhar argues[21] that the solutions (worked out by S. Chandrasekhar and Basilis Xanthopoulos) for both the Einstein vacuum and the Einstein-Maxwell equations had upset the then held conventional belief that the collision of waves would lead on to the development of curvature singularities. Indeed, in Professor Chandrasekhar's words,[22] "One found instead that event horizons formed; and a further domain which included hyperbolic arc-like singularities reminiscent of the Kerr and the Kerr-Newman black holes." Actually this situation is conceptualized in a delightfully different context by Lewis Carroll (the pen-name of the nineteenth-century Oxford mathematician Charles Lutwidge Dodgson) in his celebrated work *Through the Looking Glass* which is meant for children. In fact, Professor Chandrasekhar creates an ambience, at once mathematical and literary, which suggests Alice's intimations of Space-Time *Through the Looking Glass*: "It (the passage through the Looking Glass House) is like our passage as far as you can see, only you know it may be quite different on beyond".

Among the most remarkable features of Einstein's General Theory of Relativity is its vitality. For the consequences of the General Theory can be glimpsed in a number of disciplines ranging from literary criticism and aesthetics to the astrophysics of black holes, colliding gravitational waves and the non-radial oscillation of stars. For example, Professor Whitehead states in his *Science and the Modern World* that the great Greek tragedians Aeschylus, Sophocles and Euripides are the pilgrim fathers of the modern scientific imagination. Indeed, in a celebrated argument, Professor Whitehead recreates the dramatic significance in the very staging of that historic meeting of the Royal Society which enabled him to witness the Eddington verification of the General Theory of Relativity in a Newtonian ambience. For, he explains that the essence of dramatic tragedy is not unhappiness, but that remorseless inevitableness that pervades scientific thought.

Commenting on Professor Heisenberg's aesthetic criterion that "Beauty is the proper conformity of the parts to one another and to the whole", Professor Chandrasekhar says[23] that it is complementary to the aesthetic criterion of Francis Bacon: "There is excellent beauty that hath not some strangeness in its proportion." Chandrasekhar argues that the General Theory of Relativity has some strangeness in the Bacon-Heisenberg sense. For "It consists primarily, in relating, in juxtaposition, two fundamental concepts which had, till then been considered as entirely independent; the concepts of space and time on the one hand, and the concepts of matter and motion on the other." Thus, "in the fusion of gravity and metric that followed, Einstein accomplished in 1915 what Reinmann had prophesied in 1854, namely, the metric field must be causally connected with matter and its motion." And Chandrasekhar concludes that the "greatest strangeness in the proportion consists in our altered view of space-time."

In his discourse[24] "The Role of General Relativity and Astronomy: Retrospect and Prospect", Professor S. Chandrasekhar remarked that "the General Theory of Relativity is a theory of gravitation . . . and its natural home is in astronomy in the sense that its manifestations, whatever they may be, must be in the realm of astronomy." Again, no astrophysicist has made a greater contribution in propelling General Relativity to its 'natural home' in astronomy. Furthermore, just as Professor Whitehead had introduced a literary criterion to explain one of the consequences of the General Theory of Relativity as a contribution to the shaping of the concept of tragedy, Chandrasekhar has made use of the Bacon-Heisenberg aesthetic criteria in understanding the beauty of the framework of General Relativity. And in extending this argument, Chandrasekhar presents a bifocal view of the landscapes of Einstein's General Relativity and Monet's impressionistic paintings.

Professor Chandrasekhar has adorned Einstein's "Natural home" — which is astronomy — with the landscapes of Relativistic Astrophysics and Monet's Impressionistic Paintings. Actually the landscapes of General Relativity based on some mathematical structures, such as Chandrasekhar's mathematical theory of black holes, the Chandrasekhar-Xanthopoulos field equations relating to the collision of impulsive gravitational waves and electromagnetic shock waves and the Subrahmanyan-Chandrasekhar-Valeria Ferari work on the non-radial oscillation of stars can be interpreted as an interplay of entropy, geometry and gravity. Similarly, Monet's Series Paintings can be interpreted as an interplay of light, colour and aesthetics. Also, these paintings which range across the shimmering colours of the Haystacks, the beautiful patterns of the Poplars and the effects of Sunlight on the Foliage and Water, during the early morning at Argentueil near the Seine have been rightly described as the "Sistine Chapels of Impressionism". For these permutations and combinations of contoured beauty create different illusions of three-dimensional shapes in which the Haystacks, the Poplars, and the River Seine , can move, as it were, at different wave-lengths of aesthetic perception, thus reminding us of the art of Michelangelo in an Impressionistic world. And it is clear that just as matter implies gravity in a Relativistic setting, Chandrasekhar's bifocal view of the landscapes of Relativity and Monet's Impressionism reinforces the well-known scientific criterion that negative entropy implies creativity, scientifically as well as aesthetically.

Ananda Coomaraswamy's theory of painting understood historically Leonardo da Vinci's Holistic Theory of colour, interpreted artistically Newton's *Opticks*, viewed mathematically Professor Raman's holistic perception of colour, understood aesthetically Professor Bohr's holistic theory of Complementarity also known as the Copenhagen Interpretation of Quantum Mechanics, viewed philosophically Professor Penrose's holistic theory of physics, psychology and Neurophysiology, visualized mathematically Professor Chandrasekhar's bifocal view of the landscapes of Relativistic Astrophysics and Monet's Impressionistic paintings and, interpreted artistically, constitute a part of what Professor Robert Oppenheimer[25] termed as "the life of the human spirit". Indeed, according to Professor Robert Oppenheimer,[26] "An understanding of the complementary nature of conscious life and its physical interpretation appears to me a lasting element in human understanding and a proper formulation of the historic views called psychophysical parallelism . . . The wealth and variety of physics itself, the greater wealth and a variety of natural sciences taken as a whole, the more familiar, yet still strange and far wider wealth of the life of the human spirit, enriched by complementary, not-at-once compatible ways, irreducible one to the other, have a greater harmony".

No account of the interaction of colour with the elements – which explains how the varied colours in Nature arise from the diverse responses of the electrons in Matter to the different wavelengths of the incident light – will be complete without an assessment of Professor Gell-Mann's contribution to the physics of elementary particles.

While reflecting on a theoretical framework into which the newly created particles could be arranged, Gell-Mann discovered that most of the particles could be classified as families or multiplets, which revealed geometrical patterns that were reminiscent of Lie groups. For these patterns had been originally worked out by a brilliant Norwegian mathematician Sophus Lie. Again when the Lie reasoning was applied to Particle Physics, it resulted in a new sophisticated theory which could explain not only the properties of the particles in the multiplets, but also predict the existence of new ones a la Mendeleev. Interestingly enough, Gell-Mann termed this theory 'the eightfold way' (named after the eight attributes of the Buddhist philosophical system) owing to the fact that some particles were grouped into families having eight members. This theory, also known as SU (3) Symmetry was independently formulated by an Israeli physicist Yuval Ne' Eman. More importantly, Gell-Mann's theory has been rightly compared with Dmitry Mendeleev's celebrated classification of the Periodic Table of the Elements. And while arriving at this grouping, Gell-Mann defined a new concept known as the strangeness quantum number, S, which is linked with the multiplet charge.

Just as the Russian chemist Mendeleev had predicted the specific properties of the elements which would fill those gaps left by him in his Periodic Table, Gell-Mann predicted the properties of those particles which occupied those empty and pre-determined spaces in his classification. In fact, Gell-Mann's theory was partly confirmed in the wake of the 1964 discovery of the Omega-Minus particle which had been predicted by him. Furthermore, Gell-Mann discovered that his theory could be explained by assuming that every strong interacting particle is derived from a triplet of particles, each possessing a fraction of a proton's electric charge. Incidentally, the same discovery was made by an American physicist George Zweig at CERN – The European High-energy Centre of Physics near Geneva. Indeed it is the SU (3) theory which inspired Gell-Mann to visualize the existence of three entities out of which all the other particles could be constructed which he termed Quarks (the literary inspiration for naming these abstract mathematical concepts could be traced to James Joyce's novel *Finnegan's Wake*: "Three quarks for Muster Mark!"

As Heisenberg explained,[27] "the conception of the objective reality of the elementary particles has thus evaporated in a curious way, not into the fog of some new, obscure, or not yet understood reality concept, but into the transparent clarity of a mathematics that represents no longer the behaviour of the elementary particles but rather our knowledge of this behaviour." For we encounter a world where the atomic quantum states have uniquely predetermined specific shapes and frequencies. Again, in order to grapple with certain statistical problems at the microscopic level, Gell-Mann had visualized colour as an 'internal', not observable, which is the famous Quantum Number in elementary particle physics. Furthermore, these hypothetically conceived fractionally charged quarks are found in six flavours — the up, down, strange, charm, top and bottom quarks — any one of which can be in one of the three colour states.

Although quarks have colour as an attribute, the physically observed particles (the baryons which are derived from three quarks and mesons based on a quark-antiquark pair) are regarded as colourless. And this concept of colour confinement has inspired a new discipline known as Quantum Chromo Dynamics which is based on abstract mathematics and indirect experimental evidence. Here one is reminded of the ancient Pythagorean idea of a "pre-established harmony". As is well-known, the Pythagorean view of the "harmony of the spheres" was based on the inherent symmetry of the celestial world of the distinguished from the terrestrial, made no sense in the Newtonian setting. However, the Pythagorean ambience of the "harmony of the spheres" can be understood in the context of Gell-Mann's use of Quantum Numbers for the representation of quantum states. Indeed every hydrogen atom in the world strikes the same 'chord' (to use a Pythagorean expression) as visualized in the Balmer formula of spectral terms. In fact the Pythagorean "harmony of the spheres" undergoes a transformation as a vibration phenomenon of confined electron waves in modern particle physics. For the spectrum of frequencies of an atom reflects a typical set of values or rather the characteristic 'chord' of the atom, contributing to the re-emergence of "the harmony of the spheres" in the world of atomic physics. In fine, the ancient Pythagorean "harmony of the spheres" can be rediscovered, as it were, in the electron orbits of the atom which have triggered off the new Gell-Mann world of Quantum Chromo Dynamics.

Notes

1. C.V. Raman, *Why is the Sky Blue?* Lecture Community Service Centre, Ahmedabad (December 22, 1968).
2. Werner Heisenberg, *The Representation of Nature in Contemporary Physics,* Daedalus (1958).
3. N. Bloembergen, *Reflections on Light*, Raman Research Institute, Bangalore - 80 (1979).
4. S. Chandrasekhar, *The Series Paintings of Claude Monet and the Landscape of General Relativity*, Address delivered at the Dedication Ceremonies of the Inter-University Centre for Astronomy and Astrophysics, Pune (December 28, 1992).
5. Ananda Coomaraswamy, *The Technique and Theory of Indian Painting*, *Technical Studies*, Vol. III, No. 2, Fogg Art Museum, Harvard University, U.S.A. (October 1934), pp. 83, 88, 89.
6. C.V. Raman, *The Physiology of Vision*, The Indian Academy of Sciences, Bangalore (1968).
7. J.P. Richter, *The Literary Works of Leonardo da Vinci*, Oxford (1939).
8. A.N. Whitehead, *Science and the Modern World*, Mentor (1956).

9. Douglas Miller (ed. and tr.), *Goethe: Scientific Studies – Theory of Colour*, Part V, Suhrkamp Publishers, New York (1988) p. 272.
10. *Ibid.*
11. C.V. Raman, *Nobel Lecture* (1930).
12. C.V. Raman, "Anisotropy of Molecules", In *Nature*, London (1922).
13. C.V. Raman, "The Colour of the Sea", In *Nature*, London (1921).
14. C.V. Raman, *On the Molecular Scattering of Light in Water and the Colour of the Sea*, Proceedings of the Royal Society, London (1922).
15. S. Ramaseshan, "Introduction", to the Scientific Papers of Prof. C.V. Raman, In *Colours and their Perception*, Vol. VI, Indian Academy of Sciences, Bangalore, (1988).
16. David Malin, "A Celebration of Colour in Astronomy", In *Current Science*, Bangalore, Vol. 60, No. 1 (1991).
17. C.V. Raman, *The New Physics*, Philosophical Library, New York (1951).
18. Niels Bohr, *The Unity of Human Knowledge and Essays 1958-72 on Atomic Physics*, John Wiley, New York (1963).
19. C.V. Raman, *The Molecular Diffraction of Light*, Calcutta University Press (1922).
20. Roger Penrose, *The Emperor's New Mind: Concerning Computers, Minds and the Laws of Physics*, Vintage, London (1990).
21. S. Chandrasekhar, *How one may Explore the Physical Content of the General Theory of Relativity*, Proceedings of the Yale Symposium in Honour of the 150th anniversary of the Birth of J. Willard Gibbs, The American Mathematical Society and the American Physical Society, (1990), pp. 227-51.
22. *Ibid.*
23. S. Chandrasekhar, *Beauty and the Quest for Beauty in Science* (July 1979).
24. *The Role of General Relativity and Astronomy: Retrospect and Prospect*, Invited Discourse at the Seventeenth General Assembly of the International Astronomical Union, Montreal, Canada, *J. Astrophys. Astr* (1980) 1, pp. 33-45.
25. J. Robert Oppenheimer, *Science and the Common Understanding*, Simon and Schuster (1953) pp. 80-82.
26. *Ibid.*
27. Werner Heisenberg, *The Representation of Nature in Contemporary Physics*, Daedalus, (1958).

4

Holistic Science and Consciousness

S. C. Malik

Today, in science the basic oneness of the universe is clear. It has given rise to many unified field theories (such as symmetry, gauge symmetry, and supersymmtery, gravity and supergravity, strings and superstrings), suggesting that the constituents of matter are interconnected, interrelated and interdependent. The basic phenomenon may be understood not in terms of any isolated entities, but only as integrated parts of the whole. For example, space-time and energy are seen to be inseparable aspects of a single reality, as are energy and matter, wave and particle. Without going into each theory, and not being competent to do so, one may yet say that the physical universe is proving to be a seamless texture of inseparable events and entities, organised in accordance with a universal principle that specifies itself in innumerable forms. These may then be deduced from it, once it has been discovered. Moreover, coherence, elegance, and symmetry, the criteria of beauty and truth sought by the mathematician and the theoretical physicist, seem now to be within the reach even of the experimentalist (Gandhi:1990).

Physical sciences refer to certain well-known unifying theories in terms of processes that are mathematically describable by linear (and thus soluble) equations. But other, even more extraordinary, testimony to wholeness comes from a new quarter: the investigation of complex dynamic systems (or turbulence), which require for their description non-linear equations. This has given rise to a new department of science embracing mathematics, physics, and numerous fields — what has become known as the science of Chaos (Gleick:1987, Prigogine: 1980,1984). New mathematical revelations have demonstrated in quite unexpected fashion that chaos is simply a superficial mask of the most intricate and entrancing forms of order and pattern, and that its occurrence in nature is determined mathematically. These revelations have been made in the course of new developments in the study of complex systems. In other words, the most important contribution of chaos, in seeking the whole, the overall structure, is to end the reductionist programme in science.

The world picture implied in the theories outlined above is one of a single unbroken whole, governed by a principle of organisation universal to a self-generating system. It specifies itself in a scale, a series of forces and entities, ranging from the simplest to the most complex and opening the way to further development on a higher level of organic wholeness. Thus at the microlevel, there is a continuous scale of 'complexification' from space-time to those forms transitional between the inorganic and the organic. It is a dialectic scale of opposing, yet overlapping, specific forms, which differentially exemplify a single universal principle of order in continuously increasing degrees of complexity and integral wholeness. But this is only half the picture, which is paralleled by the other half — the macrocosm of the expanding universe, of stars and galaxies which apparently stands in contrast to the microcosmic level. But the two scales are complementary to each other, inseparable and indispensably linked to each other forming one systematically integrated totality. In its absence, there would be no planets like the earth, no life, no biosphere, and no observers. In short, the microscopic sequence from hydrogen atoms to macromolecules depends intimately upon the macrocosmic sequence of stellar evolution — ranging in scale from planets, stars, galaxies, galactic clusters, continuous right up to the final hypersphere. Space-time continuum itself is created by the pervasive activity of energy and its complimentary matter waves.

Obviously, this physical base is intrinsic and has indispensable characteristics to the existence and support of living beings, intelligent creatures capable of observation and reflection; thinkers able to ask questions about themselves and their environment, and so on. We are aware that we do exist here and now, and are apprised of this fact by our awareness. There is no astonishment to hear this necessary interconnectedness; it is not that because we exist and observe the universe that it exists, but because it is so that we observe it and we can exist (Bohm:1980). What is of significance, not philosophically or otherwise, that physicists are discovering principles determining the structure of the universe to be so finely tuned, and the relations between its parts so minutely adjusted to one another that the emergence of intelligent life is incompatible with any other possible arrangement of things and events. Were we to find that the universe could not have been other than it is, and that its being so inseparably bound up with the emergence and evolution of life forms, that would be of the most profound importance (*Fig.* 4.1).

The recent enunciation by physicists of the Anthropic Cosmological Principle marks a new revolution in the scientific outlook (Harris:1991). The principle states that intelligent life, its existence and observation of its surrounding universe, is essentially involved in what it discovers. This principle has immense philosophical implications, says Harris, as he traces it continuously through physics, biology and psychology. In short, intelligent life is necessarily involved from the very beginning of physical reality and that the entire process of natural evolution comes to consciousness of itself in the human mind. This is what Lester Smith (1975) also stated in his book – as part of the theosophical society's theme.

The wholeness of the universe is indicated by the intricate and intimate interdependence of physical and biological facts (e.g., the integral unity of the biosphere), which is widely acknowledged today. New evidence of holism also has been disclosed by the study of turbulence and the development of fractal geometry. A contemporary concept of the universe therefore requires a logico-metaphysical theory of wholes. Harris has also thrown light on the argument for God from the fact of the design, which indicates philosophical implications also of current scientific work (*Fig.* 4.2).[2]

What is important in current scientific thinking is that there is an intelligent observer watching the universe – the scientist. The reason simply is that so far scientists had considered themselves outside the painting; that their observations impinged on the physical world without interfering with it – that it was an automation that ran according to its own intrinsic laws, without relation to observers. This is the inheritance passed down from the Copernican revolution at the time of the Renaissance and its consolidation in the Newtonian system of celestial and terrestrial mechanics. Ancient or traditional thinkers considered the universe to contain human beings, and the cosmos to be a living organism with an all-pervasive soul – the human souls being individual participants. Modern thinking removed the earth and man from the centre of the universe which was now a machine, no doubt created by God but free of any divine nature, that worked independently of the human mind. Mind and body, Descartes decided, belonged to two separate substances, which had nothing in common except their creator, God. In these circumstances it would indeed have been surprising if human being found the physical world to be such as to provide the conditions necessary for the existence within it of minds. Of intelligent observers – their existence and consciousness – were thus an impenetrable mystery unable to explain their own awareness. These were the metaphysical presuppositions of science in the seventeenth and succeeding centuries. Of course, in the mid-nineteenth century, Darwin's theory of evolution changed all this, since human beings were now considered to have evolved from non-human beings or non-living matter. A bridge between matter and mind began to be conceived albeit still in terms of chance variation and natural selection.

But it was only in the twentieth century that a revolution in physics has changed all this. The universe is no longer conceived as a machine. Life can now be more easily understood as a development continuous with the non-living. The world so observed provides the conditions for the emergence of intelligent beings. Were there no Intelligence in the universe, there would be neither observers nor scientists to pronounce their theories nor any who might question their validity. In short, we exist because the universe is the way we observe it to be, and we could not observe it otherwise. What we observe is conditioned not only by the fact of our existence, but also by the nature and capacities of our perceptive and intellectual faculties. Thus, observations reveal our own nature, more about the authors than about the subject-matter. This is selective effect, even in scientific matters that needs to be kept in mind, i.e., the limitations of the apparatus – human or otherwise.

It is well to remember that one cannot by any conceivable means transcend one's own perceptual and intellectual capacities. This suggests a subjectivism for which there is no remedy, and we cannot know true knowledge even of the physical world. But this leads to an epistemological disaster, and solipsism is all too imminent. Solipsism is however contradictory, for it asserts the existence of a self alone. But this has meaning only through a distinction from an other. In splendid isolation, therefore, no self can exist – not even God who would be neither infinite nor omnipotent without his creation of the universe (*Fig*. 4.3).[2]

If Quantum theory and Relativity undermined the classical dichotomy, it was because they involved the observer inextricably with what was observed. There is no absolute frame of reference, and the observer was a fundamental factor, affecting every measurement whether of space or of time. But observers are human beings, and human beings are animals organisms, evolved from other species under influence of environmental pressures. This is to say that the conditions of human evolution are contained in the physical world, the nature of which is known to us only through human observation itself. Science now talks of the wholeness of the universe, in which human and all other life is included, dependent on the fundamental physical constants of nature. This interrelatedness has resulted in the pronouncement of the Anthropic Principle in which the unity of the universe is a basic feature – this wholeness (Harris: *Ibid*).

Wholeness

When one says that anything is a whole, it implies that one is not speaking of mere congeries of disconnected and separable items, or even just a loose collection. It also implies that it is a unity of coherent parts. Every whole is made up of differences that are combined within it to constitute one totality. A purely blank unity is virtually impossible to conceive. Even the simplest of wholes, therefore is a unity of differences which in some discernible way intermesh, interlock and interrelate systematically. In brief, there is essentially an ordering principle universally determining the interrelations of the elements so that it determines likewise their intrinsic natures, for each must be adapted and adjusted to its neighbours, although they must inevitably differ from one another to avoid complete coincidence.

Of course, within the whole the elements contrast with each other, and therefore inevitably lead to internal conflict and provisional disunity. Naturally, finite elements tends to shun one another, emphasizing their respective exclusiveness in order to maintain their self-identities. Consequently, this conflict leads to relative chaos and contingency. This is soon overcome, and unity re-established, only when identity in and through differences is acknowledged. Nevertheless, each identity is defined by the mutual relations and differences, and they are inseparable from one another owing to their mutual implications. This overlap despite difference is what effects their integration into a single whole.

Thus, overlap together with integration of opposites in a wider whole involves self-enfoldment, because the wider whole includes the more fragmentary parts, each implying the other in its own self-maintenance. For example, in a growing embryo, the mutual implication of successive stages is more apparent, as is its explicit realization in subsequent phases of development, and the self-enfoldment of the earlier forms and processes to create emerging complexifications is unmistakable. Segmentation of primitive cells continues at the stage of specialization and functional differentiation, which again is repeated and internalised in each limb and organ. What ensues is a continuous succession of provisional realisations of the organising principle — in this case the mature organism for the embryo — in a series of wholes increasing in complexity and integration. In other words, elements are double-edged, in at once excluding each other in mutual opposition, and also being complementary to each other in mutual determination and dependence for their several identities. In each, the other is implicit, representing the wholeness principle in a comprehensive way. Such a system is 'open' and cannot thus be present in any one instant or at any one point. It is not a static but dynamic principle — forbidding both isolation and repetition in abstract manner. The finite element drives itself to transcend its own limits in order to persist in its own being (*Fig*. 4.4).[3]

Thus the dynamic organising principle of wholeness, inorganic or organic, is operative and directive throughout the hierarchy of forms and phases, impelling its partial elements and rudimentary phases towards completion and fulfilment. In this way it leads to the emergence in intelligent behaviour and interpretative understanding, which is the activity of awareness. It is this self-awareness which is reflected in thinking processes, and the ability to comprehend the whole as a cognitive state of coherent experiencing. In short, both ontology and teleology — dialectics and holism — are necessarily inseparable concepts.

Traditionally teleology referred to some final end. Today, however, because of the ordering principle of an organised whole, teleological explanation is one in which the parts are seen in terms of the whole and not *vice versa*. It is opposite of reductionism, requiring conscious intention and deliberate choice towards and completion and fulfilment towards a whole. Thus purposive action, described as action by design, is revealed as the endeavour to complete a whole and to bring it to fulfilment. Processes below the level of human purpose, however, may well be teleological without involving any consciousness, but are determined nevertheless by the ordering principle of wholeness, towards intelligent self-awareness. The Universe is designed with the goal of generating intelligent observers, leading logically beyond to some supra-personality. This now is exemplified and seen in the relationships between the parts, between energy and matter, between the inorganic and the organic, between body and mind (Harris:*op.cit.*).

The unity of the universe and the exact nature of the organising principle that governs its order and structure are clearly not indifferent to the emergence and the existence of life and mind. Of all this, nothing is brought home to us than our ability to discover it. It is not because we are here that the world comes to be so disposed, but rather the opposite. In other words, it is because the world is thus ordered, because the terrestrial environment is so precisely suited to the emergence of life and the development of a biosphere, that human beings have evolved and we are able to investigate the conditions of our own being. Our observation and reflection are not the efficient causes of what they reveal to us although, perhaps, they may well be its final cause.

The unity of the physical world seems, as it were, to focus itself on the implication of this intrinsic order from the very start. The point to note is the concurrence and convergence of conditions for intelligent life within a coherent system. Of course, its explanation may be attributed to a divine creator, or to natural explanation for these interrelationships even though so far no precise values of the fundamental constants has been worked out. What it does show is that there is an interdependence of fact — things — and processes that forbids any attempts to explain matters purely by analysis and reduction to detail (necessary though it maybe). We must look at the whole for an understanding of the parts. For example, one may see the unbroken continuity between the inorganic and the organic, in a way opposites yet complementary. The influence of universal is transmitted uninterrupted, through forms of growing complication and self-enfoldment, along a scale of increasing degrees of adequacy in its exemplification, which guarantees that life is the fruition of what is already potentially present in the physical. Its emergence is simply the continuation of an already-evident tendency to build more integral, more versatile, and more self-maintaining wholes.

From the Inorganic to the Organic

It is clear that the systematic wholeness of the physical world is governed by a single principle of order. However, at the inorganic level, its unity is merely implicit since the ordering principle is immanent in its elements; it is not explicit for itself and self-reflective. It comprises elements manifested in the mutual adaptation of disparate elements that register its influence, while they are not apprised of its nature, or otherwise cognizant of each other. If the unity becomes apparent to us, it is because of the fruit of our observation, inference and interpretation as we study it; it is not apprehended by the physical reality, extended in time and space, merely as such. However, the ordering principle is dynamic; beyond the physical scale of forms from elementary particles to atoms, molecules, macromolecules, and crystals, the next step is to the living cell, the organism.

An organism is distinguished from the inorganic by the manner in which the organic being maintains its identity, the effect of which is to create and sustain an individual structure. The system of the organism is an open system in dynamic equilibrium with its surroundings. It is a cybernetic system, which maintains itself in a steady state, or homeostasis, by means of a complex and intricate network of negative feedback, or servo-mechanisms. Consequently, with an organism the concrete universal has embarked upon a new phase of self-specification, at a higher level of individuation and integrity, constantly exchanging matter and energy with its environment. Some self-maintenance of form within an energetic flux has been suggested even within the purely physical realm, but the organism is the result of intricate self-enfoldment of the physio-chemical basis by spontaneous adaptation to environing conditions. It is a system containing information preserved by natural selection, which is capable of self-reproduction. This is not say that physical laws cease to apply or physical forces to operate in the organism. On the contrary, they are essential to its self-maintenance to preserve its dynamic equilibrium (Bateson: 1979).

It is still a mystery, how organic wholes of this kind originally arose within an entirely inorganic environment. Now-a-days it is often maintained that the problem has been solved by the discovery and interpretability of the genetic code. But this certainly cannot explain all regulation, because the genetic code is reduplicated identically in every cell. But this cannot account for the cell's ability to develop differently in different situations. This, it is suggested maybe controlled by something in the organism analogous to a computer programme; the source of which remains totally obscure. Programming a computer, normally, presupposes a human agent. In principle, it may said, self-reproducing, self-programming computers are possible. But even they would initially require a human or divine inventor and programmer. To contend that such genetic machines could have been evolved by random mutation and natural selection would beg the question because selection can only operate on a self-regulating organism already in existence. Can it possibly arise from an unregulated chemical processes through a series of accidental changes, however selected, at that ?

The idea of morphogenetic field has been developed in detail and with sophistication by Sheldrake (1987), of formative causation by morphogenetic fields – non-energetic cause of form, beyond physico-chemical explanations of biomorphogenesis. What is significant in all this is the appeal to the notion of field, as it has already done in physics, giving priority in explanation to the whole over the part, in opposition to reductionism. The idea of a field is primarily a structural concept, a formative whole to which the notion of force, or energy, is subordinated. If Einstein geometrised mechanics, Sheldrake's hypothesis seeks to geometrize morphogenetics. It may very well be that the appropriate type of geometry is that discovered by the scientists of Chaos, who have examined complex dynamic systems, to find them to be ordered by "strange attractors" and to exemplify fractal curves. And so on. Can it therefore not be admitted, surely, that the organizing principle of the whole is not a physical or chemical force but a different kind of effect?

Organic Evolution

The unit of life is the cell, but it in itself is a highly complex structure, differentiated into proteins and nucleic acids, cytoplasm and nucleus, and containing many other specialised organelles, ribosomes, and so on. This microcosm of life is an unceasing activity, a constant movement of concerted and concatenated cycles of chemical analysis and synthesis. Although each step is understandable chemistry, the integrative organization is not chemistry at all, but must be explained, if it ever can be, in terms of some holistic principle. It might be referred to the genetic code in the DNA of the nucleus, but whence genetic code originates, or how, nobody yet knows. It is itself an organized system the source and principle of which has still to be discovered.

At any rate, evolution of life progressed from such unicellular organisms, from relative uniformity to differentiation and specialisation of organs which represents an advance in the degree of complexity and organization, marking another step forward in the scale of forms. The accumulated evidence is so massive that living species have evolved from progenitors of different genotypes, and are still evolving, that the theory is now firmly established and its truth is automatically assumed by respectable biologists. Likewise, the evidence is ubiquitous and copious that evolution is promoted by chance mutation and natural selection.[4]

Thus, the biosphere differentiates itself, through the process of evolution, into a scale of forms that are mutually opposed, mutually complementary species, genera, orders, and classes: distinct examples of the universal organic system, in differing and progressively intensifying degrees of integrity and complex unity. But is evolution 'progressive'? Some have argued that it is not. It is simply the constant change of living forms subject to natural selection under environmental pressures. There is a general agreement among biologists that evolution has not proceeded in a straight line. There is equally widespread agreement that different species have descended from common ancestors, and that orthogenesis must have occurred in ramifying directions (*Fig.* 4.5).

At any rate, the gamut of living species constitutes a dialectical scale of forms that progressively express with increasing adequacy the principle of order and unity immanent, not only in the organism, but also in the environment – in the biosphere as a whole. The scale proceeds towards more intelligent and self-conscious forms by way of the development of yet another aspect of its evolutionary advance, namely, behaviour. Both metabolism and physiological process are continuous with behaviour, as is apparent from protozoa onwards, directed to the protection and care of the young. In later stages, the behaviour tends to become more and more gregarious, as is to be expected when it centres on the family group. With *homo sapiens* all this blossoms out into vastly more complex and significant behaviour, and only at the human level is social conduct organized in that distinctive fashion we have come to recognize as political or civilized.[5]

Biosphere, Organism and Environment

So far one has considered evolution as merely concerned only with the organism and its changing form. Life, on the other hand, is a dynamic equilibrium, maintained between organism and environment, so that there is continual intercourse between the two. They form one organic whole and cannot be strictly separated. Evolution is a process involving both together. The evidence is widespread, of this mutual interdependence between living forms and with the environment. Organic wholeness is not confined to living units. A drop of water can contain a miniature ecosystem, as does every natural pond. But no such ecosystem in turn is altogether self-contained, it is further linked to another system and so on and on. In the end, the planet as a whole is one ecological totality, changes everywhere affecting conditions everywhere else. This is limiting our context to organic earth, but one could link it further to solar system, and other stars and galaxies – the cosmos.

The earth as a whole presents the characteristics of a living being, which in the scientific tradition of the West, has been proposed by James Lovelock (1979,1988) as the "Gaia hypothesis", which is fairly well-known by now. It is the biosphere which actually is a living whole cybernetically controlling its earthly environment to maintain the conditions most favourable to its own preservation. The idea is not new both in the Eastern and Western tradition. Without giving details of this hypothesis, the evidence offered leaves one in no doubt that biosphere, hydrosphere, atmosphere, and lithosphere are all in intimate organic relationship and interchange, and that they constitute a single organic whole. If the hypothesis of Lovelock and of Sheldrake are taken together, very promising and intriguing consequences emerge.

The concepts of the Gaia and Morphogenetic fields together would contemplate a field covering the entire planet and directing all the fantastically complex interrelated levels and phases of morphogenesis, with their cybernetically controlled homeostasis. It would make the whole earth one organism with an eminent degree of autonomy and self-determination – a freely acting individual. In that case, a planetary field would be the source of all subordinate fields, and the question of origin would be pushed back to become one of cosmological evolution. As suggested above and elsewhere, the earth cannot be treated in isolation from the solar system, nor the galaxy, or the galaxy from the universe. This is what physicists suggest also, that the universe is one system and its fundamental laws and forces can be traced back to a single principle, immanent at its origins in the Big-Bang. If so, then we must presume that there is ultimately only one universal morphic field. It would be a universal morphe, pervasive over and regulating all subsidiary field – notions mentioned as metaphysical options and theories of traditional speculative philosophy, Plato's Idea of the Good, Aristotle's form of forms as eternal activity, and in itself an active reason (Malik:1989) (*Fig*. 4.6).

Evolution, given the above statement, now assumes the aspect rather of a process of maturation, in which the development in symbiotic organisms of sense-organs and perception marks, as it were, the way in which Gaia gradually, and by dialectical stages, brings herself to consciousness of her setting within the world and of her own integral unity. She brings consciousness in the mentality of her member organisms, and this is at the same time the coming to consciousness of the entire cosmos, of which Gaia herself is a specific phase. This again conforms to the account given above of the nature of the whole. It must in principle and in fact be complete, and which cannot be totally fulfilled unless it is fully and explicitly for itself (self-aware), i.e., it is in conscious knowledge – the realm of self-reflective intelligence. The unitary whole that the physicists have discovered the universe to be is now revealed as not simply physical but also alive.

To sum up, so far, the universal organizing principle has specified itself in an extended series of subsidiary and provisional wholes, from elementary particles, atoms, and molecules to viruses and bacteria, to sentient and conscious organisms, each in its own degree expressing the implicit order and exemplifying the totality of which it's a dialectical moment. In this way, the succession of phases constitutes a graded scale of overlapping, mutually implicating, and interrelated forms issuing as intelligent minds. The major divisions of the series are thus themselves continuous, each incorporating its predecessor and each, in its continuous outgrowth from its forebears, is dominated by the ordering principle. It is first manifested in the physical world, then in the biosphere, and subsequently in the noosphere, where it becomes aware of itself in explicit conscious knowledge. To achieve the capacity for more self-determined action—intentionality, and a higher degree of internality and centralization of external differences is necessary. Now, a further phase transition is required, leading to a new threshold.

Beyond Duality

If the life-world is all inclusive, and normally the world, as perceived by common sense, is regarded as 'external' to the mind, it is because at that level 'the mind' is imagined as a function of the brain and is objectified along with the body. The subsequent attempt to explain consciousness that is seen as a result of the transmission from external objects of physical impulses through the senses to the brain, therefore naturally proves incoherent. Consequently, it has brought in the history of philosophy only epistemological disaster. What has been overlooked is the self-transcendent character of consciousness, aware at once of the presented object and of its own relation to it. Thus, as it distinguishes subject from object, it also grasps their relation within the whole, which together they constitute. The mind, become self-conscious, is capable of developing the implications of such holism in philosophical reflection.

The world disclosed in observation and interpreted in science and philosophy reveals itself as dialectical scale of forms, primarily in experience, ranging from sentience through perception and reflection to comprehension. This is why we cannot get outside the consciousness that arises from primitive sentience. But why is it that the life-world is an all-inclusive whole? It is because the physical world, not speaking only of science, is indeed an all-inclusive whole — finite but unbounded – outside of which there is nothing. The experienced world is that same whole become aware of itself. What 'corresponds' to it, therefore, are simply the prior phases of its own development. These go back beyond sentience for the very reason that sentience has revealed itself as the form of the body, the reflection and registration of organismic activity, integral to the biosphere and rooted in a physio-chemical environment. The object of the mind is, therefore, its own self in becoming, and the subject is no less than the world come consciousness of itself. Subject and object are identical, and fact corresponds to theory just so far as the theory is what the fact itself has become in bringing itself to consciousness. This conclusion reveals itself in reflection upon science and experience in general at the philosophical stage.

Throughout the course of the above argument one has traced wholes in hierarchical progression, and each succeeding whole has brought with it a new form – in the scale of forms – carrying a supervening quality not displayed at previous levels. The complex wholes that appear at every level display the emergent quality and the new capacities of life, impossible at any of the prior stages. Life is the form assumed by the integrated metabolic processes.

Now, when these develop and combine as physiological processes, integrated by vascular and neural functioning at a new threshold of intensity, a further form emerges, namely, sentience. Atoms and molecules are energy systems, and it is the form of the energetic complex that displays the peculiar properties. The proposition now being advanced is that this integration of physiological processes at a high degree of complexity and intensity assumes a new form, the experience of feeling. And this new form is sentience or feeling. Perhaps it could as well be called a distinct 'state' of the system, as gaseous, liquid, and solid are distinct states of chemical substances.

This doctrine has the advantage of disposing once and for all the problems attendant upon body-mind dualism. There is indeed only one reality but that it displays itself in a series of forms with different degrees of unity and wholeness. At each successive level, the entity or entities concerned display different qualities and capacities, although they presuppose and involve all the prior forms and degrees of actualization. When we reach the level of mind, these qualities are sensory, as at every prior level they are not. In this way one may say that there is a duality of degree in intensity of integration between the exclusively physiological, and a corresponding duality of qualitative form, but there is no dualism of substantive existence. The reference is to the continuity of the dynamic principle and its energia, its organizing activity, operating at successive levels — becoming aware of itself and its own spontaneous activity at every stage structured as a scale of forms — the physical spatio-temporal field, the biotic morphogenetic field, and now the psychical field (Stiskin:1972).

Reflection and Self-Transcendence of Consciousness

In the scale of forms that constitutes the self-differentiation of the cosmic order there are two critical transitions. The first is from the physico-chemical to the metabolic, marking the emergence of life. The second is from the sentient and perceptive to the fully self-conscious and reflective. Neither of these is abrupt or unheralded. Life is foreshadowed by crystalline and organic molecular structures; reflection is preceded by immediate perception. But the crucial awakening is that of reflective deliberation, because here for the first time the universal principle of organizations, as such, begins to become explicitly aware of itself as reason.

The universal principle is dynamically self-specifying. It manifests itself first in a physical universe, then in an organic totality, and subsequently in a known world or noosphere (de Chardin: 1959). Only then is its concrete potential fully actualized, because only then does its systematic structure become explicit. It becomes aware of itself as conscious subject, reflective upon itself, upon its own experience of itself and of the world. This is what is self-transcendence awareness, that comprehends its own finite limits and its own infinite scope and potential. The miracle of consciousness is self-transcendence. It is primarily the apprehension of relations, and no relation can be grasped within the limits of any one of the terms. It must, as it were, project itself beyond itself and alienate itself from itself. Moreover, to be conscious of an object is to cognize it in a context both spatial and temporal. But to be aware of a temporal context is at once to remember and to anticipate. For instance, all consciousness of time involves such transcendence — as does space — because the succession of events can be apprehended as a succession only if the series is grasped as a whole, which means that the apprehending subject can never be confined to any one event, past, present, or future. It must be transcendent above, or beyond, all of them.

Without getting into a long and detailed debate about the self, I, self-consciousness and so on; and, while awareness happens in our nervous systems, it is not just happening there. While happenings do involve our bodies, this is like organic wholes, and the awareness of the 'happenings' is the form taken by that wholeness at a high degree of integration. It is the form of feeling, which becomes consciousness when it is organized by attention and judgment, identifying, distinguishing, and relating objects. This involves the ego, which is the whole come to consciousness of itself as 'I'. As such, it can and does distinguish itself from its objects, including its body, in which the neural happenings occur, in order to be aware of them as physiological. Indeed, I am not a separate or separable entity from my body. I am identical with it, or rather I am its identity as a functioning whole — the self-cognizant form of the principle of unity and organization immanent in it. As the self-awareness of the universal principle of wholeness in the body, the 'I' has become transcendent over the objects of its consciousness. As objects they are its other, yet it remains identical with them, the content of its sentient experience.

Awareness of self is reflective consciousness, in which the subject becomes its own object. Reflection leads to deliberation and criticism, it is essential to all morals and politics, thought and action. It is what gives rise to questioning and wonder, and so is equally essential to all science and philosophy, and because it is the root of the awareness of the distinction between the finite and the infinite, also to religion. This self-reflection is the outcome of the bringing to self-consciousness of the organizing principle of the whole through the process of its own self-specification. Consequently, its self-awareness is the awareness of that process, is its knowledge of its own concrescent nature and the way in which must specify its universality; in other words, its the knowledge of the world of nature.

The Nature of Science and Wholeness

Science begins in wonder and the interrogation of nature, which presuppose reflection; so without that there can be no science, and without science knowledge of the world remains in its infancy. The self-reflective character of science is often overlooked. The Newtonian world-view provided no mechanics of the mind, and the celestial mechanics made no room for consciousness. The scientific observer viewed the world from the outside, and within that world no provision was made for any consciousness. The fruit of this in philosophy led to materialism and dualism; but both maybe refuted by the fact that these theories would not be possible without self-reflection. Both, whether rationalist or empiricist, fail to provide a viable theory of knowledge, of how the mind, in its separation from matter, can encompass a representation of an external world, how the world can get into the mind, or how a mechanical material process can be miraculously converted into a cognitive awareness. Meanwhile, the scientific disregard of the observer leaves science itself beyond the reach of scientific explanation.[6]

Of course quantum theory, with its principle of indeterminacy and theory of probability has led some reflective scientists to conclude that physical reality may well be a welter of energy on which the appearance of order supervenes only because we impose upon it a stochastical mathematic — the universe is thus a subjective fabrication, the actual nature of which we can never discover. If that was so, how would we explain our ability to discover this, if we are emerging from an allegedly chaotic matrix?

If reality is in principle unknowable, we are left solely with what our own consciousness presents. In the history of science, a number of world-views have arisen in succession, each to be rejected by subsequent thinkers, often as palpably false and ridiculous. Instead of seeing this succession as a series of fantasies, we see it as a dialectical succession of provisional conceptual schemes, unfolding as a scale of forms, in which each progressively more adequately explicates a conceptual whole; and each scheme is itself a particular stage in the self-discovery of the actual world. Our scientific discoveries are no more than approximations, and yet each series of scientific revolutions deploys a series of world-views that increase from each to the next in coherence and unity. The cosmic whole, differentiates itself and brings itself to fruition in self-awareness. The universal principle of organization immanent in all things manifests itself in a cosmic pattern, in which it is particularized in successive wholes, constituting various scales as self-enfoldment. In this way the world comes to consciousness of itself and explicitly realizes its essential nature, in its reflective awareness and interpretive conceptualization by intelligent human beings.

This world-concept is of a universe continuous and indivisible in space and time, deployed as a scale of comprehensive phases at successive levels; physical, chemical, biotic, sentient, and noetic, within each of which there is an analogous subordinate scale. All subsequent phases embody all their predecessors, and the latest sublates the whole prior scale, which in it is brought to a higher degree of actuality and self-sufficiency. The noetic level levels reflects all the rest, for not only does it envisage and comprehend all the prior phases but also it is realized in the practical and intellectual activity of living beings, who are at the same time both organisms and physico-chemical systems, each drawing to a focus within itself its total environing world.

Conclusion — The Context of all Contexts

The most significant revolutionary effect of the physics of relativity and quantum theory has been to generate a new view of the physical universe as a single, indivisible, generate whole, in which phenomena and events are necessarily inter-determining. It is a single system governed by a unitary dynamic principle, augmented by the results of findings in biology and ecology. Any such whole is not an undifferentiated unity, a blank; its integrity depends on the interconnection of parts internally related one to another, in accordance with an organizing principle. In the dimension of time, this principle is dynamic, generating a graded scale of subordinate wholes in which it is specified. The dynamic dialectically related forms are specific exemplifications of the universal dynamic principle governing the whole. Thus a design in the sense of pattern or structure, is obviously such a whole. Its parts and elements are interrelated systematically according to some principle of order and arrangement. The whole which contemporary physics as revealed, therefore, necessarily involves the generation of its own observation by intelligent beings, in whose minds it brings itself to consciousness.

The whole or design is not ultimately fragmentary; in principle it must be complete. Deployed in scale of forms, it must ultimately culminate in a completed totality. Nor can its self-manifestation be only partial. In principle, and in fact, there must be a culmination of the scale that is both final phases and all-encompassing — an absolute, actual whole, totally self-contained and self-sufficient, and completely realised. It must sublate in itself the entire process of its self-specification, so that end and process overlap. It would be a mistake to imagine that this culmination can, or needs to, appear in time, for it must encompass all time in itself while nevertheless enduring throughout time. It does so in the same way as human consciousness transcends the present and includes at once both the present and the past while it continues to endure and participate in the flux. The culminating phase of the scale does this likewise, for it is the fulfilment of the organizing principle universal to every phase and every existent. It is immanent throughout all process, for every process is a manifestation of its self-differentiation, contributing at its specific level and in its peculiar degree to the final consummation.

Finally, there are three characteristics of the universal principle of organization that need to be emphasised:

(i) It is in principle absolutely complete;

(ii) Its completeness involves total explication in absolute self-consciousness;

(iii) The final phase, like all others, must transcend and at the same include and comprehend all its predecessors – that is, the final phase must be, and yet transcend, the sum-total of all the parts (Harris: *op.cit.*).

It must be such as no conception or existence can exceed it. This is the perfect being, totally complete, totally self-sufficient and self-sustaining – than that which a greater is inconceivable. As totally explicit in transparent self-consciousness, this consummation of the cosmic scale is an omniscient mind – the Alpha and Omega of all being. Because the universal principle is immanent in every part, it is what generates and determines the nature of every entity, and its activity is nothing more nor less than its own self-differentiation in and as the spatio-temporal world. But its ultimate realization is a transcendent comprehension and self-conscious realization of the whole. It is thus all-creative and all-powerful, as well as all-knowing and absolutely self-complete. All this is necessarily entailed by the very concept of design. If God – *Purusa* -– is conceived as the absolute universal principle of order manifesting itself – *Prakrti* – in and as the universe, and transcending all finite phases, the argument from design, as a proof of his existence, can be justified in this, its modern rendering, without requiring any inference from a contrived plan to a Supreme Architect (unless these phrases are used metaphorically). His knowing and conceiving are immediately and simultaneously his self-manifestation in and as the whole world – his creative power, his self-revelation. This conclusion has the rare advantage that it is not a resort to God as a cloak to cover our ignorance, but it is the logical consequence of the very nature of our knowledge and of the structure of the universe as discovered by empirical science – the latter however is not the eternal truth, or at least not all of it. Whatever the alternate theories which replace one another, it is still a unitary system, this universe with its dialectical series of ascending forms. Moreover, science is but one facet of a wider and more complex noosphere. It is inseparable from society and all that entails, and social sciences with philosophical systems in conjunction with science need to pursue the deeper implications of the organizing principle, alluded to above.

POSSIBLE UNIVERSAL HOLO-MOVEMENTS

Fig. 4.1

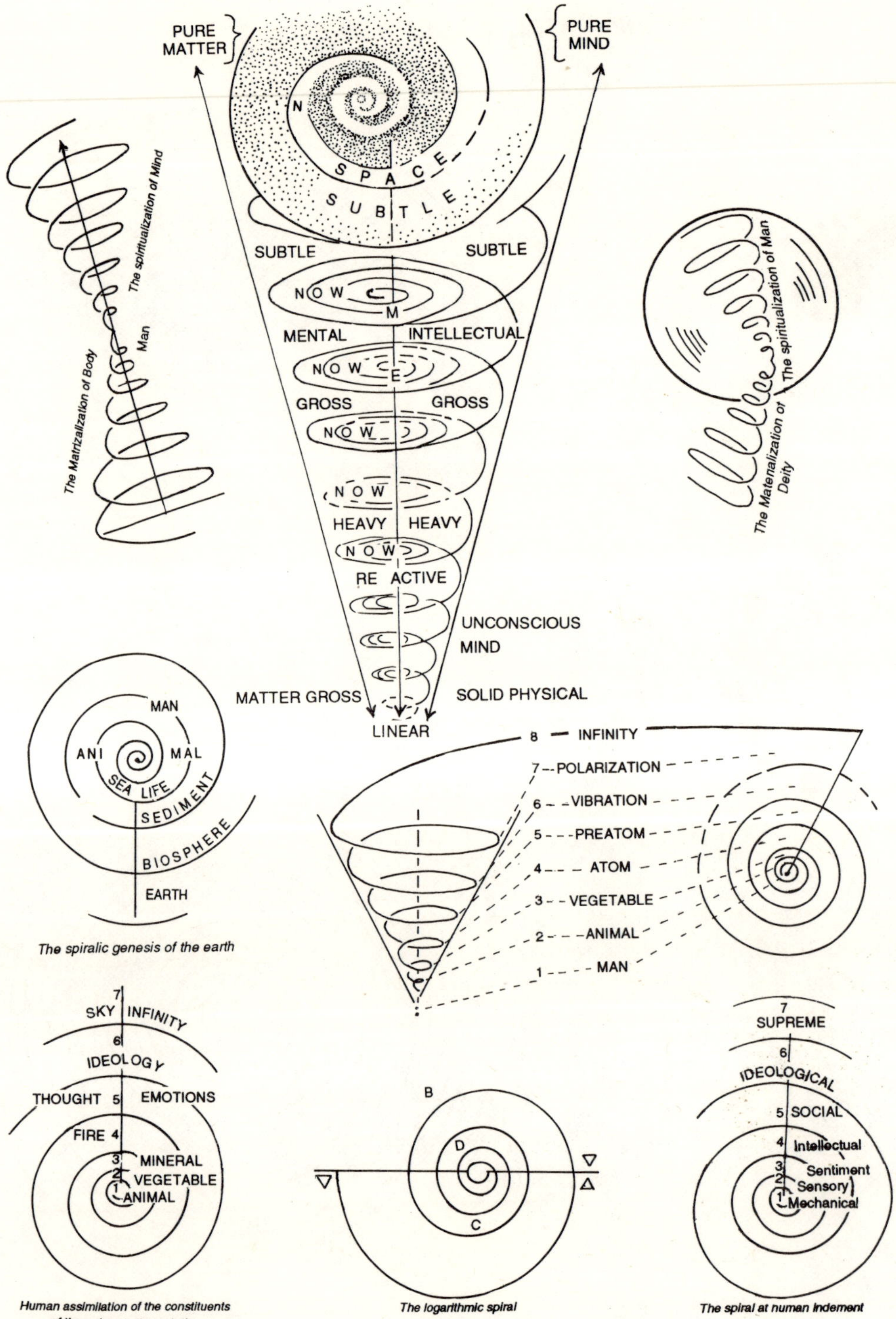

The spiralic genesis of the earth

Human assimilation of the constituents of the universe through time

The logarithmic spiral

The spiral at human indement

Fig. 4.2

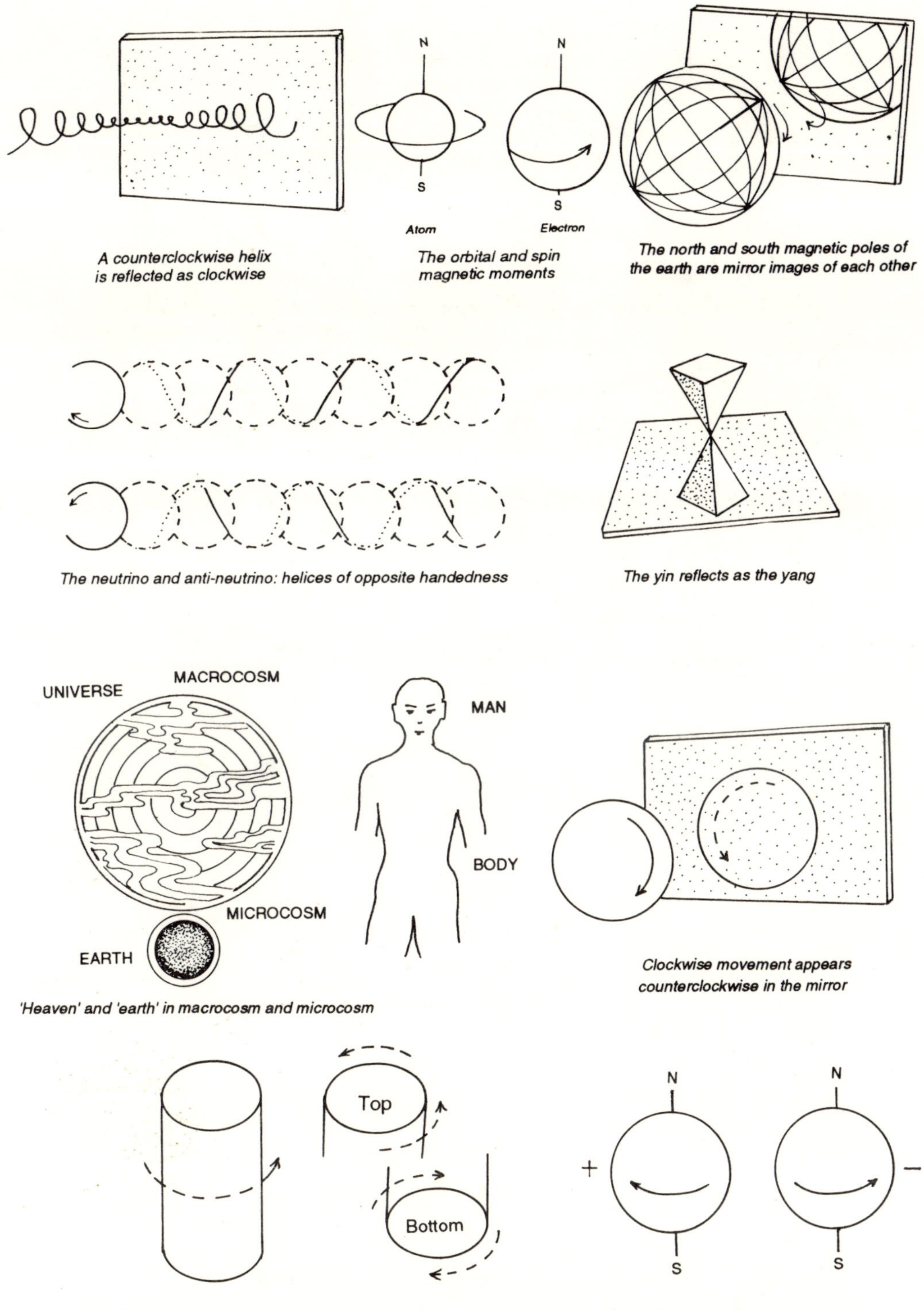

A counterclockwise helix is reflected as clockwise

The orbital and spin magnetic moments

The north and south magnetic poles of the earth are mirror images of each other

The neutrino and anti-neutrino: helices of opposite handedness

The yin reflects as the yang

'Heaven' and 'earth' in macrocosm and microcosm

Clockwise movement appears counterclockwise in the mirror

The north and south poles of a magnet are mirror images of each other

The electron and position portrayed as mirror images

Fig. 4.3

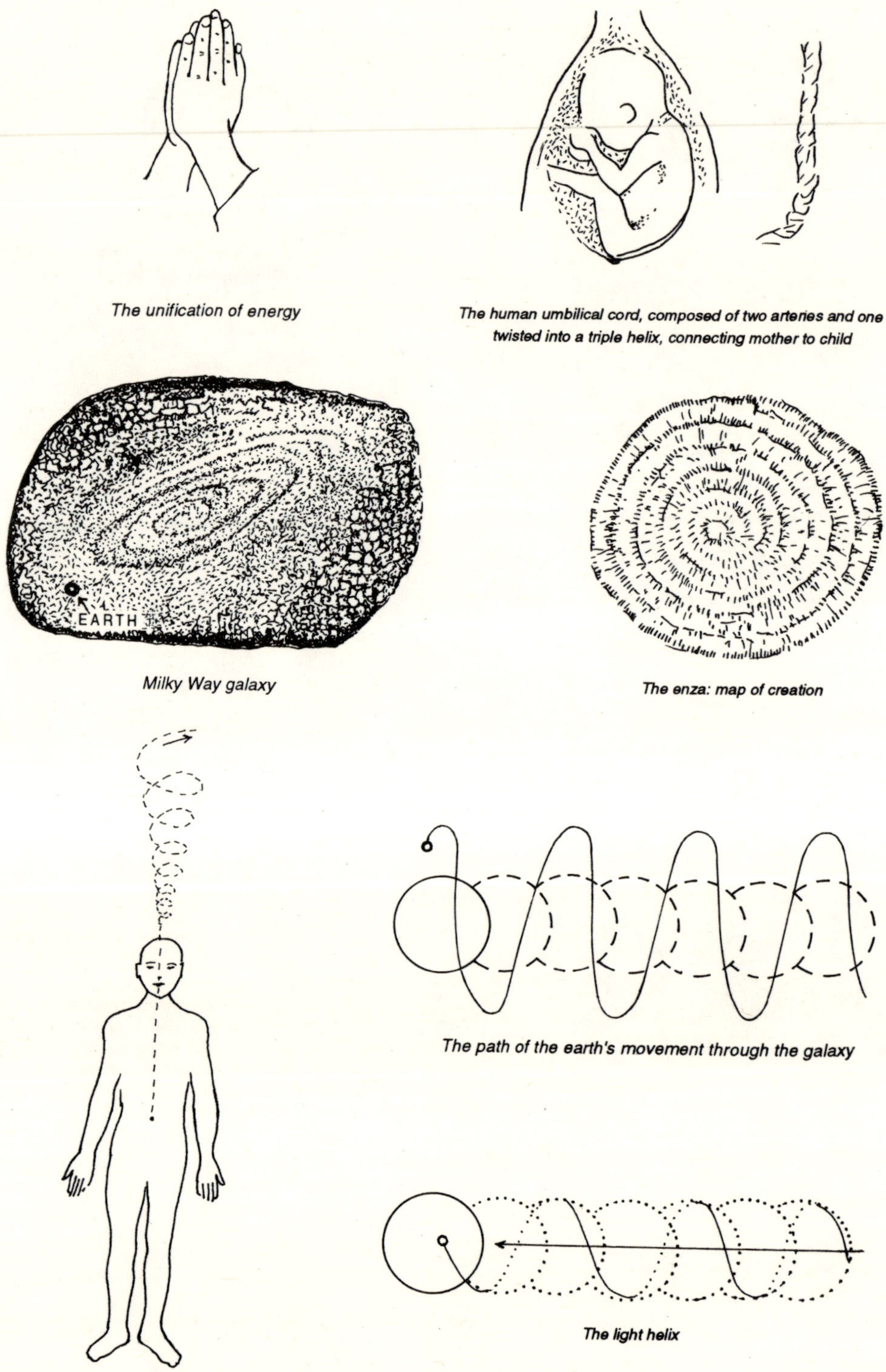

The unification of energy

The human umbilical cord, composed of two arteries and one twisted into a triple helix, connecting mother to child

Milky Way galaxy

The enza: map of creation

The path of the earth's movement through the galaxy

The light helix

Human intuition as the perception and expression of life

***Fig.* 4.4**

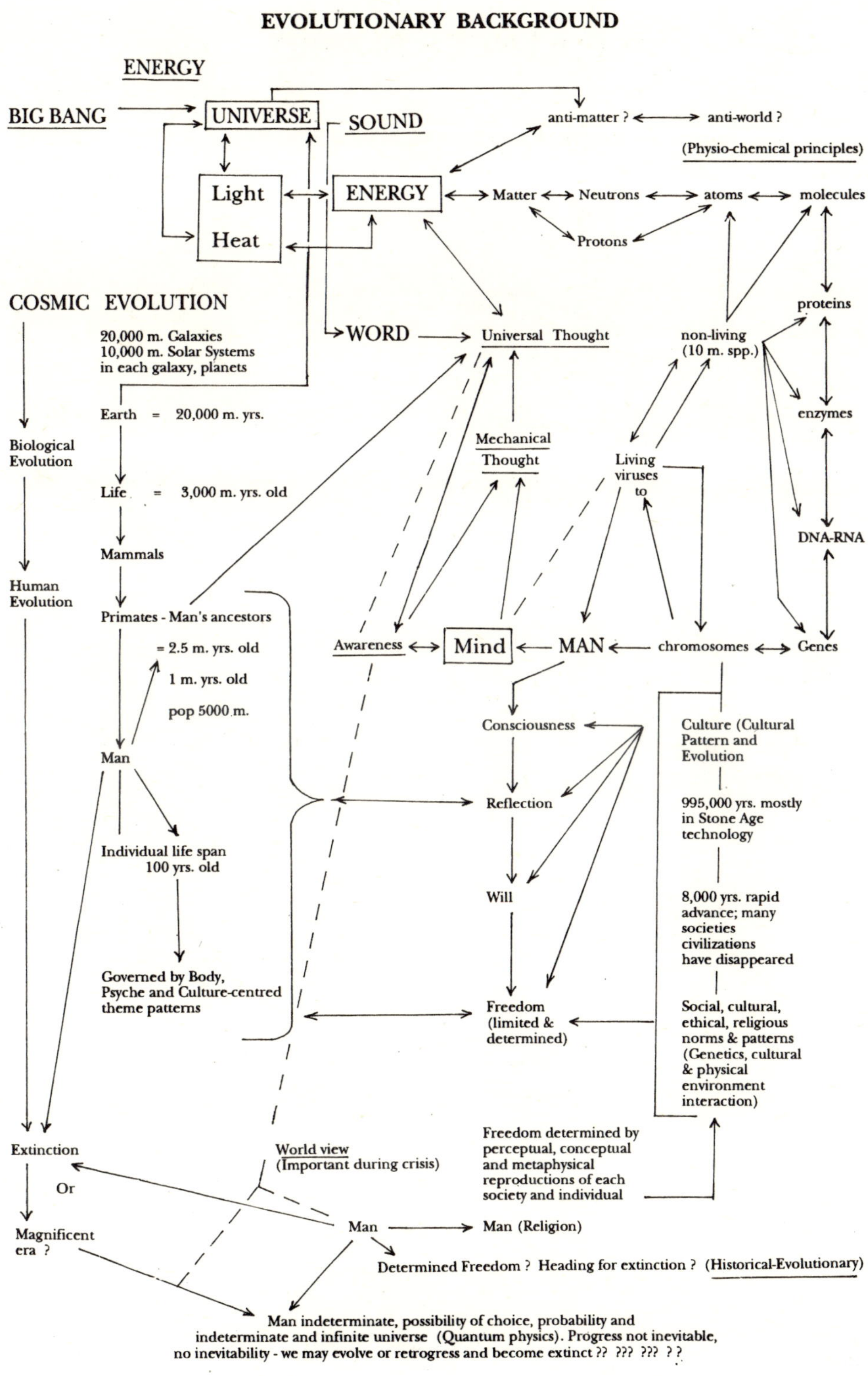
EVOLUTIONARY BACKGROUND
ENERGY
BIG BANG
UNIVERSE
SOUND
anti-matter ?
anti-world ?
(Physio-chemical principles)
Light
Heat
ENERGY
Matter
Neutrons
atoms
molecules
Protons
proteins
COSMIC EVOLUTION
20,000 m. Galaxies
10,000 m. Solar Systems
in each galaxy, planets
WORD
Universal Thought
non-living
(10 m. spp.)
Earth = 20,000 m. yrs.
enzymes
Biological
Evolution
Mechanical
Thought
Living
viruses
to
Life = 3,000 m. yrs. old
DNA-RNA
Mammals
Human
Evolution
Primates - Man's ancestors
= 2.5 m. yrs. old
1 m. yrs. old
pop 5000 m.
Awareness
Mind
MAN
chromosomes
Genes
Man
Consciousness
Culture (Cultural
Pattern and
Evolution
Reflection
995,000 yrs. mostly
in Stone Age
technology
Individual life span
100 yrs. old
Will
8,000 yrs. rapid
advance; many
societies
civilizations
have disappeared
Governed by Body,
Psyche and Culture-centred
theme patterns
Freedom
(limited &
determined)
Social, cultural,
ethical, religious
norms & patterns
(Genetics, cultural
& physical
environment
interaction)
Extinction
World view
(Important during crisis)
Freedom determined by
perceptual, conceptual
and metaphysical
reproductions of each
society and individual
Or
Magnificent
era ?
Man
Man (Religion)
Determined Freedom ? Heading for extinction ? (Historical-Evolutionary)
Man indeterminate, possibility of choice, probability and
indeterminate and infinite universe (Quantum physics). Progress not inevitable,
no inevitability - we may evolve or retrogress and become extinct ?? ??? ??? ? ?

Fig. 4.5

FULLNESS IS VOID

NO - THINGNESS

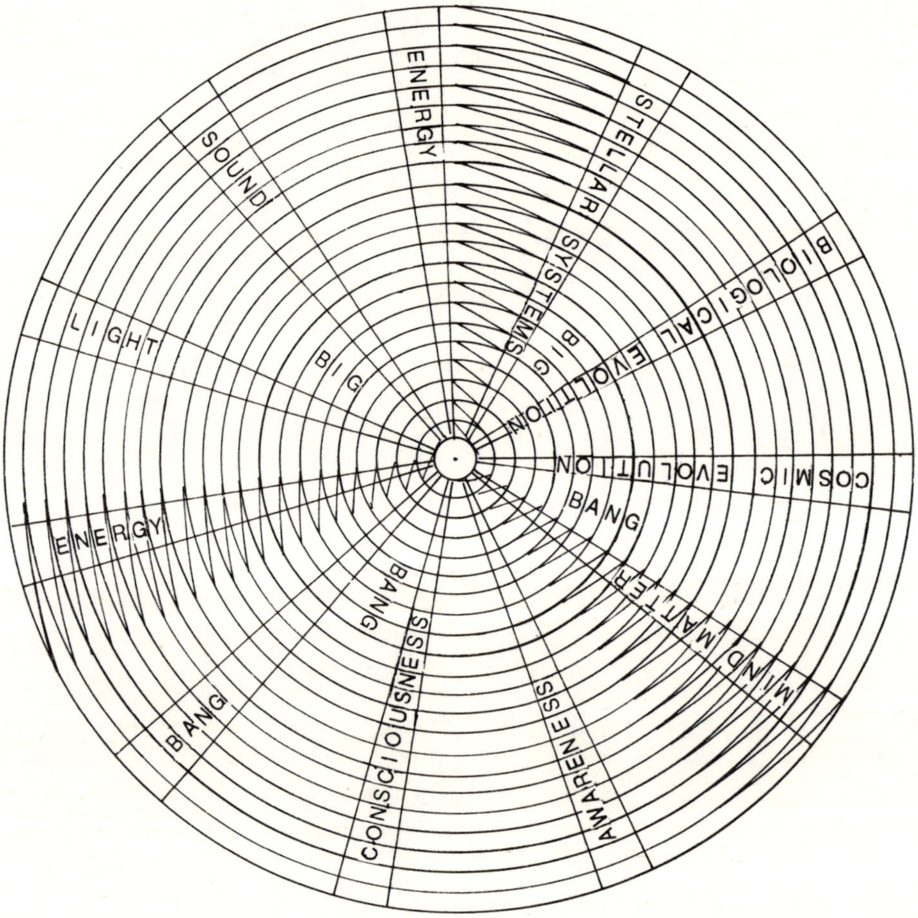

VOID IS FULLNESS
NO MIND

(DOESN'T MATTER)

Fig. 4.6

Notes

1. In recent years, physicists have suddenly discovered what they have called the Anthropic Principle, a conception that many present-day physicists regard not just as a speculative idea but as a serious scientific principle, not to be treated lightly. The principle has been stated in several forms (Harris:1991).
2. The Participatory Anthropic Principle is prompted by the Copenhagen interpretation of the quantum theory, initiated by Neils Bohr (Kothari:1990). Briefly, it follows from this that intelligent beings, through their observation and measurements, must participate in the actualisation of the universe at large. The obvious difficulty with this contention is that human bodies and their sense-organs, as well as the measuring instruments and any apparatus they may use for experimentation, are macroscopic objects made up of the microscopic entities that quantum physicists investigate. If this were the case, the physical universe could not come to be until observed; and until it existed there could be no observers because they are consequent upon the generation of life, which again dependent on the prior occurrence of physico-chemical processes. If physical reality depends on the existence of mind, and mind depends on the prior existence of physical reality, neither can exist unless both can come into being simultaneously. For, although measurement requires the coupling of the quantum system to be measured with some macroscopic instrument, once it has been so connected the entire system, including the measuring device, can be regarded as a single quantum system, indeterminate as to its state until the measurement is made and observed. But this again is a subjectivist position. At any rate, scientists have finally realised the obsolescence of the Copernican outlook with respect to human mentality, and the implications of recognising the continuity of matter with mind in a unified world (Harris, *Ibid*).
3. Every whole is a system, however primitive; every system is a whole, structured in accordance with a universal principle of order. That, in consequence, specifies itself in a scale of forms that differ consecutively in the degree of their adequacy to its explicit wholeness. But the mention here is not of abstract universals, say represented by a genus under which particulars are contained. Undoubtedly this logical schema has useful applications, but its underlying metaphysical assumption is that the real consists of a fortuitous collection of atomic particulars, mutually related externally only. This kind of assumption was encouraged by Newtonian physics, followed by the empiricist philosophers of the seventeenth and eighteenth centuries — there may be common properties but the elements are related externally only. But contemporary physics has abandoned this view, and has adopted one in which the relations between things and processes and the terms that they relate are intrinsically dependent upon one another, so that they are inseparable in a unified system. A principle of this kind is universal because its influence prevails throughout the system and is universal to its parts. There is thus immanence and transcendence in this concrete universal system.

   Relations of any kind, whether they are in this internal or are external in the sense that they fall between their terms and leave them unaffected can be apprehended only by a conscious subject, because what stands in relation must be grasped all together and as a whole. It follows that elements in relation must either be objects of some consciousness or must, as a complex totality, be conscious themselves. This is strictly correct, if by existence one means fully actualised being; but, although a relational complex is only explicit at the level of consciousness, there can be lower levels, prior to consciousness and requisite for its emergence in the order of nature — existing implicitly, having potency and latent inter-relativity. These are phases in the dialectical scale prior to mind, through which the natural whole brings itself to consciousness by its inherent nisus to self-completion (Harris, *Ibid*).

4. The reference now is to organismic genetics, for which there is enough evidence, say adaptation and adjustment to environmental conditions is inherent in the very nature of life. To be selected, a system must be better adapted for survival than others with which it competes for the available energy and sustenance. Moreover, geneticists have established that single genes do not control or determine single characteristics, but that the chromosome functions as a whole, as does, in fact, the entire genome. It is now apparent that "survival value" is equivalent to more efficient self-maintenance and more completely self-determining wholeness. What evolves is always the organic system and nothing less; and what evolution produces is increased self-determining adaptation, increased capacity for relevant variation and selective reaction to circumstances, in short, increased versatility and freedom. A whole with these characteristics is a more adequate manifestation of the self-specifying universal expressing itself in the organism as well as in the cosmos, than is any inorganic purely physical or chemical whole. Organic systems of this kind more fully reflect the nature of the principle of organization immanent in life and in the universe as such, and approach more nearly its free self-determination (Harris, *Ibid*).

5. Basically, all behaviour is instinctive, and purposive in that it pursues a definite goal characteristic of the particular instinct – eating, mating, migrating, nesting, etc. Behaviour may be characterized by relevant variation, as it blossoms in the higher species, into sensory-motor, perceptual, and intelligent learning. It is an informed activity, in terms of structural organization and perceptual enlightenment not to specific stimuli alone but a response to a total situation, which must be grasped as whole if the behaviour is to be appropriate. The inner, mental aspect of instinctive behaviour and its intelligent outcome belongs to a further phase of the self-differentiation of the universal whole; one that renders it aware of itself and its own relational structures. Behaviour is foreshadowed below the mental level in the living processes of metabolism and physiology which, as they evolve, fold back upon themselves to produce new wholes and more developed forms. When the human level is reached, the cognitive capacity of discrimination and definition, comprehension, this aspect attains to the pitch of explicit self-consciousness, thought, the principle and agency of organization – inherent from the start and is itself the immanent principle ordering the cosmos as a whole. The part played by consciousness in animal and human activity is important in order to understand behaviour in the context of evolution (Harris, *Ibid*).

6. It was at the end of the nineteenth century that the Newtonian 'paradigm' obstructing scientific progress, was broken by a new revolution, which required a more holistic approach; and this came with relativity and quantum theories. Neither of these could disregard the observer. For relativity, the relative velocity of the observer determines the value of every measurement, and for quantum theory, the observer and the measurement of specific quantities have become inseparable from the very actuality of elementary particles. The reality of elementary particles is restricted to the act of observation by means of instruments that are themselves composed of multitudes of such particles, and by observers who have evolved from organic species similarly composed. Thus the reality of the elements is made to depend on the activity of that to which they are elementary. Reference is to Copenhagen interpretation of the quantum theory – Neils Bohr, Schroedinger wave function, Heisenberg's Indeterminacy principle, Bell's Theorem, Henry Stapp's work and so on; all these works show that the unity of the universe and the apparent dependence of physical reality upon subjective experience are two aspects of a single fact). It is now being suggested that reflective awareness, in the guise of observation and interpretation, is

constitutive of the very being of the universe. It goes beyond both subjectivism (dispensing with physical reality altogether) and phenomenalism (that leaves reality beyond our ken as an unknowable thing-in-itself) (Weber:1986).

If the universe is an indivisible whole, and as such must by its very nature be complete, and if, as has been argued, the completion of a whole necessarily involves its being brought to consciousness, the danger of falling into solipsism is averted. For although hidden variables have been ruled out, the indeterminate properties of particles are admitted by the Copenhagen theories to be latent, or potential, before they are observed. In short, the actualization of what is potential at the physical and biological levels should await the activity of observation and the efflorescence of knowledge. This in no way precludes the prior reality of the physical and biological world, because the very experience of a physical and biological world as an indivisible systematic whole implies and necessitates the self-differentiation of that whole as a scale of forms, in the more elementary of which what emerges at later stages is already implicit. The existence of both macroscopic and microscopic worlds is thus established.

References

Bateson, Gregory, 1979, *Mind and Nature – A Necessary Unity*, London.

Bohm, David, 1980, *Wholeness and the Implicate Order*, London.

de Chardin, Teilhard, P., 1959, *The Phenomenon of Man*, New York.

Gandhi, K., (ed.), 1990, *The Odyssey of Science, Culture and Consciousness*, New Delhi.

Harris, Errol E., 1991, *Cosmos and Anthropos – A philosophical interpretation of the anthropic cosmological principle*; New Jersey, London.

Kothari, D.S., 1986, "Science and Values", New Delhi, Mimeographed.

Lovelock, J., 1979, *Gaia: A New Look at Life on Earth*, Oxford.

——, 1988, *The Ages of Gaia*, London.

Malik, S.C., 1973, "Human Evolution: Some Reflections on its Philosophy", In *Eastern Anthropologist*, Lucknow.

——, 1989, *Modern Civilization – A Crisis of Fragmentation*, New Delhi.

——, 1992, "Matter is Consciousness", Pune, Seminar on *The Nature of Matter*, Mimeographed.

Prigogine, I., 1980, *From Being to Becoming*, San Francisco.

——, 1984, *Order Out of Chaos*, New York.

Sheldrake, R., 1980, *A New Science of Life*, London.

Smith, Lester, 1975, *Intelligence Came First*, Illinois.

Stiskin, Nahun, 1972, *The Looking Glass God*, Canada.

Weber, Renee, 1986, *Dialogue with Sages and Scientists*, New York.

5

Nature and Life

Old Ideas New Questioning

Ananda Wood

Traditional Knowledge — Problems of Interpretation

In traditional society, before the use of printing and other modern media, knowledge was expressed and interpreted in a way that is rather different from what we are used to today.

First, traditional forms of expression tended to be rather intensive and condensed: compressing a great deal of thought and perception into the relatively few short aphorisms and verses and other forms of expression that could be passed down by oral memory and personal transmission from generation to generation.

And second, traditional learning was didactic and authoritarian. It was taught through bare assertions and prescriptions that were hard to understand at first, but had to be accepted on authority. On the part of a student, this required an attitude of obedience and trust: in order to accept and painstakingly learn the condensed and often difficult forms of traditional expression, before interpreting them and arguing from their authority.

Because traditional expressions of knowledge were so condensed, they require special interpretation. Accordingly, within each tradition, knowledge was often explained and developed through commentaries on the classic texts of that particular tradition. Such traditional commentaries are obviously useful and have to be taken into account; but, from a modern point of view, they have an unfortunate limitation. They tend to argue from authority, in a way that is no longer appropriate. In particular, they tend to argue from the authority of divine revelation in special states of mystical experience, metaphorically described and esoterically cultivated through traditional disciplines of ritual and religion and meditation.

In the modern world, through the widespread use of printing and other media, recent advances in education and science have significantly developed our ability to reason directly from common experience. Our education no longer requires us to think in mythical, religious and mystical metaphors that must be accepted on the authority of tradition. Instead, we are educated to question accepted ideas and beliefs, on the basis of our own experience. And, through modern scientific enquiry, we are educated to question directly, by abstract and analytic reasoning about the common principles of experience that underlie different appearances: perceived at different times and by different people, from different points of view.

Thus, traditional knowledge needs to be reinterpreted, by approaching it in a new way. It is no longer appropriate to prescribe thought didactically, through an authorized creed of mythical, religious and mystical metaphors. Instead, traditional conceptions are open to question, to ask what they might mean, through a direct, analytic enquiry into common experience. That is the approach attempted in this paper.

Nature and Consciousness — Objective and Subjective

The English word 'nature' comes from the Latin *natus*, meaning 'born' or 'produced'. This derivation reflects the sense of creativity and dynamism that is associated with the concept of nature. On the one hand, the concept refers to *underlying* nature, from which arise the changing phenomena or appearances that are perceived in the created world. And, on the other hand, the concept also implies the creative *activities* of nature, through which perceived phenomena or appearances arise.

Essentially the same meaning is carried by the Sanskrit word *prạkrti*: which is a compound of the word *krti*, meaning 'activity', and the prefix *pra-*. This prefix has an interesting richness of meaning. It carries the meanings of both the English prefixes 'pre-' and 'pro-'. It means not only 'prior to' or 'before', but also 'continuing on' and 'going forth'. Thus, on the one hand, the concept of *prakrti* refers to an underlying something which comes logically before activity or appearance, and which continues on beneath activities and appearances as they take place. And, on the other hand, the concept of *prakrti* also carries a sense of 'acting forth', thus including the manifesting activities and appearances through which underlying reality is perceived.

In short, the concepts of 'nature' and *prakrti* both refer to that part of experience which underlies perceived appearances and which contains activities that produce the phenomena and appearances we perceive. This is the part of our experience that we call 'objective'; because we think of it in terms of objects which act upon each other.

In modern physical science, nature is conceived as an external world, outside the minds of human beings and other living creatures. For the specialized purposes of physical science and technology, this conception has obviously proved its use; but, for the broader and subtler needs of living experience, it has its limitations, as our present environmental and human crisis is beginning to show. The trouble with this narrowly physical conception is that it creates an artificial opposition between mind and nature: making nature seem a lifeless collection of dead objects to be manipulated and dominated by our minds.

In traditional religion and philosophy, nature was conceived to be 'animate'; and hence it was taken to include not only physical objects but also living actions, perceptions, thoughts and feelings. In other words, mind and mental functions were taken to be a part of nature and its objective activities through which perceived phenomena and appearances arise.

But this raises a delicate philosophical question. How can the mind and its activities be known objectively as a part of nature's functioning? Viewed from a person's mind, consciousness appears to consist in a stream of perceptions, thoughts and feelings, which come and go in mental experience. This mental appearance of consciousness is obviously changing and is personal: it changes from moment to moment and is different from person to person. But, if one asks how the changing appearances of mind are known, then it becomes clear that there must be an underlying basis of consciousness which continues at the background of experience, while perceptions, thoughts and feelings appear and disappear in the limited focus of attention on the surface of the mind.

For example, suppose that I come out of a warm house on a cold day, and previous perceptions of relaxing warmth give way to rather different perceptions of invigorating or numbing cold. How do I know this change and variation of differing perceptions? Clearly, I do so on the basis of an underlying consciousness that continues through the change, thus enabling differing perceptions of cold and warmth to be compared and co-ordinated into a coherent knowledge of temperature. Without such an underlying basis of consciousness, knowledge could not continue through time, and different perceptions, thoughts and feelings could not be put together in coherent knowledge.

Moreover, each time we form any conception of other people, with minds other than our own, we can only do so by assuming a basis of consciousness which we share in common with them, and upon which we form whatever conception we may have of their perceptions, thoughts and feelings. Thus, there must be an underlying basis of consciousness that is shared by different persons; otherwise there could be no communication between people, no knowledge of other minds, and hence no notion of other people at all.

In short, the changing activities and appearances of mind can only be known on the basis of an underlying consciousness which is unchanging and impersonal: in the sense that it is shared in common by different moments of time and by different people, beneath the variations of time and personality.

In the *Vedanta* and *Samkhya* traditions of Indian philosophy, the word *purusa* is used to describe the changeless, impersonal principle of consciousness that underlies each changing personality. In ordinary Sanskrit usage, the word *purusa* means 'a man' or 'a person'; but in its special philosophical usage, the word *purusa* refers to changeless and impersonal consciousness as the underlying principle of personality that is the true essence or the real self of each person. As it is put in the *Brhadaranyaka Upanisad,* 4.3.7:

katama atmeti; yo'yam *vijnanamayah pranesu* *hrdyantarjyotih purusah;* *sa samanah sann ubhau* *lokav anusancarati,* *dhyayativa lelayativa; . . .*	'What is the self?' 'It is this *purusa*, which is just consciousness in living faculties, the inner light of heart. 'Staying the same, it journeys through both worlds, seeming to think and move . . . .'

The central question here is the identification of a person's self. There is a widespread and usually unquestioned tendency to identify the self as a personal ego, consisting of body, senses and mind, which manifestly change over time and vary from person to person. If this personal identification is taken for granted, as it so often is, then of course the subjective or knowing part of experience must appear to be changing and variable, and the word 'subjective' must be taken to mean 'personal'.

But the word 'subjective' does not just mean 'personal'. More precisely, it refers to the self as the knowing subject of experience; and it thus distinguishes the knowing self from the known or objective part of experience. In order to know the world correctly, it is necessary to know the body, senses and mind, for these are the instruments through which each person knows the world. But, to know the mind, it must be included in the known or objective part of experience; and hence the knowing self must be detached from it.

Can the knowing self be detached from the mind? One way of doing this is to think of the mind as the activity of creating mental appearances, of creating the apparent perceptions, thoughts and feelings that come and go in each person's experience. If a person's mind is conceived in this way, it becomes part of the objective activity of nature; and nature thus includes all the physical and mental activities through which it is manifested in experience. This is essentially the traditional conception of nature as the animate principle of all activities which produce the phenomena that appear in the world of our experience.

If nature is thus conceived to manifest itself in a person's experience, what is the knowing self before which the manifestations of nature appear? It is pure consciousness without any activity in it, for all activity has been included in objective nature. It is consciousness which does not act, but only knows, as it continues through a person's experience, illuminating the perceptions, thoughts and feelings that appear and disappear in the mind. This illumination is not any kind of act that consciousness starts doing at some time and stops doing later. Instead, it is the essential being of consciousness, which shines and illuminates appearances simply by being what it is. In the same way, by merely being what it is, as it continues unchanged at the background of experience, it provides the underlying, impersonal basis upon which people communicate and put together perceptions, thoughts and feelings in coherent knowledge.

As perceptions appear and are interpreted by thoughts and feelings, they are absorbed by understanding into this knowing basis of consciousness at the background of experience from which arise further feelings, thoughts, actions, perceptions and interpretations. When current conceptions and theories fail in their descriptions and predictions of observed phenomena, so that people enquire back to underlying assumptions which have been taken for granted at the background of experience, then it is from this same subjective and impersonal basis of consciousness that clarifications and more accurate conceptions arise.

In sum, traditional conceptions of nature and consciousness can be interpreted as a philosophical division of experience into objective and subjective parts. The objective part is nature as a self-manifesting whole, including all physical and mental activities in the perceived world, and also all the perceiving activities of the body, senses and mind through which the world appears in a person's experience. Thus nature manifests itself before consciousness, through perceived and perceiving activities that together result in the stream of appearances which come and go before consciousness in each person's experience. With all activities of the perceiving personality thus taken into the objective part of experience, the subjective part remains as pure, impersonal consciousness, which continues unchanged throughout experience, illuminating the changing appearances that come and go.

This distinction of consciousness and nature is explicit in the *purusa-prakrti* conception of *Samkhya* and *Vedanta* philosophies; and it can also be found, explicitly or implicitly conceived, in other traditions as well. In Aristotelian philosophy, nature is conceived as 'self-moving';[1] and there is thus a delicate contrast here with the conception of the 'unmoved mover', which is used to describe God in the external universe and the essence of soul in living creatures.[2] In mythical, religious and mystical traditions in general, the objective principle of nature is represented by conceptions of divine immanence in the changing manifestations of creation; and the subjective principle of consciousness is represented by conceptions of a transcendent spirit, both as a transcending God in the macrocosm of the external universe, and as an inner or spiritual essence of soul in the microcosm of individual experience.[3]

Life — The Expression of Consciousness in Nature

If objective nature is taken to contain all physical and mental activity, and subjective consciousness is taken to be pure, impersonal illumination, then what is the relationship between these two parts of experience? In particular, how do the activities of nature relate to the impersonal and unchanging illumination of consciousness?

This question is answered by the traditional concept of 'life' as the vital breath that animates the activities of nature. Clearly, this conception of living breath does not refer only to physical respiration. Instead, the physical respiration of living bodies is used here as a metaphor. In modern terms, traditional concepts of life as 'vital breath' or 'breathing spirit' or 'aspiration' or 'inspiration' are metaphors for the expression of consciousness in living behaviour.

In Sanskrit, the ordinary word for life is *jiva*. In particular, the word applies to the living personality of an individual creature. The *jiva* or living personality expresses consciousness; but this expression is part of nature's activity and is thus to be distinguished from the impersonal principle of pure consciousness that is each creature's real self. The distinction between consciousness and its expression in living personality is described in the *Mundaka Upanisad,* 3.1:

dva suparna sayuja sakhaya	Two birds, in close companionship,
samanam vrksam parisasvajate	are perched upon a single tree.
tayor anyah pippalam svadvatty-	Of these, one eats and relishes the fruit,
anasnann anyo abhicakasiti	the other does not eat, but just looks on.

The two 'birds' are *jiva*, the living personality, and *atman*, the self. The living personality expresses consciousness by acting and by tasting the fruits of action through its mental activities of perception, thought and feeling; but the self is only consciousness, unconditioned by the physical and mental activities that express it.

A parallel is sometimes noted here with the biblical story of Adam and Eve. The name 'Adam' comes from the Hebrew *adam*, meaning 'a human being' or 'a man'; and hence it could be interpreted to represent the essential principle of consciousness in each human being (just like the Sanskrit word *purusa*). The name 'Eve' comes from the Hebrew *havvah*, meaning 'life' or 'living'; and hence it could be interpreted to represent the living faculty of expression, which makes consciousness seem conditioned and thus produces the tempting, but false appearances of personal ego in the physical and mental activities of personality.

However, if life thus expresses consciousness in objective nature, a further question arises. What is this special activity of living expression, and how can it be understood? In Sanskrit, this expressive activity of life is described by the concept of *prana*: which is derived from the word *ana*, meaning 'breath', and the prefix 'pra-', meaning 'prior to' or 'continuing on' or 'going forth'. As before (with the word *prakriti*), the prefix *pra-* creates a characteristic richness of meaning. On the one hand, the concept of *prana* implies an underlying principle of consciousness that comes before and continues through all living expression. On the other hand, the same concept is used to describe the activity of life that goes forth from consciousness to its living expressions in nature. As it is put in the *Kausitaki Upanisad,* 3.3:

. . . atha khalu prana eva	But then, in truth, life in itself
prajnatmedam sariram	is consciousness, the (real) self,
parigrhyotthapayati, . . .	which holds this body all around
	and causes it to rise alive.

Here, the word *prana* has been translated as 'life'. The essential principle of life (*prana eva* — 'life in itself') is consciousness, which is the supporting basis and the unchanging cause of the living activities of the body. This is, in essence, the same conception as Aristotle's 'unmoved mover'.[4]

Thus, the living faculty of expression (traditionally called *prana* or 'the breath of life') is a special kind of activity that rises from consciousness. It is not an action of one object towards another, for it does not start from any object. Instead, it starts from consciousness, which is not an object and which neither acts nor is acted upon.

But, if the living expression is not the action of one object upon another, then how can it be understood? A little reflection shows that we do in fact understand our experience in two rather different ways. On the one hand, experience is understood in terms of objects and their actions and relationships towards each other. On the other hand, experience is understood as an expression of consciousness.

For example, a human face can be understood as a configuration of features activated by underlying muscles; but it is also understood as expressing thought and feeling, and hence consciousness. Similarly, a map can be understood as a configuration of marks and lines and colours, printed by a machine; but it is also understood as an expression of perception and meaning, and hence of consciousness. Or, a landscape can be understood as a pattern of geographically formed features;

but it can also be understood as an experience of meaning and beauty, and hence as an expression of consciousness.

These two ways of understanding experience can be described as 'objective' and 'subjective'. In the objective approach, attention goes out from understanding and accepted assumptions towards objects and events and the actions and relationships between them. Here, thought and reasoning are used to formulate descriptions of objects and their relationships, to calculate predictions of events, and to prescribe actions towards desired objectives.

When experience is approached subjectively, attention is reflected back towards underlying consciousness, from which feelings, thoughts and actions express meaning in perceived objects and events. This involves a reflection from objective perceptions to background assumptions and understanding, on the basis of which perceptions are interpreted and assimilated into knowledge. Here, thought and reasoning are used to interpret perceptions, to question and correct assumptions, and hence to clarify the understanding through which further expressions of consciousness will arise and further perceptions will be interpreted and assimilated into knowledge.

These two approaches, objective and subjective, are complementary. Together they form a repeating cycle that progressively develops knowledge, by reflecting back and forth between the objective world and consciousness as illustrated in the following diagram:

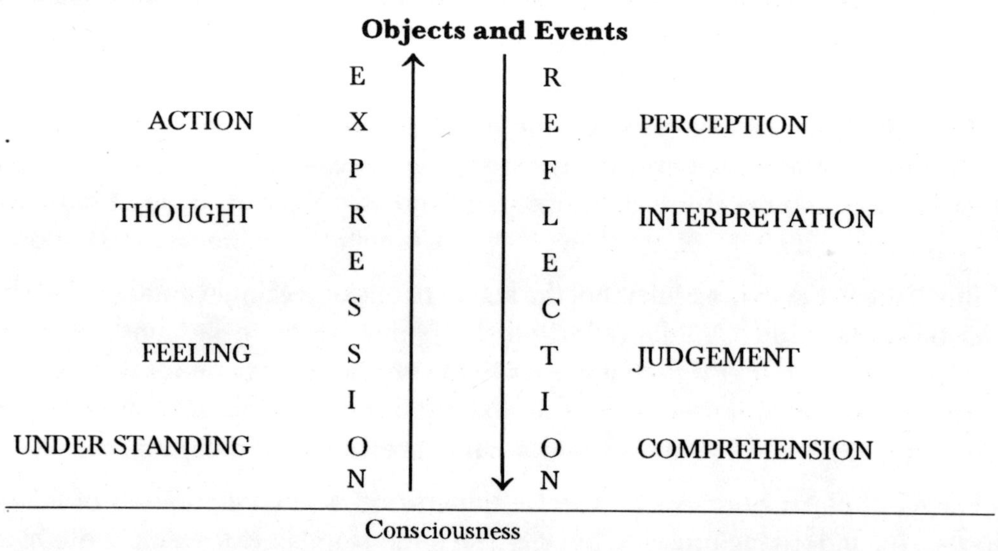

Through understanding, feeling, thought and action, consciousness is expressed in objects and events; and this expression continues on through perception, interpretation, judgement and comprehension, which reflect back to underlying consciousness, as perceptions are assimilated into understanding. Through the new understanding that is thus achieved, consciousness is expressed outwards again; and the cycle repeats so that understanding can be progressively clarified, and knowledge of the world can be progressively developed in the course of continued experience.

Unfortunately, there is a habitual and somewhat unexamined prejudice that identifies the subjective with the personal and the objective with the impersonal. This prejudice makes it seem that impersonal truth cannot be approached by subjective reflection, but only by looking out towards objects and events. Accordingly, scientific theories are reduced to the status of calculating machines for predicting events and prescribing technological action. In this view, it is only prediction and technological effectiveness that determine the truth of a theory. Conceptual intelligibility is a secondary matter, left to the personal taste of individual scientists.

This objective view is useful up to a point, when focusing on the predictive and technological aspects of modern physical science. But it is a one-sided view; and taken to extremes, it is clearly absurd. When it is claimed that scientific reasoning can only be tested by making predictions which come true, and when people are convinced that modern science is true just because its technology can work seeming miracles, then this is just fortune-telling and miracle-working pretending to the status of truth.

Even in the physical sciences, an excessive bias towards prediction and technology has its limitations, as developments in modern physics are beginning to show. In particular, quantum theory has made many startling predictions that have turned out to be extraordinarily accurate, and it has also proved very effective technologically; so it is widely accepted, despite serious problems of conception and intelligibility. But, because of these problems in quantum theory, the conceptual vacuum beneath its complex mathematical formalism has become a somewhat mystical free-for-all; with no underlying basis of intelligibility to show how quantum physics might be reconciled with the general theory of relativity, or with other ways of understanding experience.

And further, in sciences of life and mind, the bias toward objectivity has been a major road-block. The problem is that any expression of life or mind can only be understood by subjective reflection back to underlying consciousness, from which the expression comes. As a result, the study of life and mind has tended either to be relegated to the realm of poetry and imagination, or to be reduced to physical and behavioural science. Hence the continuing obsession with the mind-body problem, and the futile attempts to describe the relationship between consciousness and the body as though it were an action of one object upon another.

The only way out of these difficulties is to question our habitual identification of the subjective with the personal. Must consciousness be identified with the personal activities of perception, thought and feeling in our bodies, senses and minds? Or, beneath the changing appearances that come and go at the forefront of personal attention, does consciousness not continue at the background of each person's experience as the unchanging, impersonal basis from which changing appearances of perception, thought and feeling are known? If such an impersonal basis of consciousness can be understood, then impersonal truth can be approached through subjective reflection; and reason does not have to be reduced to mere calculation of objective consequences. Instead, reason and science can also be used to clarify understanding and develop knowledge of life and mind, as expressions of underlying consciousness.

The World and Individual Experience

How can nature be understood as a single whole, beneath the differing activities of the world and personality that manifest it in our experience? This question underlies the traditional conception of a 'macrocosm' of the external universe, corresponding to the various 'microcosms' of individual experience.

Like individual personality, the universe as a whole was conceived to express meaning and consciousness, and hence to have a life of its own, beyond the minds and bodies of particular individuals. What are we to make of this traditional idea of a living macrocosm, which expresses a universal consciousness? Must the idea be dismissed, along with a major part of traditional thought, as an essentially unscientific personification of impersonal reality? The answer depends upon how consciousness is identified. If consciousness is identified as a personal activity of the body, senses and mind, then of course it is an unscientific personification to think that the world outside the body, senses and mind could express consciousness in its own right. But, if it can be understood that consciousness is not just personal, then a major part of traditional thought is opened up to impersonal, scientific investigation.

In modern physical biology, life is conceived as the property of a specially complex kind of matter, found in plant, animal and human bodies. This conception is based on a distinction between living and non-living matter; and the distinction is made in terms of molecular and behavioural complexity. As molecular biology and behavioural science have shown, this conception can be useful as far as it goes, but it suffers from two limitations. First, since all matter is more or less complex, it is somewhat arbitrary exactly how and where the boundary between non-living and living matter is drawn in the progression of increasing complexity that leads to evident life. So the basic distinction of living and non-living matter is inherently relative and can never be entirely clear. And second, without a consideration of meaning, it is not clear how any amount of complexity can express consciousness.

When it comes to a consideration of meaning, our modern conceptions tend to be inconsistent and confused. Objectively, meaning is conceived as the representation of one object (or one complex of objects) by another, through similarity of form: as for example when a map represents a territory. However, this objective conception does not apply to our subjective experience of meaning, as expressing consciousness; because it is not at all clear how objective form is related with the stream of changing appearances in our minds or with underlying consciousness. For example, how could physical forms of expression on a person's face be objectively similar to expressed feelings of happiness and unhappiness, or to the continuing basis of consciousness that knows such differences of feeling?

In our experience of living personality, we obviously perceive some sort of relationship between the body, mind and consciousness, but we have no clear idea as to what the relationship is. So we try to keep this confusion away from our knowledge of the external world, by conceiving that mind and consciousness are somehow confined within the body (or the nervous system or the brain), to which objective signals come from the external world. However, this kind of isolationist conception can never work completely, for an obvious and simple reason. If mind and consciousness were entirely confined within the body, then of course the external world could not be known at all.

In fact, in our perceptions of the external world, we do have subjective experiences of order, purpose, meaning, value and continuity; and all our objective conceptions of structure and function arise (historically and logically) from these subjective experiences. We acknowledge this subjective aspect of knowledge by conceiving that the external world has only objective structure and function in itself, but people attribute subjective order and purpose and meaning and value to it. However, a little reflection shows that there is a curious contradiction here. The concepts of structure and function cannot be entirely objective, but only relatively so. Beneath their objective exterior, they are founded on subjective perceptions of order and purpose that are expressed from the perceiver's consciousness. If subjectively perceived order and purpose and meaning are not there in the world, but are only attributed to it by personal perception, then all our concepts of objective structure and function are founded on lies.

Traditional conceptions of life and world took a broader, more systematic view, beneath their variety of ritual and religious metaphors. The English word 'person' comes from the Latin *persona*, meaning 'a mask'; and as this derivation suggests, the outward personality was conceived as the apparent surface of an underlying, inner principle of life. Thus, traditional conceptions of 'living' and 'non-living', or 'inner' and 'outer', refer essentially to different levels of experience, not to territorial divisions. Life was not essentially conceived to be confined within the personality, territorially divided from a non-living world outside. Nor was life essentially conceived by a territorial division between living and non-living kinds of matter.

Instead, matter was conceived as the objective surface of appearance at which life expresses consciousness, both in the individual personality and in the external world.

In this sense, traditional conceptions take matter in itself to be lifeless and inanimate, as described by the Sanskrit word *jada*. Matter is living or animate only to the extent that it expresses consciousness. And this expression of consciousness is a relative affair. It is not all or nothing, but only more or less. Consciousness is expressed only partially imperfectly by human beings, but more by human beings than by animals, more by animals than plants, and more by plants than earth and stones.

The human expression of consciousness is characterized by reflective discrimination (*viveka* in Sanskrit), which questions apparent knowledge so as to distinguish truth from falsity. Animals lack human reflection, but express consciousness through instinctive motivation. Plants lack animal motivation, but express consciousness through purposive growth and functioning. Seemingly inanimate objects like stones lack purposive growth and functioning of their own, but even they express consciousness to some degree through the part they play in the ordered functioning of an intelligible universe. The ordered functioning and intelligibility of the world was conceived as a universal **expression of consciousness**[5] which is not so obvious as the expression of consciousness in living creatures, but which requires a more delicate and subtle interpretation.

However, if the functioning of the world is conceived to express consciousness, an immediate question arises: Whose consciousness is expressed, and how is it to be understood? In mythical and religious beliefs, this question was somewhat metaphorically answered by conceiving a variety of gods and spirits, or a single transcendent God, by whose divine purposes and will the universe was taken to be ordered and ruled. Such divine purposes and will were mystically described, as beyond the limited comprehension of the ordinary human mind; and so they were not meant to be questioned, but instead propitiated and accepted through ritual worship and religious devotion.

Though traditional conceptions were thus popularly expressed in mythical and religious belief, they were founded on a more philosophical enquiry into universal reality and individual experience. Broadly speaking, this enquiry of traditional philosophy can be described in three stages.

First, an enquiry is made into the changing character of the external world and individual personality. At this stage, it is skeptically observed that everything ultimately changes, in both world and personality; so all their seeming continuity is only relative and cannot provide any final basis of unshifting certainty upon which truth could be securely known. Accordingly, understanding is sought by a knowing detachment, from the changing character of all worldly and personal things. In the Indian tradition, this philosophy of change is generally associated with Buddhist philosophers. In the European tradition, essentially the same position is associated with the early Greek philosopher, Heraclitus.[6]

When it is accepted that everything in the world and personality is subject to change and difference, the question of continuity remains. On what continuing basis can differences be compared, so that changes can be known and understood? This question leads to a second stage of philosophical enquiry, where change and difference are associated with appearances. All changing world and personality are conceived as differing manifestations of the common reality of underlying nature, which thus manifests itself in changing appearances before unchanging consciousness. This is of course the philosophical dualism of nature and consciousness which this paper has already been describing. Here, understanding is sought through a complete distinction of objective nature from subjective consciousness so that nature is known in all its completeness, and no trace of personal partiality remains in the knowing consciousness. Both in the external world and individual experience, nature is conceived to express consciousness by a very special and delicate relationship between the two. In Aristotelian philosophy, the self-moving nature was conceived to act for love of the 'unmoved mover'. In *Samkhya* philosophy, nature (*prakrti*) was conceived to manifest itself 'for the sake of consciousness' (*purusartha*).

But, if all nature thus expresses consciousness, does it not follow then that consciousness is the underlying reality which is manifested in all of nature's appearances? Such questioning leads to a third stage of philosophical enquiry, where consciousness is investigated as the underlying reality of all that is known. The resulting philosophy is called 'non-dualism', because it concludes that there is really no duality between that which knows and that which is known.

The non-dualist position can be described as follows. When knowing consciousness is completely distinguished from the partial and changing activities of personality, then the underlying reality of nature is known truly and impartially, from the impersonal basis of consciousness that continues through each person's experience. But, in each person's experience, all appearances of the world arise from this underlying basis of consciousness, and no appearance of the world can exist apart from consciousness. Thus, it finally turns out that consciousness is the entire reality which is shown by all appearances.[7] Consciousness and reality are identical, as that one unchanging principle which is common to all the different appearances that come and go in our experience. When this underlying principle is sought subjectively, by reflecting back into individual experience, it is called 'consciousness'. When it is sought objectively, by looking out into the external world, it is called 'reality'. The two words are thus differing names which result from different approaches to the same thing.

From this non-dualist position, it is much easier to understand the traditional conception of a living macrocosm that expresses consciousness. If the consciousness that underlies individual experience is identical with the reality of the whole world, then this consciousness is the world's own underlying reality, and it is only natural that the world should express it. Quite simply and naturally, it is the perceiver's own consciousness that is thus expressed in the perceived objects and events of the world. But here, it must be clearly understood that the perceiver's own consciousness is neither personal nor changing nor varying. Instead, it is the impersonal, continuing principle of reality that is shared in common with other perceivers and with the perceived world. Thus, understanding and knowledge are sought in two ways. First, by reflecting back to the impersonal basis of consciousness that underlies individual experience; and second, by looking out from this impersonal basis, to see the whole world as an expression of consciousness.

In India, this non-dualist position is represented by the philosophy of *Advaita Vedanta*. In the European tradition, essentially the same position is associated with the early Greek philosopher, Parmenides, who described reality as an indivisible, unchanging unity, where knowing and being are identical.[8]

How can such traditional conceptions be related to modern physical science? Through the correspondence conceived between macrocosm and microcosm, a major part of traditional knowledge is concerned with the expression of consciousness in the world and personality. Where this is so, a great deal of confusion could perhaps be avoided by distinguishing different levels of knowledge, through each of which reason enquires towards impersonal truth.

At the level of physical science, the world is described by conceiving theoretical systems of interacting objects and interrelated events. Once these theoretical systems have been conceived, knowledge is used and tested by calculated descriptions and predictions of objects and events. When descriptions and predictions fail, there is a change of direction, from objective calculation to subjective reflection, as scientists question the underlying assumptions and understanding that they have been taking for granted. From this subjective reflection, understanding is clarified, assumptions are corrected, and new conceptions and theories are formulated to be used and tested again by objective calculation. Thus, modern physical science is directly used and tested by objective calculations, which indirectly depend upon an underlying level of subjective reflection.

However, where knowledge is more directly concerned with meaning that expresses consciousness, subjective reflection is more directly used. By its very nature, such meaning is perceived by subjective reflection, in particular, where meaning is perceived in human and living behaviour. Where this kind of meaning is under investigation, we are engaged in a level of enquiry that underlies and complements physical science. We are no longer concerned merely with actions and relations between objects and events, but with the meaning that is perceived in these actions and relations, by reflecting back into the basis of consciousness that underlies our minds. At this level, knowledge may be conceived to reflect back to a common, impersonal reality which is shared in common by perceiver and perceived, but which appears differently in different minds and at different moments of time. Here, knowledge is used and tested by interpreting perceptions so as to clarify understanding, and by expressing new understanding in further feelings, thoughts, actions, perceptions and interpretations.

Modern conceptions tend to be rather confused about this second level of knowledge to which a great part of traditional knowledge belongs. For our modern sciences of life and mind, and for our understanding of the world as a living environment, it might be useful to attempt a little more open-minded questioning of our current confusion. And such open-minded questioning could perhaps lead to a better understanding of the wealth of experience that has accumulated through long traditions of philosophical enquiry into a non-dual reality that underlies both the perceived world and the perceiving personality.

The Elements — Divisions of Experience

Where modern physical science is primarily concerned with a world of external objects and events, traditional conceptions tend to be more philosophical beneath their didactic and metaphorical manner of expression. They are more philosophical in the sense that they are more primarily concerned with an underlying unity or truth of experience, which appears differently through different aspects and at different levels of experience. However, these different aspects and levels were somewhat metaphorically represented by the constituent principles and elements that were didactically asserted to make up the traditional cosmos. In this philosophical context, traditional principles and elements can often be interpreted as divisions of experience into different aspects and levels.

As already described, experience was divided into objective and subjective aspects with nature as the objective aspect, including all physical and mental activity, and with consciousness as the aspect of pure, impersonal knowledge.

In *Samkhya* and *Vedanta* philosophies, nature (*prakrti*) is divided into three further aspects, called the three *gunas* (literally 'qualities'). The most objective aspect, called *tamas*, is characterized by inertia and obscurity. It can be interpreted as describing the objects of nature that are acted upon. The second aspect, called *rajas*, is characterized by stimulation and energy. It can be interpreted as describing the motive forces that act upon the objects. The third aspect, called *sattva*, is characterized by harmony and clarity. It can be interpreted as describing the underlying order and expression of consciousness that nature acts for.

It can also be noted that these three aspects, *sattva*, *rajas* and *tamas*, form an ascending hierarchy of levels in the expression of consciousness. Consciousness is most directly expressed in the clarity and harmony of nature's underlying order, less directly expressed in the stimulation and energy of motive force, and most indirectly expressed in the inertia and obscurity of objects.

In both European and oriental traditions, nature was also considered to be constituted of five elements: 'earth', 'water', 'fire', 'air' and 'ether'. Though they are called 'elements', they are often described as a series of increasingly subtle levels on the appearance of the world. On the one hand, in a progressive enquiry towards underlying reality, each element is found to overlie the next (in the above order).[9] On the other hand, in cosmological accounts of creation, the same elements arise in reverse order, as a progression of increasingly gross levels through which reality appears.[10]

'Earth' was the traditional element of solidity, whereby objects maintain their separate identities. 'Water' was the traditional element of fluidity, whereby the separate identities of particular objects are formed and transformed. 'Fire' was the traditional element of propagating and consuming energy which causes the formation and transformation of objects. 'Air' was the traditional element of transparent tangibility, through which energy is propagated (as by wind, sound, radiant heat and light in the physical atmosphere). 'Ether' was the traditional element of pervading continuity, which underlies the subtle qualities of 'air', the propagating energy of 'fire', the changing fluidity of 'water' and the separately identified objects of 'earth'.

Accordingly, from a more modern philosophical point of view, the five elements could perhaps be interpreted as a division of experience into five levels along the following lines:

EARTH

When the world is perceived through body and mind, it seems at first to be made up of different objects and events. At this initial level, an element of differentiation and particularity appears in experience. This could well be symbolised by the traditional element 'earth' in the sense that earth is found differentiated into particular objects, like clay is found fashioned into different pots (to use the traditional analogy).

Traditional element	*Element of*	*Level of experience*	*Correspondence with modern physics*
'Earth'	Differentiation and particularity	Particular objects	Places of matter
'Water'	Change and transformation	Changing forms	Moving configuration
'Fire'	Representation and propagation	Intelligible meaning	Propagation of energy
'Air'	Qualification and conditioning	Relative characteristics	Fields conditioning space and time
'Ether'	Underlying continuity	Continuing background	The space-time continuum

WATER

If particular objects are perceived to exist, then how do their differences and particularities arise? How are objects told apart, and how are they formed? Such questioning leads to an underlying level of experience, where change and transformation become apparent as that element of experience which forms and shapes the world. This could well be symbolized by the traditional element 'water' in the sense that water flows in changing shapes and forms.

FIRE

What do change and transformation show, and how do they take place? What is shown by changing forms, and how are they transferred from one object or one place to another? Such questioning leads to another underlying level, where representation and propagation become apparent, as that element of experience which gives meaning to forms and enables them to move from place to place. This could well be symbolized by the traditional element 'fire' in the sense that fire consumes and illuminates (like meaning consumes its representations to illuminate what is represented), and fire also propagates (by burning its way through things and radiating energy).

AIR

How do representation and propagation work? What represented qualities are shown by meaningful forms, and what characteristic qualities and conditions travel along with forms that move identifiably from place to place? Such questioning leads in its turn to a further underlying level, where qualification and conditioning become evident as that element of experience which gives relative character to varying objects and localities in space and time. This could well be symbolised by the traditional element 'air' in the sense that air or atmosphere is an enveloping medium of relative qualities and conditions (described, in one traditional metaphor, as that which can be 'felt but not seen').

ETHER

How is experience qualified and conditioned? On what continuing basis are varying conditions and characteristics compared in different objects and localities differently situated in space and time? Such questioning leads to a fifth level of experience, where a basis of underlying continuity is understood at the common background of experience, which enables differing characteristics to be contrasted and compared, and which thus enables objects to be discerned apart and related together again. This background continuity could well be symbolized by the traditional element 'ether' in the sense that the 'ether' was conceived to pervade (and thus to continue through) all objects and all localities in space and time.

The above division of levels is very general and abstract; and hence it can be applied in somewhat different ways to many particular fields of experience. In the above table, an illustration how it might be applied in two ways is given: first to experience in general (including physical and mental aspects), and second to modern physics (where the physical aspect of experience is isolated and focused upon).

In traditional thought, the *pancikarana* distinction of five elements has in fact been applied somewhat differently in different fields of experience: as for example in the five elements (*panca mahabhutas*) of the external world, five levels of personality (the *panca kosas*), five levels of mind (*ahankara* — ego or personal identification, *citta* — will, *buddhi* — intellect, *manas* — qualitative mind or sensibility, *antahkarana* — the 'inner faculty' or understanding), five vital functions (*pranas*), five senses (*jnanendriyas*), and five external functions of action (*karmendriyas*) in the enveloping spheres of Aristotelian and medieval European cosmology (with the sphere of 'earth' progressively enveloped by spheres of 'water', 'air', 'fire', 'ether': all finally enveloped by the infinite reality of God),[11] and in other ways.

If the three *gunas* are compared with the five elements, an evident correspondence emerges. *Tamas* (inertia and obscurity) evidently corresponds to 'earth', since both correspond to objects of action. *Rajas* (stimulation and energy) evidently corresponds to 'fire', since both correspond to motive energy. *Sattva* (harmony and clarity) evidently corresponds to 'ether', since the harmony and continuity of nature imply one another. Through a little further interpretation, 'water' and 'air' can also be seen as aspects of *rajas*. 'Water' can be interpreted as the element of fluid tranformation, brought about by the motive energy of *rajas*. 'Air' can be interpreted as the element of relative conditioning, through which the energy of *rajas* is propagated. Hence the five elements can be interpreted as arising from the three *gunas*, by a further division of *rajas* (into 'water', 'fire' and 'air').

A progressive division of experience ending with the five elements can thus be summarized in *Fig.* 5.1.

Divisions of Experience

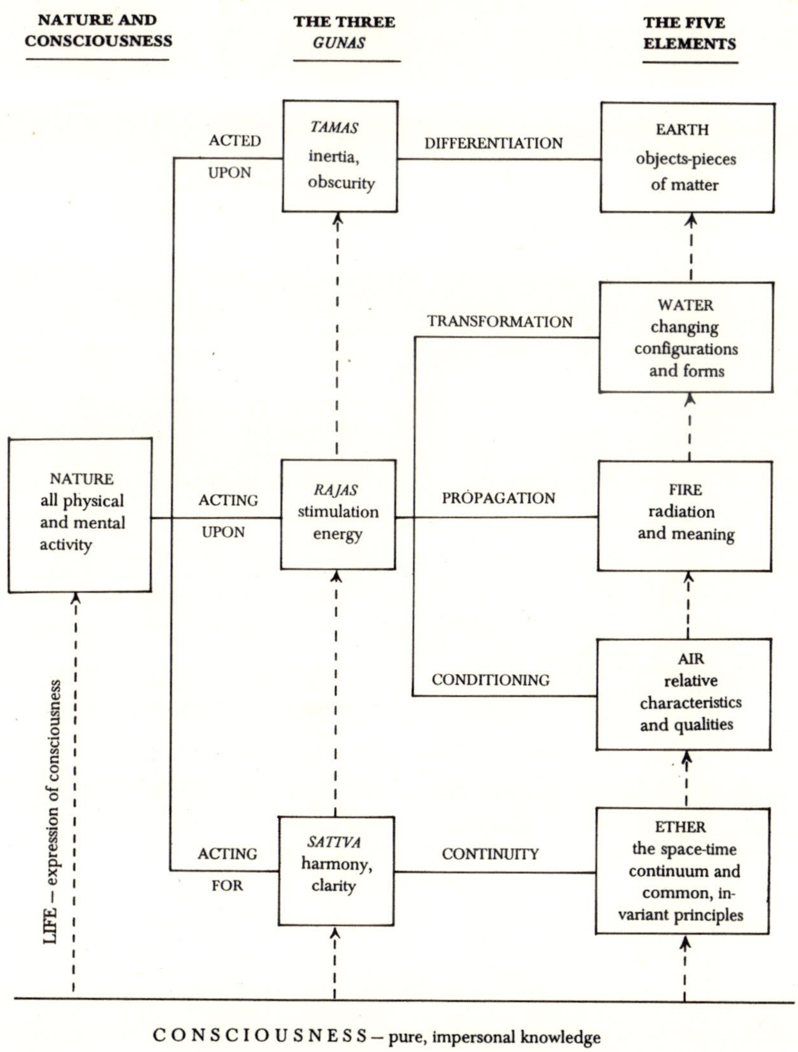

Fig. 5.1. Divisions of Experience

Appendix

An interpretation of traditional philosophical enquiry

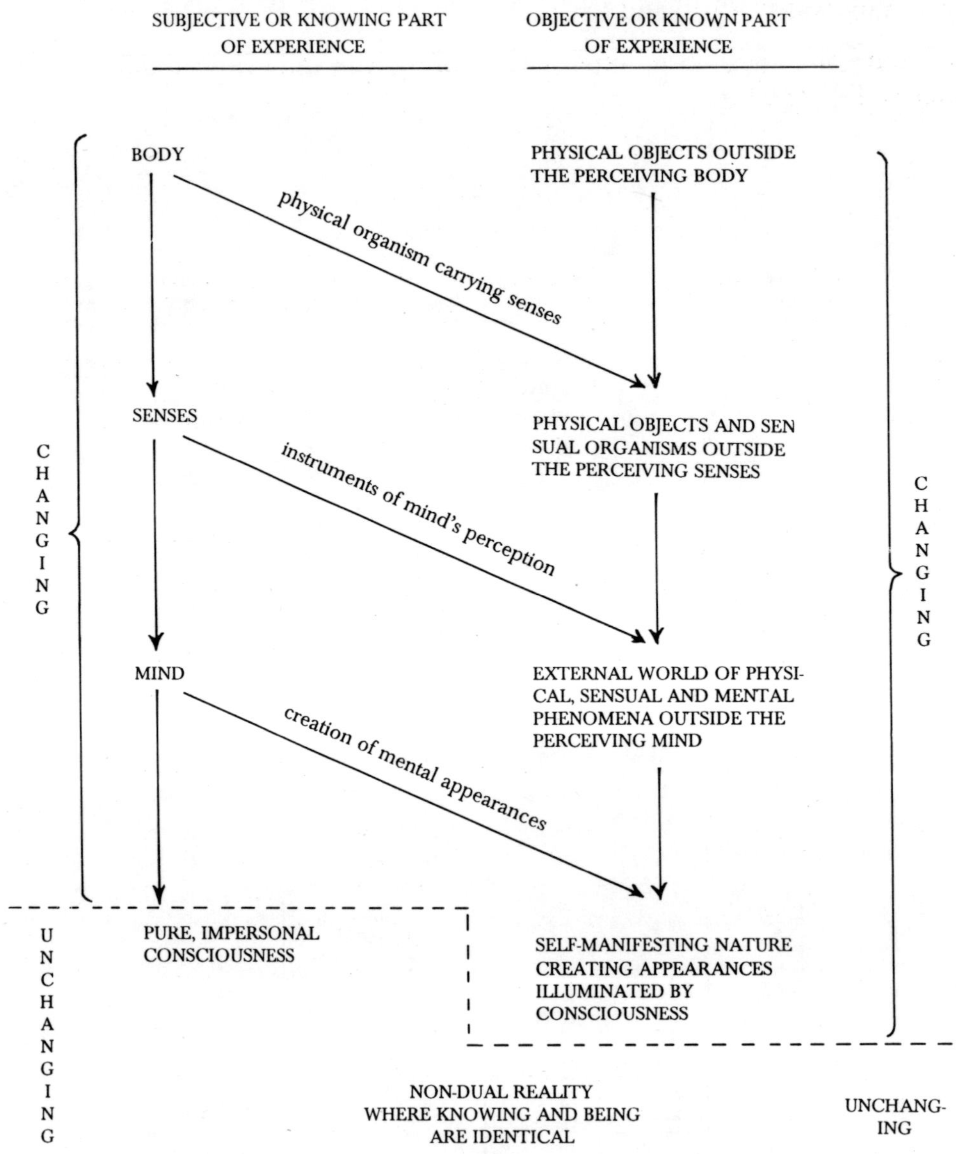

Fig. 5.2.

The above diagram shows a series of levels, at which experience is differently divided into subjective and objective parts.

At the uppermost level consciousness is attributed to a person's body, and thus the physical body is taken to be the knowing part of a person's experience. From this point of view the known or objective part of the experience consists in the physical objects with which the body interacts.

However, a little reflection shows that the body itself contains a knowing part and a known part of the experience. The knowing part consists of the five senses: sight, sound, smell, taste and touch. The known or objective part of the body is a physical organism which carries the senses. The apparent consciousness of the body comes from its perceiving senses, and it is thus more accurate to identify the senses as the knowing parts of the experience.

This leads to the second level of the above diagram. At this second level (as shown by the slanting arrow that comes down from above) the body as a sensual organism is taken into the objective part of the experience, which is thus expanded to include sensual organisms as well as physical objects.

A little further reflection shows that the senses are the objective instruments through which the mind perceives an external world. The apparent consciousness of the senses comes from the selective attention of the mind, and thus it is more accurate to identify the mind as the knowing part of the experience.

This leads to the third level of the above diagram. At this third level (as shown by the slanting arrow that comes down from above) the senses as instruments of the mind are taken into the objective part of the experience, which is thus expanded to include the mental as well as the sensual and physical phenomena in the external world outside the perceiving mind.

When the mind in its turn is reflected upon, it too can be seen as an objective instrument, which functions to create the changing appearances of perception, thought and feeling that come and go in each person's experience. These changing appearances of the mind are known by underlying consciousness which continues at the background of the experience, while perceptions, thoughts and feelings appear and disappear at the surface of the mental attention. Thus, the apparent consciousness of the mind comes from its underlying basis of continuity at the background of the experience where consciousness is not mixed with any appearance of objects, nor with any personal activities of the body, senses or mind. Instead of attributing consciousness to the changing and personal activities of the mind, it is more accurate to identify the pure, impersonal consciousness as the knowing part of each person's experience.

This leads to the fourth level of the above diagram. At this fourth level (as shown by the slanting arrow that comes down from above) the mind's function of creating appearances is taken into the objective part of the experience, which is thus expanded to conceive nature as a self-manifesting whole, containing within itself the creation of appearances that manifest it before the pure, impersonal illumination of consciousness.

But now, if it is asked what common and continuing reality underlies the differing and changing appearances of nature, it turns out that there is no way for distinguishing this objective reality from subjective consciousness, because both are always present together at every moment of each person's experience. Neither has any existence independent of the other; and they are just different aspects of a single, non-dual reality, where knowing and being are identical.

Notes

1. For Aristotle's concept of nature as self-moving, see R.G. Collingwood's *The Idea of Nature*, first published by Clarendon Press, Oxford, 1945, republished by Oxford University Press

paperback, (1960). Collingwood points out the opposition implied by the classical Greek concepts of nature (*phusis*) and artifice (*techne*). As opposed to the artificial objects of technical manipulation, the things of nature 'have a source of movement in themselves'. 'When a Greek writer contrasts *phusis* with *techne* (i.e. what things are when left to themselves with what human skill can make of them) . . . he implies that things have a principle of growth, organization and movement, in their own right and that this is what he means by their nature; and when he calls things natural he means that they have such a principle in them.'

2. For Aristotle's conception of 'soul as the source of movement but not itself moved', see Brett's *History of Psychology*, edited and abridged by R.S. Peters, (George Allen and Unwin, London and Macmillan, New York, 1962). Peters quotes Aristotle as saying: 'Nor is it correct to speak of the soul as being itself moved, as in anger. It is even scarcely correct to say that the soul feels anger; for that would be like saying that the soul weaves or builds. We should rather not say that the soul pities or learns or thinks, but that the man does so with the soul; and this too not in the sense that the motion occurs in the soul, but in the sense that motion sometimes reaches to, sometimes starts from the soul.'
3. For a mythical conception of underlying nature as divinely immanent in change, and manifesting itself through change, see the 'Mutabilitie Cantos' at the end of Edmund Spenser's *The Faerie Queene*. In cantos VI and VII, Spenser describes nature allegorically, as manifested through the Greco-Roman gods and other spirits; but, in the brief canto VIII, he ends with a sudden invocation to the Christian 'God of Saboath hight': who transcends nature, in sharp contrast to the Greco-Roman gods and other spirits through whom nature is manifested. In medieval and Renaissance Europe this was a common and prevalent contrast. On the one hand, there were the Greco-Roman and other gods and spirits through whom nature was mythically and allegorically described. And on the other hand, there was the transcendent God of Christianity, who was the pure and supreme spirit to whom people must turn for the sake of the immortal soul.
4. See note 2 above.
5. This is described in the *Brhadaranyaka Upanisad* as follows:

From 3.8.9

etasya va aksarasya prasasane,	Under the guidance of this
. . . suryacandramasau	same changeless principle, . . .
vidhrtau tisthatah;	the sun and moon are kept in place, . . .
. . . dyavaprthivyau	heaven and earth are kept in place, . . .
vidhrte tisthatah;	moments, hours, days, nights,
. . . nimesa, muhurta,	fortnights, months, seasons, years
ahoratrany ardhamasa, masa,	are kept in place . . . .
rtavah, samvatsara iti	
vidhrtas tisthanti, . . .	

From 3.8.11

tad va etad aksaram . . .	This is that same changeless principle
adrstam drastr, . . .	which is not seen, but is the see-er, . . .
avijnatam vijnatr, . .	which is not known, but is the knower . . .

6. 'You cannot step twice into the same rivers; for fresh waters are ever flowing in upon you.' (Heraclitus, fragments 41 and 42, as translated in John Burnet, *Early Greek Philosophy*, Black, 4th edition, England, 1930)
7. In modern academic philosophy such a conclusion is often dismissed as a 'solipsist' fallacy

on the grounds that the consciousness of a person's body and mind is only a small part of a much larger world. But here it is taken for granted that consciousness is a personal activity of body and mind. So the dismissal does not apply to non-dual philosophy, where the personal identification of a knowing self is questioned and found to be false. As the *Chandogya Upanisad* puts it:

From 8.1.3

. . . *yavan va ayam akasah,*
tavan eso'ntarhrdaya akasah.
ubhe asmin dyava-prthivi
antar eva samahite,
ubhav agnis ca vayus ca
surya-candramasav ubhav,
vidyun naksatrani. . .

. . . Just as great as the space
(of all the world) is this
inner space within the heart.
In itself, contained within,
are both heaven and earth,
both fire and air, both sun and moon,
lightning and the stars . . .

From 8.1.4

. . . *yadaitaj jara vapnoti*
pradhvamsate va,
kim tato'tisisyata . . .

. . . When this (personality)
ages or is destroyed,
what remains of that (reality)?

From 8.1.5

. . . *nasya jarajaitaj jiryati,*
na vadhenasya hanyate.
. . . *esa atma* . . .

. . . By the ageing of this (personality),
it does not age.
By the killing of this (personality),
it is not killed . . .
it is the self . . .

8. See Parmenides' composition, On Nature. In John Burnet, *Early Greek Philosophy* (see note 6 above), Parmenides is translated as saying: '. . . it is the same thing that can be thought and that can be' (On Nature, 5.). From Burnet's footnote, it seems that an alternative translation might be: '... it is the same thing that is for knowing and for being.' (By translating *noein* and *einai* as 'for knowing' and 'for being' respectively.)
9. As described in the *Brhadaranyaka Upanisad,* 3.6 and 3.8.
10. As for example in the *Taittiriya Upanisad,* 2.1.1.
11. For a lively account of the first four elements in European thought, see Edmund Spencer's *The Faerie Queene*, 'Mutabilitie Canto VII', stanzas 17-25. (The fifth element 'ether' of underlying continuity is the implicit subject of the 'Mutabilitie cantos', but Spencer does not explicitly describe it as the element 'ether'.) For a more general account of all five elements in European thought, see any standard account of Aristotelian cosmology and C.S. Lewis, *The Discarded Image: An Introduction to Medieval and Renaissance Literature*, (Cambridge University Press, England, 1968-70).

6

Nature as Feminine
Ancient Vision of Geopiety and Goddess Ecology

Madhu Khanna

The Feminine conceptualization of nature occupies very significant place in Indian religious history. The image of the earth as a goddess, known variously as *Prthivi*, *Dharatimata*, *Jagadddhatri* is ancient and all-pervasive. Almost all the geographical features of the natural environment are personified as goddesses. Mountains, caves, rocks, forests, trees, plants, healing herbs, rivers, streams, lakes were conceived of as potent symbols of feminine power, inherent in nature. From the *Vedas* down to the *Puranas* nature personifications are mediated through the symbol of the divine feminine. In the *Rg Veda*, for example, the crimson streak of day-break is portrayed as Usas, the Mistress of Dawn whose brilliant effulgence spreads out piercing the formless black abyss (*R V*, 10.127). Night and day are the two celestial sisters that bring rest and awakening to the world. In their lap, gods recline and enact their roles. The much celebrated mother of the gods, Aditi who claims as many as sixty hymns in the *Vedas* is the infinite and the womb of the cosmos. Goddesses such as, Kuhu, Sinivali, Anumati and Raka are lunar divinities symbolizing the waxing and waning of the lunar-cycle. The rivers Ganga, Yamuna and Sarasvati mentioned in the *Vedas* are goddesses who preside over the facundating waters of life. The hymn dedicated to *Aranyani* (*R V*, 10.146) or the forest goddesses (*Vanadevis*) celebrated the spirit of the forest and groves. They are joined by an innumerable number of goddesses who preside over village territories and specific sacred centres (*Ksetradevis*). The life sustaining foods also have their goddesses in the personifications such as, Annapurna, Sataksi and Sakhambari. Thus from the sky wandering celestial bodies to the sprouting plant were conceived of as a manifestation of the feminine principle. In later literature these personaifications culminate into the composite vision of an all-inclusive cosmic from (*virat svarupa*) of the goddess, where mountains, rivers, celestial bodies, vegetation and stratums of space from various parts of her body:

> They (the gods) saw the goddess's superanal cosmic Form. The *Satyaloka* is situated on the topmost of Her head; the Sun and Moon are her eyes; the quarters, Her ears; the *Vedas* are Her words; the Universe is Her heart; the earth is Her loins; the space between earth and sky is Her navel; the asterisms are Her Thighs; the *Maharaloka* is Her neck; the *Janarloka* is Her face; Indra and the Devas and then *Svarloka* is her arms; the sound is the organ of Her ears;. . . . The fire is within her Face; day and night are like her two wings; the mountains are Her bones; the rivers are Her veins, and the trees are the hairs of Her body. O King ! youth virginity, and old age are Her best gaits, the two twilight are Her clothings; the Moon is the mind of the Mother of the Universe.
>
> [*Devibhagavata Purana,* VII. Chap. 33.1-21ff]

Energy, Synergy and Consciousness

All the forms of nature personifications of the goddess invariably converge into the abstract notion of *Sakti* or Energy and its inherent power of synergy. All the visible forms of nature, despite their outer appearances, mountains streams, rivers, fields, vegetations, etc. is said to be endowed with an invisible energy of *sakti* that constitutes its substle nature.

> Riverse and mountains have a dual nature. A river is but a form of water, yet it has a distinct (subtle) body. Mountains apper as motionless mass, yet their true from is not so. We cannot know, when looking at a lifeless shell, that is cantains a living being. Similarly, within the apparently inanimate rivers and mountains there dwells a hidden (feminine) energy (*sakti*).
>
> [*Kalika Purana,* 22.10-13]

The hidden feminine *sakti* inherent in nature stirs the seeds to fructify as the universe. Nature's *sakti* is visible everywhere in the cyclic movement of germination, growth and decay of life. *Sakti* is the energetic feminine potency of the Earth Mother, the life line of the living earth. The earth is an animated and live organism with an efficient network linked to the biological vision of the ecosystem. The world-body of the great goddess is a whole organism — a 'holon' — in which each part in related to the whole.

From very early times, India employed the image of the loom to explain this interrelated web of life. The universe is imaged as a woven fabric the warp and woof of which form intricate interrelated patterns. The *Brhadaranyaka Upanisad* (2.1.19) employs the metaphor of a spider sitting at the centre of its Web, issuing and reabsorbing, its threads in concentric circle. The spider's web symmetrically expand into a visible circumference, and though there are divergent lines, all the threads interrelate and can be traced back to the central point of the web. The sacred geography of the land is the reflection of this interrelated web. Earth, water, plants, animals and human life are inter-dependent and interrelated in the grand design of creation. These interrelationships operate within the expanding and contracting cycle of the seasons. As the wheel of time turns, the products of nature transmute, change, decay, and are born a new. Her ongoing rhythms web together the waters, vegetation, and the earth. It is for this reason that nature gets humanized and is treated with extreme reverence in India. No part of nature is desecrated as they all participate in the animated play of *Prakrti*. The fundamental motive behind the ancient perception is the belief that nature is conscious (*cit*), alive and animated. Text such as the *Yogavasistha* have dealt with the inherent consciousness that underlies creation. Consciousness or *cit* resides in everything just as 'vibration resides in air, or void in space, as water in whirlpool' (*YV*, VI *Uttara* 211.23).

Nature goddesses thus, do not stand in opposition to the natural powers of the earth, of life, of death, or regeneration, but are ever in harmony with the natural law of cyclic order in creation. They operate as unifying participants in essence of life : as a self-containd fusion of energy and synergy. Just as water, soil, light/heat and vegetation are in a constant symbiotic relationship, similarly, the feminine personifications, as the symbolic projections of nature, are interlinked to one another. Earth and water goddesses interact to create vegetation, the moon orbits sustains the sap of the plants, roots and trees. The goddesses manifest as primal *relational* powers of nature, connecting all elements of life in a single biotic web.

Our seminal concern in this essay is to revision the nature heirophanies from an ecological perspective. The interpretive model that I adopt will attempt at comprehensive analysis on the conceptual understanding of the feminine principle. There are countless number of goddesses and innumerable local varients. This essay will focus on two of the most important nature personifications : the earth and the waters of life. It will illumintate the concept of the earth mother as expounded in the *Atharva Veda*; and trace the timeless myth of the Descent of the Ganges in the light of ecological concerns. By viewing the Feminine Principle as an integral symbol of nature one may gain insight on the ecological implications of the symbolic feminine. These ideas must be viewed in the larger context of the traditional attitude of reverence toward nature. The traditional perceptions toward nature has roused a variety of critical responses. The scriptural sources that extol such attitudes, are generally seen as a collections or primitive songs of nature worship and a reflection of archaic animinism. They are considered no more than 'half-formed myths, crude allegories, obscure gropings' and immature poetical ramblings of a very primitive stage of human civilization. Some consider the Indian passion of sacralization of nature to be an adulation in the extreme rooted in unreasoning faith. The nature hymns of the *Vedas* are conceived to be an imaginative, but subjective model of the mind that helped to develop a world-view based on emotional participation of nature.

Our hypothesis is that the descriptive, prescriptive and ecologistic passages on nature deities found in scriptural sources were a means of inculcating ecological awareness. Their significance lies in the fact that the metaphors provide that methodologies and strategies adopted in the past to sustain the imbalances and threats posed to the natural environment.

As no activity whether biological, natural, human or metaphysical can exist outside the sphere of the earth, the concept of the Mother Earth[1] assimilates a wide range of meanings. The celebrated *Prthivi-sukta* (also referred to as *Bhumi-sukta*) in the *Atharva Veda* (12, 1.1-63)[2], sums up the Vedic attitude towards earth. Our seminal concern here is to revision the Vedic concept of Mother Earth as woven into the sixty-three verses of this hymn, in the light of ecological concerns. The whole of *Rgveda* reflects a religion of nature, where man is conceived as a part and parcel of its natural dynamics. Vedic man was nature centred for whom the natural phenomena arose from a divine source. Behind the wide spectrum of gods and an immensely intricate ritual technology of the fire-sacrifice, there was an insight into the natural laws of nature. The *Rgveda* (*c.* 2000-2500 BC), resonates with praise hymns to the deities of the sky, earth and atmosphere, thunder, rain, sun and wind. In contrast, the *Atharva Veda* rings a new note. It affirms the life of man-in-the-world. The text contains incantations, magic spells, and formulas either to bless or appease, to curse or to protect the general well-being of the community.

The *Atharva* hymns, named after the fire-churning priest Atharvan, were devised to establish harmony in family and village life. Here the attention of the forest-dwelling seers has shifted, as it were, from the sky pervading nature gods to the life sustaining earth. Vedic culture, as we know, was rooted in a very high degree of material comfort. Man's life was conceived as a harmonious unit. There was neither any pessimism nor any conflict between the pursuit of *dharma*, *artha*, *kama* and *moksa*. Life on earth was considered a short sojourn or a stepping stone to higher life in other regions. From the fertile soil of this life affirming milieu sprang the most exalted vision of the real visible earth, conceived as a nurturing mother of human-kind:

> The earth on whom water flow day and night, never ceasing motion
> – the earth that is brown black and red in colour, a vast abode.
>
> [*Atharva Veda,* 12.1.9a-11b]

Prthivi : The Earth Mother

The Vedic praise hymns to the Earth Mother cover a wide range of aspects: physical, organic, metaphysical, ethical and cosmic. No aspect of existence is kept out of its fold.

The Vedic seers were moved by the beauty and splendour of the far spreading earth. The earth holds the verdent continents, lands with forests, nurtured by abundant rains and simmering warmth. Her body laced by rivers, rimmed by ocean is adorned with "gentle slopes and plains" (*A V*, 12-1.2). The earth is composed of hills, 'rock, stone and dust' and is compactly held. An essential feature of the Earth is her fragrance which pervades all the products of the earth. The herbs, water, nymphs and celestial creatures bear it. Her fragrance enters the lotus and the flowers everywhere. May this fragrance enter him, says the seer:

> Instil in me abundantly that fragrance,
> O Mother Earth, which emanates from you
> your fragrance which has entered the lotus
> where with the immortal Gods at the Sun-daughters wedding
> were redolent, O Earth, in times primaeval –
> instil in me that fragrance.
> Your fragrance that adheres to human beings
> O Earth, steep us, too deeply in that fragrance
> [*Atharva Veda,* 12.1.23-26]

The Broad One

Once Priyavrata, son of Svayambhu Manu, the first human to be born on earth, ruled the country for eleven hundred million years. One day he saw the sun travelling on one side of the earth and wondered that one side of the earth must be dark. Curious to know what lay on the other side of the earth, he rode his chariot and travelled around the earth seven times. The wheels of the chariot made seven furrows. These furrows became seven seas, the beds between the furrows became seven islands, inhabited by people (*Linga Purana,* 52.35-39). Thus, the setting of the earth mother is a limitless domain, far spreading and wide. Her immensity is beyond the grasp. Hence, she is called *Prthivi*, the Broad One:

> Your regions, earth, to Eastward and to Westward.
> Southward and Westward, may they receive me kindly.
> [*Atharva Veda,* 12-1.31]

Earth as Supporter

The earth is the eternal matrix 'on whom moves all that breathes and stirs' (*A V,* 12-

1.2). She carries on her body the four directions of space, on whose body the ploughman toils. She is the dwelling place of creatures, animate and inanimate:

> On whom the men of olden days roamed.
> On whom the conquering Gods smote the demons,
> the home of cattle, horses and of birds,
> Her upon whom the trees, lord of forest,
> stand firm — unshakable, in every place,
> this long-enduring Earth . . .
> [*Atharva Veda*, 12-1.3, 27]

It is upon her that men enact the drama of life; the animal kingdom find their homes. It is upon her paths that human's tread and its her highways that men use for their chariots. She is the unshakable One in whose bosom trees and forests stand firm. None can escape the touch of the earth, whether walking, sitting or standing, whatever postures one may take, she provides the 'couch' for all. In this way, she is the foundation and supporter of all. The word used to describe earth is *dharani* or *dharati* (derived from the Sanskrit root *dhr*, meaning to hold or bear). By reason of this, the seers realized the generosity and patience of the long-enduring earth and approached her with praise:

> O Purifying Earth, I you invoke,
> O Patient Earth, by sacred word enhanced,
> bearer of nourishment and strength, of food and ghee
> O Earth, we would approach you with due praise !
> [*Atharva Veda,* 12-1.29]

Our Relationship to Earth

The Vedic attitude toward earth springs from man's primal experience of being an offspring or a child of earth:

> The Earth is Mother, I am son of Earth.
> [*Atharva Veda,* 12.1.12b]

The earth is the supreme, loving, life sustaining mother. She is beautiful, fertile, nurturing and generous. She is close to humans as their own skin. As a person's entire existence depends upon her, man is of earth, part of earth. The earth is his home. She is a merciful compassionate mother whose benign heart pours unconditional love to all, irrespective of their talents and station in life:

> She carries in her lap the foolish and also the wise
> She bears the death of the wicked and the wise.
> [*Atharva Veda,* 12.1.48]

She is the gracious leader and protecteress of the world (*AV,* 12.1.57). Helpmate of human kind, she lives in friendly collaboration with all.

Man adores the earth, yet is smitten by her awe. Capricious and unpredictable is her rule over man. She is benevolent, but also wild, destructive, chaotic, disorderly, death-dealing. Earth is more than a material segment. Her formidable size, hidden elemental powers released from time to time besott man and make him a stranger to his environment. Although, man's relationship to the earth remains ambiguous and ambivalent the inseparability of man and earth is affirmed in no uncertain terms.

Earth as Sacred Womb

"You (Earth) germinate the seed with quickening power" (*Rg Veda,* 5.84.1). The Earth Mother is the vitality that generates growth and germination. In Her maternal womb, She nourishes the potent seed which completes its life-cycle in the tree, the flower, the fruit, and once again the seed. One association of the earth is with the food saplings that grow on Her vast body. The earth reveals Her powers in the form of Mother of Grains. Grains such as corn, wheat and barley is her bounty, simultaneously the basic source of nourishment. She is the continuous source of food and herbs valuable for healing (*AV,* 12.1.19). Just as a human mother gestates the child in her womb, similarly, the Mother Earth nourishes the seed till they ripen. There is no danger between the earth and the forms that emerge from Her. All Her birthlings remain bound to their source and their relationship is one of intimacy and solidarity. The creative and fecund nature of the earth are given so much prominence that she requires none but herself to procreate. It is for this reason that several epithets of earth are virgin mothers who were endowed with the power of parthenogenesis-goddesses who could give birth unaided by men. Durga is one such epithet who is an eternal virgin, 'the energy of all but consort of none'. In the mythological context, She has the superhuman ability to give birth to a number of goddesses who emanate from Her body, like sparks of fire. The image of the earth as a universal womb explains why vessels, hollows, grottos and caves were found to be the vulvic body of the Earth Mother.

If on one hand the Earth Mother awakens the fertility of the soil from its potential state, it also encompasses the reality of death. For, she contains the eternal condition of life and death; death in life and life in death. The mythical destiny of earth is to stand at the beginning and end of every biological form and share in the history of human destiny. Thus she mediates between the mystery of life and death. Life consists in abundant growth involving a brief detachment from the womb of the Mother Earth, death consists in a return to the eternal condition in the bosom of the earth. As said:

> You are the earth, I place you in the earth.
> [*Atharva Veda,* 12.1.11; 12.1.14]

The earth is the dwelling from which all life is born and into which it returns. That is her supreme nature. Since Mother Earth resists destruction, she is one of the most powerful images of recurring life. She is endowed with an inexhaustible capacity to organise its own energy and growth patterns. Left to its own natural devices, she creates order where there is disorder, harmony in place of disharmony, life in place of death. The earth mother in this respect is endowed with self-regenerative energy. She therefore symbolises the sacred totality of life's processes: birth, death and rebirth.

An overwhelming concept of the Earth Goddess is found in the characterization of Goddess Viraj,[3] the epitome of Earth's essence and cosmic form. She is the universe as *Prana*, *Vak*, and the creator. Viraj is the Resplendent One, who is intimately associated with the process of creation. Her most important feature is that she is imperishable and never dies. All the gods and powers of nature fear Her origin for they consider, 'She will become This All'. She spews forth as the vital energy that quickens the sap of the seed and enters the sacrificial household fires, the plants, trees, villages, and pastoral sites. She rises. She is above, below, around, everywhere. Then rebirthing Herself as the creator, for Her very own propitiation by man, to make abundant the earth, She arises, She stands, She strides fourfold and comes to the trees, to the manes, to the gods and to humans. They all slay Her one after another. She vanishes into the atmosphere, then returns into existence. Even when slain, She remains invincible and indestructible like the patient earth, who endures but never dies (*AV*, 8.10.1-33).

Earth in the Cradle of *Rta*

The entire earth by virtue of its animation is sustained by a harmonious cosmic principle. In Vedic code, this principle is known as *Rta* or cosmic order. It is the self-regulative law of harmony. It is the impersonal power, the underlying regulator of all life on earth at the natural and human level. The two functions of the earth, birth and death, are embodied in the fundamental ecological principle of interdependence. In every environment, the hilly, desert or forest, the plant and animal specie that constitute the biotic community, together with the soil, air, water are innately organized so as to form a unified life support system. There exist an intricate and extensive networks of links. If a single unit of this links is damaged, it would destroy and weaken the whole structure. 'There is no room for waste in nature's finely balanced economy'. Whatever is used is recycled once again through seasonal flux. The fundamental intuition of the cyclic order of the seasons is celebrated by the seers:

> Your circling seasons, nights succeeding days
> Your summer, O Earth, your splashing rains,
> Yours winter and frosty season yielding too spring-

may each and all produce for us milk !
[*Atharva Veda,* 12.1.36]

The processes of the earth seasonal cycles are grounded in *Rta,* the principle of universal order that holds the seasonal movements like a hub of a wheel. Earth is held by a regularity of cosmic order: the rising and setting of the sun, cycle of seasons, spring time and harvest. *Rta* is the intrinsic justice and order that sustains the eco-balance of nature.

The sense of interrelatedness, enjoined so fervently in the *Vedas* provides a norm for the ethics of the environment. The Vedic vision of geopiety considers man to be a guardian of natural resources who, replenishes the bounties of the earth rather than plunders it. Conservation, thus, means a state of harmony (*rtam*) with land, forest, waters and natural environment. Harmony is restored only when the bond between humans and nature is consistently strengthened, when man and nature are viewed as one biotic community. The earth, therefore, is worthy of adoration. The modern reductionist world-view, value-system and code of ethics are inadequate for a long term survival of our planet. Our last refuge is to revive a caring for the Mother Earth. It is said in the *Atharva Veda* (12.1.60) that the Earth was revealed to mankind for joy. In the light of this sensitive attitude, the seers had evolved a strategy to preserve the integrity and stability of the biotic community. Earth is, invoked with a feeling of great humility:

Whatever, I dig of you, O Earth,
May that grow quickly upon you,
O Pure One, may my thrust never pierce thy
Vital points, thy heart.
[*Atharva Veda,* 12.35]

Earth and Us

History records that man's attitude towards the environment has been twofold: either of exploitative dominance or pious reverence. Vedic ethos considers man/nature as twin agents who, reshape their environs for mutual benefits. The concern for the environmental conservation and protection is based on natural law of mutual dependence and reciprocity. The way we treat nature determines the way nature will treat us.

The Vedic code states that we live in a participatory universe which threads together man and his active actions in nature in a causal chain. When there is genuine caring and sharing it brings about beauty and bounty in the environs and maintains the eco-balance.

When man looks upon nature as an object of exploitation, as a commodity for trading, man is said to go against the current of life. He instigates disorder, chaos, falsehood (*anrta*), is swayed by the natural forces of darkness leading to disintegration. He acts against the natural current of life. The sympathetic bond between man and nature became a basis for the celebrations associated with the returning cycles of the seasons. These celebrations stimulated with prayer, incantations, consecration and offerings to the Earth Mother reinforce innate links with the natural world.

What is it that holds the earth together? The unequivocal claim of the *Vedas* is that the eternal bond between man and nature is nourished by the law of universal harmony (*Rta*), truth (*Satya*) and prayers:

> Truth, unyielding cosmic order, consecration,
> Ardour and Prayer and Holy Ritual
> Uphold the Earth, May she the ruling Mistress
> of what has been and what will come to be,
> for us spread wide a limitless domain.
> [*Atharva Veda,* 12.1.1]

The message of the praise hymn to Mother Earth in the *Vedas* is that the earth mediates between man and the unyielding cosmic order inherent in nature. This natural bond is one of partnership and continuous renewal.

The Goddess as the Waters of Life

The goddesses association with the waters of life is perennial. There is an enormous amount of material to show the antiquity and popularity of the intimate connection of the goddess with the waters. The *Mahabharata* (VI.10-35) invokes all the rivers as 'Mothers of the World'. In the Rg Vedic hymn, the waters, referred to as *Apah* appear as goddesses, young maidens and wives, and life-sustaining mothers, of Agni. The rivers also appear as independent goddesses (*Saptasindhavah*).

All the rivers of India that meander through the land, plains and hills embody as the fecundating element that renews life. An early invocation celebrated the river goddesses:

> The waters of the sky or those that flow (on earth), those that are dug out, or those that arise from themselves, those pure and clear waters that seek the ocean as their goal — Let the waters, who are goddesses, help me here and now. [*Rg Veda,* 7-49.2]

The texts categorically assert that there are innumerable rivers and that all are uniformly divine. They are said to have sprung from the celestial rivers that dwell in the form of clouds and rain in the atmosphere:

> The celestial river of sacred waters spring from it (the Moon), the reservoir of nectar. The river of clear transpresent water flows through the sky through the path of the wind (on earth).
>
> [*Vayu Purana,* 43. 2-3]

The waters wash away the impurities. They are pregnant with healing, life-giving and purifying properties:

> May the waters, purify us; clarifiers of *ghee*, may they clean us with *ghee*, for the goddesses carry off impurity. [*Rg Veda,* 10.17.10]

The vast landmass of India, covering an area of 3,287,782 km is irrigated by hundred of streams. Ganga is the foremost among all the rivers. She is said to have absorbed the divinity of all the rivers. Of all the rivers, it was Ganga who achieved the highest acclaim and personification. In Hindu myth she appears as a younger sister of Uma, co-wife of Sive and mother of Karttikeya. In her icons, she is frequently given human shape riding her crocodile mount. To the pious Indian, Ganga is not simply a river among many that flow across the country, she is conceived of as one who descended on this earth by some special grace. The river Ganga is one holy stream which represents all the rest. She is the mother of all rivers, is considered to be the purest and holiest water stream in India. Emerging from the Himalayan glacier, Gangotri, in Tehri Garwal, Uttar Pradesh, it makes a unique scenic fall at *Gaurikunda*, whereupon it courses its way through the length of 2,525 km to the Bay of Bengal. Our concern here is to decode a distinctive narrative pertaining to the river Ganges as an expression of primal ecology. The myth, expounds in veiled language one of the most profound ecological statement of our times.

Ganga *Avatarana* in the Light of Ecology

The myth relates to the fecundating waters of life personified as the Goddess Ganga. It expounds in veiled language one of the most profound ecological statements of our times.[4]

There are several versions of this myth. In one popular version from Vaisnava sources,[5] the descent of the heavenly waters to earth takes place from the 'foot of Visnu' (*Visnupada*). The holy river had its origin in the heavens when Visnu, in his Vamana, Dwarf-cum-Giant incarnation measured the three worlds with his three steps. His third step pierced the heavenly vault and caused the waters to flow. Through the opening in the shell of the universe, the Ganga flowed into Indra's heaven, and settled around the immovable Pole-star, Dhruva. In this form Ganga is known as *Visnupadi.* She meandered through the sky to the moon as the milky way. The milky way is often referred to as *Akasa-Ganga* and suggests the idea of a heavenly river.

The next episode of the myth describes the descent of the Ganges on earth. The story consists of long episodes which I shall not recount here. For our purpose, what is necessary is that the heavenly Ganges descended to the earth for salvic purpose, namely to animate and purify the sixty thousand son's of Sagara, who were reduced ashes by the glance of sage Kapila.

The Ganga was brought down to the earth by Bhagiratha who performed fierce austerities on the Himalayan slopes and won the favour of the Goddess. She agreed to descend but warned Bhagiratha that the earth would split under the torrential currents of Her fall. Ganga asked him to placate Siva. Siva agreed to catch its gushing waters in his matted locks before releasing the waters. The mighty river wound Her way through Siva's ascetic locks and found Her course on the mountains and plains of India.

Bhagiratha, then led the Ganges to the nether world where Her purifying 'funeral' waters liberated the sixty thousand sons of Sagara. In the nether worlds, Ganga is called Bhogavati, from which the waters were raised for Bhisma, by Arjuna who pierced the nether regions with his arrow. Bhagiratha, then conducts her to the sea. With its waters the sea was replenished. After completing Her course of the three worlds, the mother of the holy rivers returned to the heavens.

The ecological implications of the myth can be decoded and its meaning laid bare. Water's natural flow is rooted in a cyclic pattern. It continuously renews itself. Water circulates from land, seas, to the clouds by coming in link with solar heat. It returns to the land and rivers, lakes and underground streams below the soil and intermingles in the deep oceans. Being a volatile element, its flow is invisible. It is below the soil, on it and above as air and clouds. The myth preserves in metaphorical language, the vital links of the ecoprocesses of the water cycle. The Goddess Ganga is referred to as *Trilokagamini*, one who meanders through the three worlds starting from the heavens above, coursing her way to the earth down to the subterranean levels of the nether world. The course of the Ganges as depicted in the myth is in consonance with the 'logic' of the water cycle in nature.

The water is released in the heavens by the foot of Visnu, who is traditionally identified with the Sun.[6] Since the milky way follows the track of the sun, the *Puranas* often refer to the Ganges as liquid essence of matter issued from the resplendent glory of the Sun as Visnu. Is this an allusion to the melting of ice in the Himalayas by the Sun or the liquification of that element which is absorbed by the Sun?

Is it not that the origin of the Ganges highlights the complementary relationship of solar energy and water, which forms a part of the water cycle in the physical universe?

Next comes the imagery of the Ganges roaring down in torrents on the Himalayan slopes. Brahma and the gods were obviously concerned with the hydrological problem caused by her descent. For, 'the earth alone could never bear the mighty torrents travelled from the air'. In our terms it mirrors the enormous havoc caused by powerful monsoonic rains on the Himalayan slopes. If the waters were to fall directly on the naked earth the river would cease to be a life giving source. Hence, the *Itihaskaras* struck a symbolic solution and cause the waters to be tamed in Sivas locks, which in the sacred geography of India are identified with the thick forests on the Himalayas. As the eminent ecologist, Reiger has rightly pointed out. 'In Siva's hair we have a very well-known physical device which breaks the force of water coming down . . . If the forests on the Himalayan slopes were not maintained, we would foresee destruction.'[7] This episode relates to the intimate biotic connection between the waters and vegetation.

Lastly, the myth reiterates the value of *tapas* and reverence to the waters of life. This message is brought to us through the resolute character of Bhagiratha, whose only mission in life was to bring the pure waters to the earth by means of *tapas* and prayer.

It is no gainsaying that the narrative cycle of Ganga *avatarana* seems to be inspired by the observation of natural phenomena. The *Itihasakaras* of this myth had considerable insight into indissoluble connection of the pairing of the elements such as water/fire, water/vegetation, and earth/sky. Further the narrative reflects great concern for the unconditional moral order that "Truth is the base that bears the earth" (*AV*, 14.1.1). In all these respects, the story validates the seminal aphorisms of the *Bhumi-sukta* of the *Atharva Veda*.

Our brief analysis has shown that the early views on the earth mother from the *Atharva Veda* and the Pauranic myth on the Descent of the Ganges reflect a remarkable awareness of primal ecology. The nature hierophanies make a good case for a reconstruction of a 'Goddes Ecology'. The emerging vision of the earth as one organism, is only a recent image of an ancient heritage, traced to the *Vedas*. The ancient view of Geopiety and 'Goddess Ecology' contains a remarkable insight for the modern man. Its true significance will manifest when the catastropic implications of technology become more and more visible.

Notes

1. The paper is mainly concerned with the concept of the *Prthivi* as a separate divinity. The notion of Heaven and Earth together has been expounded adequately by several scholars. See for instance, Gonda J., *The Duel Deities in the Religion of the Vedas*, Amsterdam, (1974), pp. 93-117.

2. All translations from the *AV* are taken from Pannikker, Raimundo, *Vedic Experience, Mantramanjari*, New Delhi, (1977).
3. *RV*, 10.90.5; *AV*, 10.10.24; *AV*. 8.10.1-33.
4. I am indebted to Kapila Vatsyayan for this insight. For an excellent exposition on a similar theme, see: Kapila Vatsyayan, Ecology and Indian Myth, In *Indigenous Vision, India International Centre. Quarterly*, Vol. 19, Numbers 1-2 Spring-Summer, (1992), pp. 157-90.
5. *Bhagavata Purana,* 5.17 ff. *Devibhagavata Purana*, 8.7 etc.
6. *RV*, 1.154.1 and 1.154.3 etc.
7. H.C. Reiger, "Whose Himalaya? A study in Geopiety"; In T. Singh (ed.), *Studies in Himalayan Ecology and Development Strategies*, New Delhi, (1980), p. 2.

7

On Some Aspects of Bhutas During Birth-Death Passages

Gian Giuseppe Filippi

This brief study deals with the topic of the *bhutas* and their expression of the homogeneity of the human being with Nature, at least in the perspective of the gross manifestation. I have used the classic terms of the Upanisadic Tradition. With quite simple changes in point of view, it would be possible to use the terminology pertaining to any other classical Philosophy. *Samkhya*, *Puranas*, *Tantras*, among the several streams of Indian Culture. In each doctrine the description of the *pancabhutas* changes, but the concept of the continuum of Nature does not change. The apparent exception, the *caturbhutavada* of the ancient Buddhist doctrines, has been integrated only by the fifth element in the Tibetan Tradition.[1]

The problem here discussed is, in which manner the five elements[2] produce the human body starting from conception; where the elements originate; and, analogically, how the corpse is destroyed and where the *bhutas* go after death. When a *jiva* appears in this world, it rains down from the sky as a potentiality of being. In this condition it leads a vegetative existence, awaiting a body. The description of the *pancagnividya* in both the *Brhadaranyaka* and *Chandogya Upanisads* agree on this point.[3] Actually, it is evident that the *jiva* is complete in its own components, at least insomuch as it can be complete in this state of subtle latency. It does not have as yet a bodywhich will enable it to develop a human life. The body is considered as an instrument which will be used by the real being to modify its own condition or destiny. For this reason the *jiva*, without the body, is obliged to lead a vegetative life. It is so, because in this world the body is the extreme limit of human manifestation. Borrowing the terminology of the *pancakosavada* as displayed by the *Taittiriya Upanisad,* we can express the concept of limit of manifestation, pointing out that it is the last of the five envelopes worn by *Atman*. This envelope, called *annamayakosa* is the body itself. The previously mentioned doctrine of the *Taittiriya Upanisad* is very useful for our purposes. When we say that *jiva* has not yet met its body, we mean that *Atman*, at its present stage, is wearing all the *kosas*, except the *annamayakosa*. In this way, maintaining the previous comparison between the *pancagnividya* of the *Brhadaranyaka* and the *Chandogya Upanisads* and the *Taittiriya's* doctrine, we can make a connection between the *jiva* in the vegetative state awaiting the body, and *Atman* in the *pranamayakosa*.

It is evident that the body is the achievement of the whole individuality, which allows the actual development of life, as well as the actions, choices, and developing awareness peculiar to that being.

The absence of the body corresponds to the absence of the *bhutas*: the gross elements constituting the corporeity. In these terms we can infer that the *jiva* in the examined state, is provided with the other manifested *tattvas*. Then, where does the body come from? We already know that the body comprises the organic compound of the five elements. From the perspective of the *Chandogya* and *Brhadaranyaka Upanisads*, the body cannot proceed from the subtle elements because they are not its direct material causes, but only causes of the *bhutas*.[4] The solution of this problem is found in the same doctrine of the *Taittiriya Upanisad*, which defines the body as being composed of food, the *annamayakosa*.[5] It seems as if the *pancabhutas*, in order to form the body, ascend nature's ladder from the mineral, through the vegetal, to the animal realm. The description of this very delicate passage from vegetal to animal is omitted by this Upanisadic statement. How then does the food, i.e., the herbs, become a man? the *Prasna Upanisad* fills the gap: "Prajapati indeed is the food; from that indeed the semen comes; from that are born these beings."[6]

There is another point of great importance: *annarasamaya* from the aforementioned *Taittiriya* quotation, can be translated not only, as is usual, the essence of food but, instead, tasting the food. If this interpretation is correct, we can once again link this argument to the *pancagnividya*; the *rasa* from this point of view indicates how *ap*, after its fivefold oblation to the fire, comes to be known "by the word human being".[7]

To review all these concepts, the five elements are the origin of the herbs: the man eats the herbs, and his food "when eaten, becomes divided in three parts: that which is the grossest component becomes excreta: that which is the medium becomes flesh, and that which is the subtlest becomes mind".[8] "That which is this semen is extracted from all the limbs as their vigour. He holds that self of his in his own self, when he sheds it into his wife, then he procreates it".[9]

Here we take for granted two topics. The first is the philosophical argument that herbs are not the *jiva* itself, but only its abode. This argument is discussed extensively in the *Brahmasutra Bhasyas*.[10] The second one is that the same process of assimilation of the food becomes blood or ovum in the women, as well as semen in the man. This subject is discussed in detail by Ayurvedic texts.[11] These arguments are basic, but they could distract us from the primary points that the author wishes to pursue in this paper.

The body of the new being begins its development with the fusion of the seed and the ovum. "Uniting the semen and the blood, the embryo arises . . . .";[12] "One night after the union in fertile period, arises a nodule (*kalila*); after seven nights it changes into a bubble (*budbuda*); in half a month arises the embryo (*pinda*) . . . ",[13] and so on. The conclusion of the same *khanda* is important for our subject. This is because it is stated that the *prana* "grows well on the food and drink received from the mother, which arrive by means of a cord, in the form of vein".[14] It is demonstrated, at least in brahmanical thought, that the five elements which are changed successively into food, semen and ovum, constitute the first nodule, the first abode of a new *jiva*. From this moment the nodule begins to grow, nourished by the food eaten by the mother, that is to say by the five elements that the mother receives from outer ambience. And after his own birth as a human being – as well as other different beings – what does he do? He continues to eat, eating food or, more accurately, the five elements. This is the central reason which the gross body (*sthula sarira*) composed of the five elements is called *annamayakosa*. If one does not eat, one is no longer able to replace one's burned or excreted components and, at last, one dies.

After death the constitutive *bhutas* of the corpse undergo an analogic process, but in opposite directions. The body's components return to Nature.[15] Every individual element merges into the general external element. ". . . When the voice of the dead is merged in fire, the smell in the air, the sight in the sun, masses in the moon, hearing in the cardinal points, the body in the earth, the internal *akasa* in the external *akasa,* the hair of the body in herbs, the hair of the head in trees, the [female] blood and the [male] seed in water, where is the man?".[16] To answer this question we can state that he is no longer here. He has moved to another more subtle level of Nature, the *pranamayakosa*. This may take place only after having returned the *pancabhutas* to the gross level of Nature.

It is evident that the ancient seers of India have demonstrated and described the space-temporal continuum (*sarvavapi*) with scientific rigour. The *bhutas*, before the conception of the human being – and not only human ones, are herbs which serve as food for the man. In the last stage the gross body composed by *bhutas,* becomes food once again: food for the fire of the cremation pyre; or food for the earth, fertilizing the earth and provoking stimulating the growth of herbs; or food for animals; birds, fish, insects etc; becoming the constituents of their organisms.

This recalls to our mind the classical and incontestable example of the *satkaryavada:* the goldsmith gives to gold the form of rings, armlets and necklaces. These products differ but are identical in their Nature.[17] Gold, in fact, is the space-temporal continuum which sweeps away temporary and local differences. We can, in this way, express how it is possible to have an authentic and genuine contact among living beings. For example, I can see the flower because I have fire (*tejas*) in my eyes and the flower also contains the fire. The *tejas* of the sun assists the growth of the flower by means of the sun-rays which reach and nourish it. The flower, with his own *tejas* recognises and worships the blazing sun, following with respect the sun's movement in the sky. There is no cessation or gap for the fire between my eyes, the flower, the sun. Moreover I can listen to you because you have ether (*akasa*) in yourself producing your words, there is ether between us, and I have ether in my ears. There is no cessation of ether between your mouth, the space between us, and my ears.[18]

Nature is, of course, not limited to the gross manifestation. There are several increasingly more subtle levels. Using the same example employed to illustrate the continuum of ether, we can note that with the addition of a rational message to the sound of the voice, the human being is able to express his thought to the outer environment. In this way the thought is received and understood by other human beings. This is possible because there is *manas* in the person who speaks, *manas* in the listener, and *manas* in the space between them. No cessation of *manas* is between them. Nature is the universal substratum of the Cosmos,[19] and it is in this way the continuum is, and this Indian holistic doctrine of the *Prakrti* overlaps the concept of *Natura naturata* in Spinoza's Philosophy.

Notes

1. This element, called *nam-mkhah* in Tibetan, corresponds to the *akasa* and is the substance of the universal consciousness.
2. Sometimes one finds the body is composed of only three elements, i.e., earth, water, fire. Actually this assertion cannot be in total opposition to the others of the *sruti*. The passages describing the body as composed of only three elements are found on the doctrine of the *pancakosa*. In fact the *Taittiriya Upanisad* (*TU*) differentiates two kinds of nutrition: food and drink (*annarasa*), and the respiration of the *prana*. With the first nutrition the body gets its solid components. Breathing the body gets its dynamic motor. See *TU,* II.ii-iii. *The Garbha Upanisad* (*GU*) expresses both points of view in a statement which unites them. "This body is composed of five because five elements are: earth, water, fire, wind and ether. What is earth, what is water, what is fire, what is wind, what is ether? Here, that which is solid is earth, that which is liquid is water, that which is hot is fire, that which moves is wind, that which is hollow is ether." *GU*, I; G.G. Filippi, "The Secret of the Embryo in the *Garbha Upanisad*", In *Annali di Ca'Foscari,* S.O., XXXI, 3, 1992, p. 303.
3. *BAU*, VI. ii. 1-15; *ChU*, V. iii. 1 - x. 9.
4. *Ahamkara* is the cause of the *tanmatras*, as well as these are the material causes of the *bhutas* (*Isvarakrsna*, *Samkhyakarika*, 3). *Ahamkara*, through the subtle elements, manifests the *bhutas* in the beginning of the cycle. The *bhutas* aggregating among them, produce the ambience: in this way the *bhutas* are transformed into food, the food into seed and ovum,

then into body. In this manner the *jiva* (or *ahamkara*) in transmigration, performing as Prajapati, prepare the worldly ambience from where it will seek its own body's constituents. This is the meaning of the statement "*Ahamkara* manifests the world". At the same time it is arbitrary to maintain that the *jiva* produces its body's *bhutas* starting from the moment of its conception. Arbitrary it is but not wrong, because that was the way for the human beings to be born during the *Satya Yuga*: "Sexual intercourse, O leader of the Bharatas, was not necessary to procreate. Their offspring came into being through the mere wish, without fear of death." *Ramayana,* XII.207.38

5. "... from that, which is the *Atman* has been *akasa* from *akasa vayu*, from *vayu agni* from *agni ap* from *ap prthivi* from *prthivi* the herbs, from the herbs the food, from the food the man. This man is done by *rasa* of the food ...". *TU*, II. i. 1.
6. *PU*, 1.14.
7. *ChU*, V. iii. 3. Sometimes one translates *purusavacasah* into with human voice: this possible translation doesn't contribute to clarifying the meaning of the text.
8. *ChU*, VI.v.1.
9. *AU*, II.i.1.
10. *BS*, III.i.24. About this subject see our *Post mortem et liberation d'apres Shankaracharya*, Arche, Milano 1978, p. 17.
11. "The stages produced by the nutrition are the formation of the body, the growth, the continuity of breathing, the satisfaction, the increase and the energy." *Caraka Samhita* (*CS*), IV.3.12: also *Susruta Samhita* XIV.2-13.
12. *GU*, II. See G.G. Filippi, "The Secret...", p. 304, Cf. *SS*, *Sarira Sthanam*, V. 2 and *CS*, IV 4. 7.
13. *GU*, III. G.G. Filippi, "The Secret ...", p. 304.
14. *GU*, III. About the umbilical cord see G.G. Filippi, "The Secret ...", p. 302.
15. Very interesting are both the possible etymologies of the word body, *sarira*, that is from the root *sri* "which is hot", or from *sr* "which is corruptible."
16. *BAU*, III.ii.13. Also in the decomposition of the corpse, as well as for the formation of the body – in opposite directions – the corporeal components don't return to the *tanmatras*, but in the ambience, becoming food for the transformation of different beings. Only some kinds of saints are able to transmute their corpse directly into *bhutas* and to lead them back to the *tanmatras*. In this case the death is announced by the disappearance of the corpse. The tales of the death of Kabir, Dattatreya and other *sants* are well-known in India.
17. *BAU*, IV.iv.4. Actually, it maintains the same doctrine, the interpretation of the material cause depends because of the differences in the *darsanas*: in the case of *Samkhya* gold should be a symbol for *Prakrti* in the case of *Vedanta* a symbol for *Parabrahman.*
18. All these considerations are personal developments of the *Nyaya Sutras*, III.i.41-43, where the *sutrakrt* explains the necessity of existence of fire in the eye, in the ambience, in the object.
19. "The body produced by father and mother falls and dissolves in the earth and in the other objects which correspond" (*Isvarakrsna*, XXXIX). Finally all the objects will be reduced in the *bhutas*, and these will merge in the *tanmatras*. What about these principles? "During the *pralaya* the mind, the *tanmatras* and the *indriya* dissolve in Nature" (*Isvarakrsna*, 40).

8

Akasa, From Space to Spacelessness
Medieval Indian Mystics' Concept of Akasa

S.G. Tulpule

What is *Akasa*, the last among the five elements? It is certainly not the sky, which is the region of space visible from the earth. The sky consists of atmosphere which extends hundreds of miles above the earth. Its colours result from the scattering of sunlight by the gas molecules and dust particles in the atmosphere. This description of the sky does not apply to *Akasa* which exists even beyond the atmosphere and is colourless. Then what is *Akasa*? It is certainly not ether; this is supposed to be a subtle fluid filling and pervading the whole universe and becoming the peculiar vehicle of life and of sound. *Akasa* is also not just vacuity. *Akasa* exists, while vacuity does not exist.

Thus, the term *Akasa* slowly enters the field of the mysterious. But we get a clue to its mystery in compounded words like *hrdayakasa* and *mahadakasa*, *ghatakasa* and *mathakasa*, which indicate *akasa* bound and unbound, or limited and unlimited. Jnanesvar speak even of *Gitakasa*, the *akasa* of the *Bhagavadgita*.[1] But that is only a poetical image and nothing more. The compound words I have mentioned tend to suggest that *Akasa* is space — space confined or not confined. Considered this way, the term *Akasa* may be said to be a partial synonym of the term *avakasa*. In fact, Jnanesvar has used these two terms synonymously, e.g.,

aghavam akasi jaise |
avakasu houni akasa ase | |

Just as *akasa* becomes and exists as *avakasa* in all spaces.[2]

We have thus to interpret the term *akasa* as space and this interpretation befits the peculiar position of *Akasa* in the fivefold scheme of the *mahabhutas*, or the Elements. The other four elements are cognizable, some even perceptible. But *Akasa* is different. As space, it continues in all directions and has no known limits. It is wrong to say that space begins where the earth's atmosphere ends or is too thin to affect objects moving through it. That would be equivalent to saying that space begins about 100 miles (or 160 km) above the earth, a statement that negates the very definition of space. Writers on astronomy have divided space into different parts, such as Cislunar space, or the space between the earth and the moon; Interplanetary space, reaching far beyond Pluto, the planet most distant from the earth; Interstellar space, or the space between stars, reaching unimaginable distances; and Intergalactic space, or the space between galaxies. Now, such a division of the contiguous space might have its practical advantages, but the very idea of dividing space into different strata seems strange.

The doctrine of *Akasa*, or space, as the origin of all things, came rather late in the history of Upanisadic thought. Also in Greek philosophy, the concept of space as the arche of things appeared very late. With Thales, Anaximenes, Heracleitus and Empedocles we meet the conceptions of water, air, fire, and earth, either individually or collectively. It is only when we come to the time of Philolaus that we get to the notion of space as the arche of all things. The first four elements, namely *Prthivi*, *Ap*, *Tejas* and *Vayu* are more or less tangible; but for *Akasa* to be regarded as the origin of all things requires a higher philosophical imagination. That we find in the *Chandogyopanisad* in the answer given by Pravahana Jaivali to the question: *asya lokasya ka gatih*? What is the final habitat of all things? He answered, it was space: *akasa iti havaca*. He further clarified his statement saying: "All these beings emerge from space and are finally absorbed in space; space is verily greater than any of these things; space is the final habitat": *sarvani ha va imani bhutani akasadeva samutpadyante, akasam pratyastam yanti | akaso hi eva ebhyo jyayan, akasah parayanam* | |[3] This passage from the *Chandogya* is corroborated by another passage from the same *Upanisad* where we are told that "space is really higher than fire. In space are both the sun and the moon, the lightning and the stars. It is by the space that man is able to call. In space and after space are all things born. Meditate upon space as the highest reality": *akaso vav tejaso bhuyan | akase vai suryacandramasavubhau | vidyunnaksatranyagnih akasenahvyati | akase jayate | akasamabhijayate | akasamupasveti* | |[4]

Thus, space is regarded as a higher entity than any of the conceptions that have hitherto been reached. In fact, space is, to put it in the words of the *Chandogya* itself, *tajjalana*, a cryptic term the *Upanisad* uses to name that from which all things spring, into which they are resolved and in which they live and have their being.[5] This analogous development of cosmogony in Greek and Upanisadic philosophical thought can best be explained, as Ranade suggests, by the theory of Independent Parallelism.[6]

Seen on this Upanisadic background, the contribution of the mystics of medieval India to the conception of *Akasa* looks significant. Almost all of them interpret *Akasa* as space and use it as an imagery to give expression to their mystical experience. Jnanesvar, for example, explains the identity between the *Nama* and the *Nami* on the analogy of *Akasa* which is its own support.[7] In his most poetical commentary on the phrase *Acaryopasanam* of the *Bhagavadgita* (13.8), Jnanesvar says that after physical death, a disciple merges into the space inside his heart, into the space where his *Guru* lives.[8] Tukaram, in his famous *abhanga* beginning with the words *anuraniya thokada*, recited most meaningfully by Pandit Bhimsen Joshi, declares that he has become smaller than an atom and as spacious as the sky. The poem is a masterpiece of his mystical experience and I feel here tempted to render it into English thus:

> Smaller than an atom, Tuka is as vast as the sky.
> He swallowed up his own body
> which was but an illusory form.
> Then all kinds of trinities dropped down,
> and the lamp was lit inside.
> Tuka now lives only to oblige the world.[9]

Ramadas has a novel way of explaining the term *Akasa*. It is called *Akasa* because, according to him, it lives in all the five *bhutas*: *pancabhutamadhye vas | mhanini bolije akasa | |*.[10] This definition of *Akasa* brings out its nature and meaning very clearly. But Ramadas is also aware of the danger of *Akasa* being identified with the *Brahman*, or the ultimate Reality. A metaphor like *Kham Brahma* is well-known. It tries to bring out the similarity and not the identity between space and Reality. But the metaphor is so often used and the similarity so often shown that one finally identifies the two. When all is said and done, *Akasa* still remains a *mahabhuta*, a great Element, but thinking, or rather poetising, gives it the status of the highest Reality. Ramadas has taken great pains to disprove this imaginary identity between space and Reality. A whole sub-section of his *Dasabodha* is devoted to distinguishing between *Akasa* on the one hand and *svarupa*, or *vastu*, or *brahman*, all identical terms, on the other.[11] The *Dasabodha* is written in the form of a dialogue between the *Guru* and his disciple – *a guru-sisya samvada* – and the sub-section I am referring to begin with a statement of the *Guru* to the effect that *Akasa* is *avakasarupa*, it is hollow, spotless and steady; it pervades all; it is the one among the many; it contains all the other four *mahabhutas*; and it is like *svarupa*. On this is a question from the disciple: "If both are alike, why not call *Akasa svarupa*, or *svatahsiddha vastu*?" Ramadas answers as follows: "*Vastu* is *nirguna*, without quality, while *Akasa* has seven qualities: *kama*, *krodha*, *soka*, *moha*, *bhaya*, *ajnana* and *sunyatva*. Therefore, *Akasa* is a *bhuta* and cannot be equated with *vastu* or *svarupa*, or the form of the Self, which is absolute. How can a *bhuta* and *Ananta* be one? Glass-tiled floor and water look alike, but knowers know the difference". However, this argument does not silence the disciple. He is still in doubt. His next question is: "If *Akasa* is basically *arupa*, formless, then why not identify it with *vastu* (which is also without any form)? The other four *bhutas* come to an end, but *Akasa* is endless and so is *Brahman*. Then why not identify the two?" On this question of the disciple, Ramadas has an answer to give. It is this: "*Akasa* is known as *sunya* or, void, and ignorance is its characteristic. *Sunya*, or void, is *ajnana*, ignorance, and *Akasa* is typically void. *Ajnana* is mixed up with *Akasa*, and that *ajnana* is destroyed by *jnana*. Naturally, *Akasa*, like *ajnana*, is destructible, while *svarupa*, being *jnana*, is not. *Akasa* and *svarupa* look alike, but there remains the difficulty of *sunyatva*, or voidness, in identifying the two. It is like *unmani* and *susupti*, or the transcendent and the sleeping states, which appear the same, but are different. Secondly, says Ramadas, *Akasa* is seen as distinct from its seer, while in the case of *svarupa*, the seer becomes one with the *svarupa*. Thirdly, *Akasa* is experienced, but *svarupa* is beyond experience. Who is there to experience *svarupa* when one becomes *svarupa* oneself? Therefore, the two cannot be one." Here Ramadas differs from Sankara who defines the *Brahman* as *Akasa* (*akasah tallingat*) in his commentary on the *Brahmasutras*.

The gist of the whole argument of Ramadas is that *Akasa* is the most convenient and handy expression to describe the *Brahman* which pervades the universe, but it cannot be the *Brahman* itself for the reasons given above. In other words, space cannot be equated with something that is spaceless, that is the *Brahman*, or *Svarupa*, or *Vastu*.[12] It is exactly here that medieval Indian poet-saints make an absolutely original contribution to the philosophy of mysticism. They do entertain and make use of the concept of *Akasa* to describe *Brahman*, or the ultimate Reality. But on rare occasions they go beyond it and enter the field of spacelessness. It is a void, but not of the nature of an abyss or a bottomless pit, but of the nature of the vast and expansive space itself. It is this spacelessness, or infinitude, that is at the core of their mystical experience. Among the many medieval Indian mystics I have selected two, one from the North and the other from the South. Kabir represents the north and Kudaluresa represents the south. Kabir has a special term to denote the concept of spacelessness. It is *sunya*, meaning 'void'. Constructing a metaphor of the fabulous *Anal* bird who is supposed to make its nest in the air without ever touching the earth, Kabir says:

> The Anal, the fire-bird, has made its nest in the air,
> he dwells forever in between;
> from earth and sky he remains aloof;
> his confidence needs no support.[13]

This concept of 'void' seems to be a favourite of Kabir's:

> Crossing the boundary, I entered the boundless,
> I made my dwelling in the void.[14]

Even this 'void' is transgressed by Kabir as can be seen from the following couplet:

had had par sabahi gaya, behad gaya na koya |
behad ke maidan men ramai kabir soya | |

> All have gone up to the boundary, but no one has crossed the boundary. Kabir plays in the *maidan* which is the open space of *behad*, the limitless.[15]

Here Kabir uses the term *had* to denote bounded or limited space. *Behad* is an antonym of *had* and means unbounded or unlimited. According to Kabir, we are all living within the limits of space. As the girl in the German film 'Ein stuck Himmel' can see only a very small patch of the sky and not the whole sky, in a similar way our experience of the Divine is limited or bounded by our worldly existence. It is only a mystic like Kabir who can transgress the limit and become the Infinite. We see on the television screen astronauts walking in space. But Kabir is a super astronaut. He not only walks but also plays, and that too not in space, but in the spaceless. Elsewhere he has used the phrase, *avinasi ki god* "the lap of the eternal", to denote the idea of spacelessness.

A parallel to Kabir's experience of the *behad* is found in a poem by Kudaluresa from Karnataka.[16] It begins with the words *nodiri brahmanatava* 'Behold the sport of *Brahman*', and goes on describing this sport in the Upanisadic fashion. Kudaluresa concludes the description of his experience of the Reality in very significant words, I quote from the original: *bayalige bayilu nirbayilu tanadaddu* "This God is shining in the spaceless space". Now, *bayalige bayalu nirbayalu* is a very special idiom in the Kannada language. The Kannada word *bayalu* means space. There is space beyond our space, *bayalige bayalu* and that which transcends this space is *nirbayalu*. What Kudaluresa means is that for him God fills the whole of the existence, and the whole of the non-existence. These concepts of these two mystics, *behad* of Kabir and *nirbayalu* of Kudaluresa, would remind a student of Greek philosophy of the *Apeiron* of Anaximander against the *Peras* of Pythagoras. The *Peras* is a small conception, but the *Apeiron* brings us quite near to the infinitude that is portrayed in the manifestations of the sublime. The experience of the sublime seems to be almost transcendent and baffling even for the imagination to reach. Anaximander, therefore, regarded the *Apeiron* as his most fundamental category. It is this aspect of the element of Divinity in all cases of Infinitude which is at the basis of the *behad* of Kabir and *nirbayalu* of the Kannada mystic.

It is a long journey from *sima* to *asima*, from *had* to *behad*, from *bayalu* to *nirbayalu*, from *peras* to *apeiron*, from space to spacelessness. The concept of *Akasa* takes one ultimately to *nirakasa*, the spaceless. It is not only from *Guha* to *Akasa* as Bettina Baumer says in her valuable paper bearing the same title, but from *guha* to *akasa* to *nirakasa* as well.[17] It is here that the medieval saints like Jnanesvar and Kabir and

Kudaluresa shine with a mystical lustre all their own. They have raised a *mahabhuta* like *Akasa* to the status of the *Brahman*, the ultimate Reality, just by making it void of space, or spaceless. The Sanskrit root *akas* has two meaning: (1) to shine, and, (2) to view, to recognize. It is this second meaning which conveys the sense of consciousness that is spaceless. Thus, consciousness and spacelessness are one, the one *Samvid*, *Samvid* of the Self. Dimensionless space is much more than Eternal Silence. It is Consciousness which reminds us of a Chinese saying which states that void is mind itself and mind itself is void.

Spacelessness takes us to timelessness. For space and time are like two sides of the same coin. Both are the world's deepest mysteries. If we can imagine a world without space, then we can also imagine it without time. It was formerly believed that if all material things disappeared out of the universe, time and space would be left. According to the relativity theory, however, time and space disappear together with other things. That is why a mystic like Kabir can say that he has gone beyond the bounds of time and space. To say it in the words of Ramadas,

> There is no factor of time in the formless *Brahman*,
> Time appears only when the formless takes a form.
> Otherwise, there is no room for time.
> It exists only so long as there is change.
> When change comes to a halt, when one becomes *nirvikara*,
> time ceases to exist.[18]

Kabir has given expression to his timeless state in his usual cryptic manner:

> Kabir has taken his posture in the *gagana mandala*
> and *Kal* beats his head in despair.[19]
> Kabir's soul clings to the feet of Ram,
> where Kal's hands cannot reach him.[20]
> The salt has dropped from its container,
> and got mixed with water;
> it cannot fill the container again.
> Consciousness has merged in the Eternal Sound,
> and *Kal* is silenced.[21]

Kabir finally declares that he is leaving for his *nija-ghar*, his own Home, where *Kal* has no entrance: *kah kabir niya-ghar chalim, jahan kal na jahee.*

Thus, there is a fusion of time and the three dimensions of space which gives us the concept of space-time, also known as 'the fourth dimension'. The *mahabhuta Akasa*, therefore, has a very different interpretation for the medieval mystics whose approach to it is both spacial and temporal, culminating finally in the unitive experience of the *samvid*, or Consciousness, that lies beyond the 'impassable Pass' and where all duality is forever abolished.

We can conclude in the words of Kabir in their English translation by Charlotte Vaudeville, a great scholar of Kabir.

> He who walks between boundaries is a man;
> he who goes beyond them is a saint.
> But he who transcends the limited and the limitless,
> his state of mind is unfathomable.[22]

This may be an answer to the question poised by Keith Critchlow: "Space: Plenum or Abyss?": in the volume on Space mentioned above.

Notes

[The author is grateful to Dr Kapila Vatsyayan for the volume on *Concepts of Space (Ancient and Modern)*, edited by her (New Delhi 1991), which gives an overall view of the concept of Space.]

1. *Jnanesvari*, 18.1643.
2. *Ibid.*, 11.527.
3. *Chandogya*, I.9.1.
4. *Ibid.*, VII.12.1.
5. *Ibid.*, III.14.1.
6. R.D. Ranade, *A Constructive Survey of Upanishadic Philosophy*, 2nd ed., Bombay (1968), p. 74.
7. *Jnanesvari*, 17.400.
8. *Ibid.*, 13.434.
9. *Tukaram Gatha* (Govt. ed.), No. 993.
10. *Dasabodha*, 9.9.21.
11. *Ibid.*, 8.5.
12. For *Vastu*, see S.G. Tulpule, vide *Bhakti in Current Research*, Berlin (1983), pp. 403-11.
13. Ch. Vaudeville, *Kabir*, Oxford (1974), p. 263, No. 8.
14. *Ibid.*, p. 203, No. 21.
15. R.D. Ranade, *Paramartha Sopana*, Sangli (1954), p. 290, No. 35.
16. Padma Kulkarni, *Kannada Paramartha Sopana*, Bombay (1992), p. 136, No. 9.
17. Bettina Baumer, *From Guha to Akasa* (vide, *Concepts of Space*, New Delhi, 1991, pp. 105-22).
18. *Dasabodha*, 12.8.1-5.
19. Ch. Vaudeville, *op.cit.*, p. 254, No. 6.
20. *Ibid.*, p. 255, No. 8.
21. *Ibid.*, p. 290, No. 34.
22. *Ibid.*, p. 262, No. 6.

9

Amrtamanthana
The Vedic Sources of Hindu Creation Myth

Natalia R. Lidova

The *Mahabharata* presents the *Amrtamanthana* myth – one of the essential in Hindu mythology – as a detailed and consecutive narration, though the earlier tradition has not yet revealed its precedents. Vedic literature do not mention the cosmogonic act, which divided the soil from the water, stated a new order of things and created fabulous treasures. Many hypotheses sought to explain this conspicuous gap, one by G. Dumezil,[1] major student of Indo-European mythology, who drew on Scandinavian, Celtic, Greek, Latin and Persian materials to reconstrue the archetypal basis of the myth, which he traced to the archaic rites of spring, widespread among Indo-Europeans. He derived the idea of the elixir of immortality to the sacral drink used at festivals – wine in Greece, and *soma* or *haoma* with Indo-Aryans. In the extremely extensive mythological context used by Dumezil, the *Mahabharata* myth is a mere example to illustrate global structures. The scholar saw it as old enough to reflect archaic Indo-European ideas, and sought to demonstrate that the conspicuous silence of the *Vedas* did not prove its comparative novelty, with Vedic sources generally standing aloof to narrative myths. Not that his explanation of its absence sounds convincing enough. At any rate, it does not cancel further search for the source of this particular epic tradition.

The hypothesis at which K. Geldner came in his Rgvedic studies was far more concrete.[2] As he points out, the *Veda* attaches the idea of *amrta* to *soma* and *havis*, sacrificial butter – the two basic ritual offerings – with the myth of the churning rooted in the *havis* poured into the ritual fire. He thinks the ability of clarified butter to divide into parts as poured into fire (*amrtam viprkvat*) is analogous to the stratification of the primal Ocean as it was churned, citing the mention of the sacred horse appearing "from the ocean, this primal source" in Hymn 163 of the first *mandala* as auxiliary proof (*RV*, I.163.1). The scholar also singles out another stanza of this hymn, which points out that the steed was not merely born in the primal ocean but was "half divided from *soma*" (*asi somena samaya viprktah*) (*RV*, I.163.3). Thus, the hymn includes the motif of oceanic birth, salient in the epic myth, and specifies its way, 'division' designated by the verb describing the stratification of *havis*.

As we see it, Geldner proposes the correct approach – *Rgveda* really offers the archaic precedent to the *Amrtamanthana*. However, we discern an even closer Rgvedic parallel to this monument. By *amrta*, the *Veda* means specially made *soma* juice, also granting immortality, no rarer than *havis*. We think it was this circle of *amrta* ideas that the myth of "The Churning of the Ocean" actualized. Symptomatically, the epic myth closely follows the Vedic idea of *amrta* as *soma* juice. As the *Rgveda* specifies, the potion of immortality is to be found in water, and combines with medicines:

> There is *amrta* in the waters,
> There is a remedy in the waters,
> Be valiant, ye gods, for their glory.
> (*RV*, I.23.19)

This is a direct indication of the water provenance of *amrta*:

> From the ocean rose the honeyed wave,
> Together with the *Soma*, it acquired the properties of *amrta*.
> (*RV*, IV.58.1)

The epic myth also mentions *amrta* concealed in water, to be separated by churning or powerful mixing. When the great Ocean was churned, "the gums of various trees and herbs mixed with the waters of the Ocean. And the celestials attained immortality by drinking the waters mixed with these gums vested with the properties of *amrta*".[3] Thus, the myth also presupposes the idea of herbal juices diluted with water – the heart of the Vedic rite of *amrta* making. The third component of *amrta* – milk – is also present as part of the Ocean water turned into it when churned. Only *soma*, the principal ingredient of the elixir, is absent from the description, but the logic of the myth allows clear allusions to it with oblique characteristics instead of naming it. Among these oblique indications is the semantic renaming of *soma* into *amrta*, and the untrivial device by which actual *soma*-squeezing rites are presented at the mythological level.

Many Rgvedic hymns mention the regalia of the ceremonial *soma*-making ritual, performed solely by priests. Only once does the *Veda* come across the rite of simple or urgent *soma* juice squeezing (*anjahsava*) to be performed by any householder with his wife (*RV*, I.28). As we see it, the practical details of this Vedic rite, re-appraised as mythic events, lie at the basis of the *Amrtamanthana*. Here is the Rgvedic description of the quicker rite:

There where the broad-based stone is raised on high
to press [the juices] out,
O Indra, swallow [the juices] squeezed by the mortar.

There where the woman performs now the pulling,
now the pushing [of the churn-staff],
O Indra, swallow [the juices] squeezed by the mortar.

There where they tie the churn-staff
as reins to drive [a horse],
O Indra, swallow [the juices] squeezed by the mortar.*
(*RV*, I.28.1-4)

Coded in metaphors, this hymn, however, clearly points at devices and utensils which allow us to re-create the *soma*-squeezing process. A stone press was put to the bottom of a wooden mortar, with *soma* containing herbs on it. The churn-staff was tied with a rope, the head of the household and his wife gripping each end to pull at it in turn, thus making the staff rotate and mash the herbs, whose juice trickled into the mortar.

Notably, scholarly literature has never yet described this rite, and translators of the hymn mostly interpretate the word *mantha* as pestle[4] meaning that the herbs are not mashed but crushed – seemingly, a minor difference. In fact, it gives a different reconstruction of the quick *soma*-squeezing rite, based not on staff rotation but the up-and-down movements of the pestle as it is lifted and pushed down with an effort.

Be this as it may, the precise meaning of *mantha* is churn-staff, not pestle, as specially indicated by Sayana, author of the most authoritative *Rgveda* comments. As he stresses, *Pada* 4a of this hymn means the staff usually "used to mix milk [with *soma*]". Characteristically, the Vedic rite very rarely used pure *soma* juice. More often, it was diluted with water or cow milk by pouring the juice, water and milk into a wooden *vat* and violently mixed with a churn-staff for the ritual potion. According to Sayana, the quick squeezing rite used the same utensils – evidently, with one difference – a pressing slab in the bottom. The rope fixing the *mantha* serves as another proof. This fixation is necessary for a staff, more than that, is the basis of its work – while there is no point in tying a rope to a pestle. Symptomatically, the verb

---

* *yatra grava prthubudhna urdhvo bhavati sotave |*
ulukhalasutanam aved indra jalgulah ||

yatra nary apacyavam upacyavam ca siksate |
ulukhalasutanam aved indra jalgulah ||

yatra mantham vibadhnate rasmin yamitava iva |
ulukhalasutanam aved indra jalgulah ||

vibandh, used in this hymn, implies not mere tying but fixing on both ends.[5] In other words, the rope was to have both ends loose, with a special knot in the middle which tightly embraced the staff. The *Rgveda* compares this rope with reins tied to steer a horse – meaning that the staff was brought into motion with a rope. The wife of the master who performed the rite took one end, and he the other. Thus the utensil demanded not one person, as a pestle, but two.

Though there's a wealth of difference between *soma*-squeezing in a little home mortar, and the cosmic scope of *amrta* churning in the huge Ocean, it isn't hard to see that the resulting potion was practically the same. The myth we regard has the Ocean for the ritual vessel; associates the King Tortoise, who lies on the sea bottom giving his shelled back for the job, with the slab on the broad mortar bottom; and replaces the small churn-staff with the giant Mount Mandara, and the rope with Vasuki. Like in the *anjahsava* rite, the grandiose Ocean contraption is set in motion by a rope pulled on both ends in turn.

Symptomatically, the word *mantha*, used in the Rgvedic hymn we use for comparison, comes up here as a generic notion bringing together all actions involved in churning. Thus, The *Mahabharata* repeatedly refers to Mandara as *mantha-giri*, Mount Churn-staff, to Vasuki as *manthani-krta*, the Churner, and to water, as churned into milk by gods and demons, as *manthodaka* (i.e., *mantha-udaka*). The act of Ocean churning comes up as *manthana* – the word form used in the *Amrtamanthana*.

The imagery of the epic myth is also close enough to the Rgvedic. As the *Veda* has it, *soma*-squeezing in a mortar is a very noisy process:

> If, O mortar, thou art set in every home,
> There sound the loudest,
> Like the drum of conquerors!*
> (*RV*, I.28.5)

Another sound effect accompanies the procuring of *amrta* from the Ocean. When the gods and *Asuras* were churning the Ocean with Mandara, a great noise rose like thunder coming out of monstrous clouds.

In the *Mahabharata*, gods and demons turned Mandara at an amazing speed as they pulled now at Vasuki's head, now tail. Similar movements made a churn-staff rotate on the bottom slab:

---

* *yac cid dhi tvam grhegrhe ulukhalaka yujyase |*
iha dyumattamam vada jayatam iva dundubhih ||

These [both] who acquire by means of a sacrifice,
and obtain the best reward,
Rush loudly about, like two bay horses,
Devouring the herbs [of *soma*].*
(*RV*, I.28.7)

The aerial turbulence produced by the rapid staff rotation is likened unto the wind. Likewise, the staff itself is addressed as a mighty tree:

O Lord of the Forest,
The wind bloweth round thy top.
For Indra, press out, O mortar,
The *soma* to drink.**
(*RV*, I.28.6)

With flames and smoke, the winds accompanied Ocean churning to gather clouds round Mandara and pour rain on the heads of the tired celestial denizens.

The Rgvedic hymn shows how widespread the quick *soma*-squeezing rite was, performed "in every home" (*RV*, I.28.5). We can thus assume that it was well-known to all Indian social strata in the Vedic time – and the early epic period, judging by the persistence of Indian traditions. In other words, the mortar with a slab in the bottom, the churn-staff and the rope clearly indicated a particular *soma* rite. The mythic allegory was also meant to discern household utensils in the fantastic attributes of the cosmic churning, identical to them in function – the Tortoise with its rounded back corresponding closely enough to a slab; Mount Mandara, broad at the foot and peaking toward the top like a churn-staff; and Serpent Vasuki, strong and elastic like a rope.

So, as we see it, the *Amrtamanthana* reinterpreted the *soma* related Vedic cult ideas. *Vedas* practically omitted mythological treatment of the *soma* cult, giving pride of place to its ritual aspect. The *Amrtamanthana* gave a new mythological interpretation, based on the initial Vedic symbolism actualized, to practical parts of the Vedic rites – *soma*-squeezing and mixing the juice with water. *Soma* entered the epic tradition as *amrta*, on the one hand, bringing out its unity with the Vedic symbol and, on the other, emphasizing its properties as immortality elixir.

---

* *ayaji vajasatama ta hy ucca vijarbhrtah* |
havi ivandhamsi bapsata ||

** *uta smate vanaspate vatah vi vati agram it* |
atho indraya patave sunu somam ulukhala ||

Soma and *amrta* figured as partly interchangeable concepts in Hinduism, interconnected through the moon — the vessel preserving the immortality potion, and at the same time, identified with Soma the moon god. This form of the Soma cult was not characteristic of the Vedic era. Thus, Vedic texts most often name the moon Candra, not Soma. On the other hand, already the later Vedic time knew a widespread moon-Soma connection. Thus, the rather late Rgvedic nuptial hymn, of *mandala* X (*RV*, X.85), associated Soma with the moon; the *Atharvaveda* says that "the moon feeds on this [*soma*] potion, which consists of *amrta*" (*Ath*, 3.31.6); the *Satapatha-Brahmana* steadily names the moon god King Soma, the celestial food granting immortality, and the moon "the highest celestial glory of Soma" (*SBr.*, VII.3.1.46). The *Satapatha-Brahmana* directly indicates that "the moon is none other than King Soma, the food of gods" (*SBr.*, XI.1.4.4). The *Aitareya-Brahmana* (*AitBr.*, 7.11.5) and many other *Brahmanas* and *Puranas* offer a similar concept of the Soma-moon.

We see this concept of the Soma-moon-*amrta* in the myth of "The churning of the Ocean". According to tradition, Soma-moon, the firstborn of the cosmogonic creation, came out of the Milky Ocean and rose to heaven. At the end of the myth, after they win the battle for *amrta*, the gods put it in a formidable vessel and give it to Krtin-Nara to keep. The *Mahabharata* does not directly allude to the moon as this vessel, which it became as it emerged out of the churned Ocean. The later tradition, however, specified it as the vessel for the precious elixir. According to *Puranas*, the night time luminary was regularly filled with *amrta* to be drunk by gods in the light half-month and *Pitrs* in the dark. The interpretation of the Soma god as moon god and keeper of the *amrta* was widespread in Hinduism, whereas the ritual hypostasis of *soma* as sacrificial juice lost all topicality. This change of symbolism was objectively due to the gradual obliteration of the *soma* cult in the later Vedic era. The epic time gave up rites of the *Somayajna* type, and even forgot the plant with its hallucinogenous juice. The sacral ideas of *soma* — the oldest kernel of the Indo-Aryan ritualism — were, nevertheless, holy enough in themselves to be fully forgotten. Probably, this was why the rites of *soma*-squashing and mixing with milk and water, though leaving out the everyday ritual system, received a mythological interpretation as the events that gave rise to the *Amrtamanthana*.

Thus, the epic myth succeeded to many essential aspects of the Vedic *soma* concept, though its Vedic reminiscences are not limited to it. There is the motif of the god-demon battle — the central in the Vedic mythology. As *soma* embodied the principal Vedic rite, so the theme of gods-*Asuras* opposing was the principal Vedic myth. The *Rgveda* saw Indra as warrior god, and presented his duel with *Asura* in many versions of one and the same pattern. Essentially, *soma* was its indispensable attribute. *Soma* or *amrta* is often presented as temporal possession of Indra's enemy, whom the god challenges to take over the precious elixir. Even more often, Soma is treated as Indra's ally promoting his victory (*R V*, IV.1-5). More than that, Indra always drinks *soma* before the battle and so comes out on top (*RV*, I.32.3). We can easily notice all these motives actualized in the *Amrtamanthana*, where the fight starts for the wondrous potion, of which the gods partake before it, unlike the demons, to become deathless and the strongest, and thus rout out their enemies.

As experts on Vedic mythology conclude, the *Rgveda* treated Indra's heroic fight with the *Asuras* as a creative act in which a harmonious Universe emerged out of the primogenital stagnant Chaos.[6] The Vedic time also gave rise to the idea of a world born out of primal waters – the beginning of all things that exist (*SBr.*, IV.7.4.3-5; IV.8.2.3-5). An analogous cosmogonic interpretation is met in the epic myth. Here, only the creative method is unique. The earlier tradition never mentioned a cosmos set in order by churning, which first coagulates the waters, then lending fabulous treasures and setting a new world order. The cosmogonic aspect of the *Amrtamanthana* determined its outstanding impact on post-Vedic culture, which promoted it to the status of the pivotal Genesis tradition.

As we trace the links of this myth with Vedic mythology, we can't omit the motif of a woman stealing the magic elixir. The epic legend attaches pivotal significance to this act on the borderline between the two major events regarded above – the preparation of, and the battle for the *amrta*. Curiously, this central episode is also borrowed from the Vedic mythic circle. The *Brahmanas* include a legend of *soma* guarded by *Gandharvas*, and the gods gathering in conference to discuss how to get the potion. They recurred to many means, but to no result. At last, they said: "The *Gandharvas* are fond of women. Let us send *Vac* (Speech) to them, and she returns to us together with *Soma*." This scheme proved a success as *Vac* stole the elixir for the gods (*SBr.*, III.2.4.1-4).[7] This plot-turn almost fully coincides with the *Amrtamanthana*, where gods want to obtain *soma* from their rival friends and finally get it, using the mighty power of the feminine charm. The epic legend makes this plot more complicated. It is not a goddess but Visnu Narayana figuring as a female who steals the immortality potion from the *Asuras*. The protagonist of the myth, he is addressed by gods for assistance at the critical instances of the churning. Notably, the female hypostasis is unique among the many *avataras* of Visnu, and connected with this myth alone. Possibly, his transformation into a beautiful woman was necessitated by a particular Vedic mythologeme according to which *soma* was stolen by a goddess.

As we see it, the epic *Amrtamanthana* is a synthetic, artificially modelled myth which brought together the key ritual and mythological ideas of Vedism. The time of its origination remains a topical issue. As pointed out above, it was never registered in manuscripts of the Vedic era. Neither the *Vedas* nor the later *Brahmanas* literature of the eighth and seventh centuries B.C. ever mentioned it. We first come across this legend in the opening book of The *Mahabharata*, whose mythology experts trace up to the oldest epic layer from about the mid-first millennium B.C.[8] To all appearances, this date is a precise enough indication of the time when the myth emerged. Really, it appeared on the borderline of two eras—the later Vedic and the early epic. Notably, the type of mythological concepts and imagery are here closer to the old *Veda* texts than the *Brahmanas* and *Upanisads*. The later Vedic writ preserves the theme of the god-*Asura* fight, but does not attach a cosmogonic content to it. The rivalry is treated with less solemnity, and the idea of struggle brought down. Thus, the Upanisadic prose, historically the closest to the earlier epic, tells of gods fighting demons with the help of *Udgitha*, the peculiar ritual singing. The *Brhadaranyaka-Upanisad* has this to say: "Prajapati gave birth to two kinds of beings – gods and *Asuras*. The gods were the younger, and *Asuras* the older. They grappled for these worlds. The gods said: 'Let us vanquish the *Asuras* by *Udgitha* during a sacrifice'" (*BrUp.*, 1.3.1).[9] The later Vedic era promoted this situation to an archetype. In fact, the gods' triumph now directly depended on their knowledge of Brahmanic dogmatic norms and rites, in which they surpassed the *Asuras*. It is easy to see that the myth of *Amrtamanthana* has nothing in common with this esoteric ritualized tradition. More than that, later it negates this later, to an extent. The comparatively young *Mahabharata* legend reflects another world-view and contains an artificially revived archaic myth-making power.

Notes

1. See: J. Dumezil. 1924. *Le festin d'immortalite. Etude de mythologie comparee indo-europeenne.*
2. See: K.F. Geldner. *Festgruss an Rudolf von Roth.*, S. 192, Stuttgart, 1893. We did not take into consideration the most disputable concepts as, for instance, Slater's hypothesis of the Egyptian impact on pre-Aryan Indian culture. In *Amrta*, he saw an Egyptian palm juice drink imported via Mesopotamia in the Dravidian era and later inherited by the Aryans (G. Slater. *The Dravidian Elements in Indian Culture*, L., 1924, p. 78).

   For a comparative analysis of the many versions of the *Amrtamanthana* myth see: K. Ruping. *Amrtamanthana and Kurma-Avatara. Ein Beitrag zur puranischen Mythen- und Religionsgeschichte.* (Wiesbaden, 1970).
3. *Adiparva*, p. 80.
4. Cf. Elizarenkova's translation of *Rgveda* (*Mandalas* I-IV. Translated, compiled, preface and annotated by T.Y. Elizarenkova. Moscow, 1989, in Russian).

   > There where the pestle is tied
   > like reins for driving . . . . (*RV*, I.28.4)

   See also the translation by R.I.H. Griffith: *The Hymns of the Rigveda*: Translated with a Popular Commentary. (Benares, 1896, 2nd ed.).

   > There where the woman marks and learns the pestle's
   > constant rise and fall . . . (*RV*, I.28.3)
5. Our attention was attracted to this fact by L.I. Kulikov, to whom we express gratitude for priceless linguistic consultations as we translated the *Rgveda* and other texts from the Sanskrit.

6. See: W. Norman Brown, 'The Creation Myth of the Rig Veda', In *Journal of the American Oriental Society*, (1942), vol. 62, pp. 85-98; F.B.J. Kuiper, "Cosmogony and Conception: A Query", In *History of Religions,* (Chicago, 1970), Vol. 10, No. 2, pp. 91-138; and *Ancient Indian Cosmogony*, (Delhi, 1983).
7. In some other versions of this myth, *soma* was stolen from the gods by another celestial maiden – for instance, Gayatri, personification of the Vedic verse metre. Cf.: "*Soma* was there. The *Devas* sent Gayatri, saying, 'Bring that *Soma*' ", Quot. from F.B.J. Kuiper. 'An Indian Prometheus? – *Asiatische Studien, Zeitschrift der Schweizerischen Gesellscaft fur Asienkunde.* XXXV. (Bern, 1971), S. 95. See also: *AitBr.*, III.25.1; 26.1-3.
8. See: E.W. Hopkins. *The Religions of India*, (New Delhi, 1970), p. 408; and 'Epic Mythology', – *Grundriss der Indo-Arischen Philologie*, (Strassbourg, 1915), Bd.III, H.1.
9. The translation was made with the help of: *The Brhadaranyaka Upanisad* with the Comment. of Sankaracarya, tr. by Swami Madhavananda, (Calcutta, 1958, 3rd ed.)

10

Elements of Nature and the Order of Culture

Baidyanath Saraswati

On the origin of human culture there are two incompatible maxims – *cultura ex cultura* and *cultura ex natura*.[1] Culturalists grant cultural phenomena as autonomous efficient agents of themselves. Naturalists, on the other hand, attribute cultural forms to nature. The object of this paper is to suggest that the order by which both culture and nature are bound is the same.

What are the elements of nature? How are they related to the elements of culture? Do nature and culture follow the same law? Or is the order of culture unique? What, essentially, hold nature and culture together? How does cosmology pattern human culture?

These questions demand explanations from both cultural and cosmological viewpoints. As anthropologist my concern and capability are limited to the cultural explanation, quite understandably, away from scientific cosmology.

To this group of questions different answers would follow, depending on the kind of intellectual tradition we refer to. I am here attempting to characterise the indigenous vision of traditional cultures. Within this category there are two different but related traditions known as the 'oral' and 'textual'. The textual tradition offers a full and systematic analysis of the universe. Reflections of the oral tradition are more concentrated in practice than systematic in explanation. The difference is, essentially, epistemological.

The Transcendent Order of Nature

The Indian textual tradition has produced a unique contribution to thought that characteristically look inward upon the universe. A splendid example of this is the theory of Elements. The basic assumption in this is, that, like the rest of the material world man is made up of Elements which at death disintegrate and dissolve into nature. The Elements have been spiritually identified and metaphysically debated for thousands of years. Traditions differ in respect of both identification and enumeration of Elements.[2] At the most general level there are nine *tattvas* or Elements: Earth, Water, Fire, Air, Sky, Time, Directions, Mind and Soul. Of these the first five are called *bhuta* and the last four *dravya*. The gross and the subtle aspects of Elements are recognised. Traditional vision, then, leaps over the dichotomy. The reality of the subtler plane is said to be responsible for the grosser plane, and at a higher level of realisation the distinction between the gross and the subtle gets totally obliterated.

In the tribal oral tradition there is no categorical term that may equal *tattva* or *bhuta*, but its characteristic attitude towards nature is the same.

If we set out to examine the theory of Elements, as discussed in classical texts and described in the oral tradition, we should soon realise that Elements of nature are subject to a fivefold order: (1) origination, (2) binding, (3) interlocking, (4) overlapping, and (5) transcending.

ORIGINATION

Tribal cosmogony[3] refers to a state of nothingness. But that nothingness was not an absolute vacuity. Everything was Water or Cloud, or nothing, nothing at all but two Eggs shining like gold. As the Eggs broke open, from one came the Earth, from the other the Sky. Metaphorically speaking, when the Sky made love to the Earth every kind of things and beings were born. In another story, the Earth, the Cosmic Mother, died of her own accord and every part of her body became the part of the world. These myths can be parallel in the textual description of *Hiranyagarbha*, the golden germ, and the sacrifice of *Purusa,* the Cosmic Person.

Elements originated in phases. Water, Earth and Sky came first; aquatic animals and bird second; land third; Air or Wind fourth; and finally Fire.[4] Variations occur in the structured sequence, particularly in respect of the first element.

Another curious feature of tribal cosmogony is that there is no single creator of the universe. There are creators for each specific element.

In the early phase there does not seem to have any real distinction between man, animal and spirit. Things and beings multiplied inter-specieswise.

Thus, three apparent ideas emerge: (a) a break in the radical solidarity gave origins to male-female principle; (b) heterogeneity is a fundamental aspect in the origin and development of species; and (c) the built-in order of cosmic unity is 'one-to-many'.

BINDING

Elements of nature have a binding-ability. Each Element has a form, a location, and a dependent-relation with another Element. Living Forms of nature are self-originating, self-organizing, and self-sustaining. Form is predetermined; it is filled by perishable matter. Life is formless, self-existent and, essentially, indestructible. As form and life come together, the process of origination begins. Life activates matter that constitutes form, but in itself is not a material substance.[5]

Elements of nature constitute human and other forms, both individually and collectively. Each major organ is said to have its own builder. Head and ears are associated with the Sky; neck and chest with Air; stomach with Fire; and body with Earth.[6] Five fingers, from the little finger to the thumb, are associated, respectively, with Earth, Water, Fire, Air and Sky.[7]

Elements are also known to have caused the origin of bio-social types. The ironsmiths relate themselves with Earth, carpenters with Water, coppersmiths with Fire, sculptors with Wind, and goldsmiths with Sky.[8]

Elements' binding-ability is expressed in life-processes. As the *Garbha Upanisad* describes,[9]

> One night after the union in a fertile period, arises a nodule (*kalila*); after seven nights it changes into bubble (*budbud*); in half a month arises the embryo (*pinda*); after one month it becomes solid; when two months have passed the head appears; after three months the formation of the feet is completed; at four months happily originates the sex, the abdomen and the hips; at five months the back forms; after six months form the mouth, nose, eyes and ears, and after seven months the individual soul concludes the unification. At eight months all the parts are complete.

If tribal description of Elements is transposed on the Upanisadic theory, it would be clear how Elements are associated with intra-uterine formation of major organs. The liquid stage from which the embryo arises is Water; when the embryo becomes solid it is Earth; the appearance of hollow head is Sky; the formation of the moving feet is Wind; the origination of sex and abdomen is associated with heat or Fire.

This sequence of embryonic development roughly corresponds with the origin of the universe: from primeval Water to Earth and Sky, and from these two Wind and Fire. It also supports the general theory of man as microcosm.

INTERLOCKING

Form and life are cross-linked. By entering into a form, the formless life acquires qualitative distinctions. It gives different expressions to different forms or species. Accordingly, it is called by different names. As a transcendent substance, life gets involved in the threefold cosmic process of formation (origination), affirmation (preservation) and negation (dissolution) of Elements. Interlocking of life and form help realise the existential changes; it makes cosmic order visible.

Interlocking of Elements[10] is described metaphorically. Earth and Sky are universal parents; Fire and Wind are brothers just as Water and Mist are brothers. Earth and Wind, Water and Fire are negatively linked; they have always been enemies. Wind is the friend of Fire against Water and he fights the rain to drive it before him.

The more complex interlocking is perceived in the textual tradition (*Figs*. 10.1-10.4)

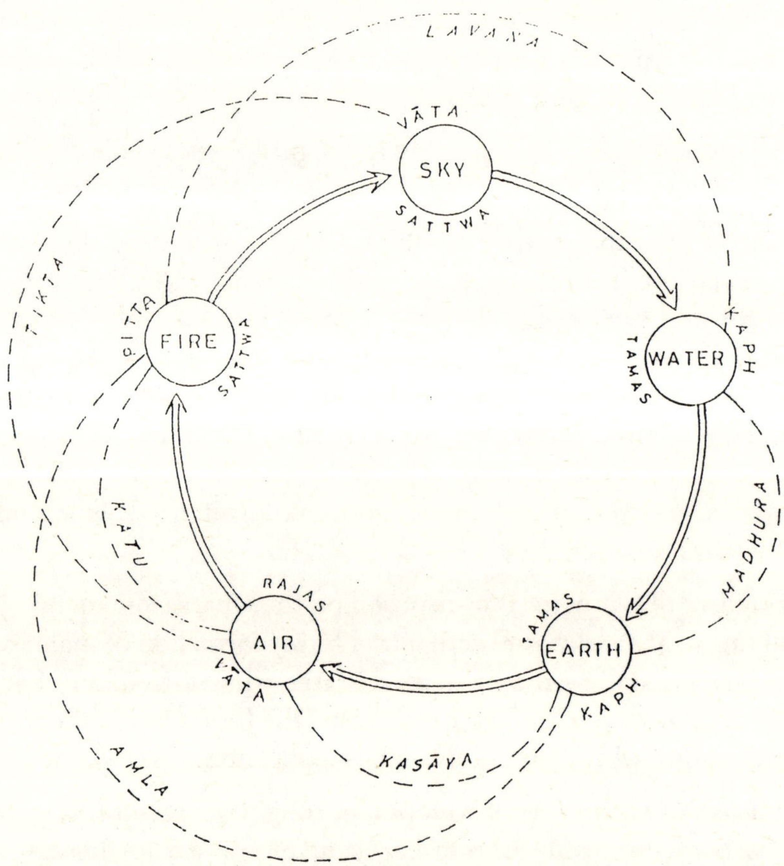

Fig. 10.1. Interlocking Elements (Ayurvedic Tradition)
5 Elements, 3 *Gunas*, 3 *Dosas*, 3 *Rasas*
⟹ Interlocking Path ----- Composition of *Rasas*

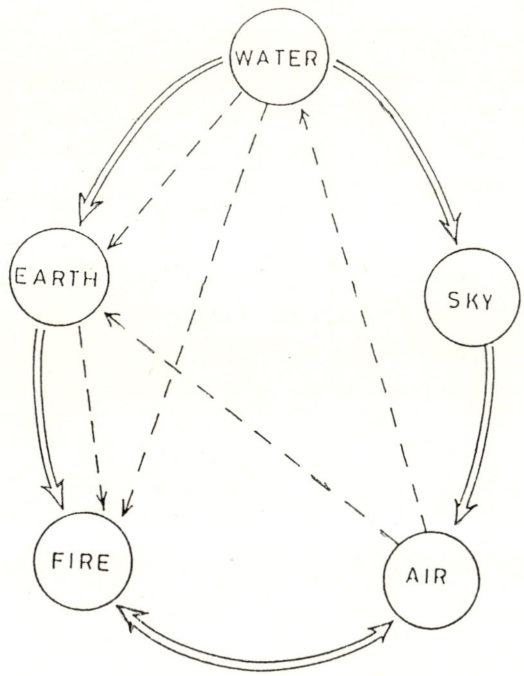

Fig. 10.2. Interlocking Elements (Tribal Tradition)
⟹ Positive - - - → Negative

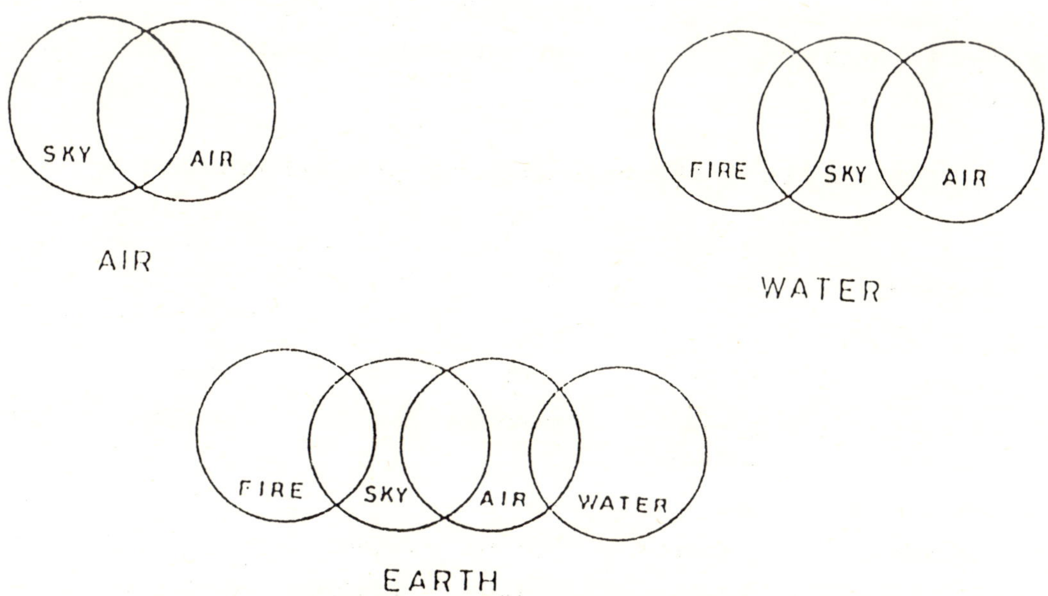

Fig. 10.3. Overlapping Elements
Eternal (*Parmanu*) Forms
(a). *dwyanuka* (b). *trayanuka* (c). *caturnuka*

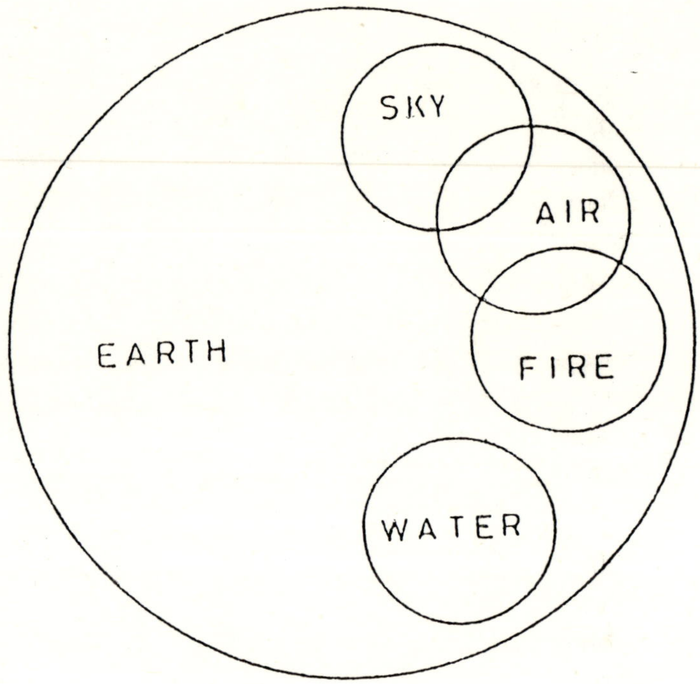

Fig. 10.4. Overlapping Elements
Gross Earth containing 50% earth and in the residue portion all the remaining four elements.

In the Indian classical text, the five primal Elements are linked with other Elements or aspects of nature such as colour, form, sense-organ, physical character, property, functions, etc.

Table A: The Five Elements as Perceived in Indian Tradition

	Five Elements	*Sky*	*Air*	*Fire*	*Water*	*Earth*
1.	Property	sound	touch	form	taste	smell
2.	Physical character	absence of resistance	movement	heat	liquidity	rough-ness
3.	Sensory organ	ears	skin	eyes	tongue	nose
4.	Functions	porousness,	lightness	colour	heaviness,	solidity,
		distinction	activity	digestion, braveness, brightness, intolerance	coldness oleaginous, semen	heavi-ness

5.	Psychological property (*Guna*)	*sattva*	*rajas*	*sattva*	*tamas*	*tamas*
6.	*Dosa*	*vata*	*vata*	*pitta*	*kapha*	*kapha*
7.	Colour	crystal white	dark	red	white	yellow
8.	Form	circle	hexagon	triangle	half-moon	square
9.	Mark	*bindu sakti* (point of power)	six points	*svastika*	lotus	*vajra*
10.	*Bija-mantra*	*haum*	*hyaim*	*hrum*	*hvim*	*hlam*
11.	*Kala*	*Santya-*	*santi*	*vidya*	*pratistha*	*nivrtti*
12.	Presiding deity	*isana*	*tatpurusa*	*aghora*	*vamadeva*	*sadyojata*
13.	*Karnesvara*	*sadasiva*	*isvara*	*rudra*	*visnu*	*brahma*

Nos. 1 to 6, as perceived in the Ayurveda (Sharma, 1976); Nos. 7 to 13, as recongnized in the Saivite system in South India (Janaki, 1988).

These Elements are also linked with psychological attributes called *gunas*. Each Element is tied with a divinity and its related aspects such as *mantra*, etc.

The Five Elements referred in the classical Chinese[11] are Wood, Fire, Earth, Metal and Water. Each of these is linked with colour, taste, season, climate, also with the human body — *yin-yang* — organs, body tissues, sensory-organs and emotions.

Table B. The Five Elements as Perceived in Chinese Tradition

Source : Butt and Bloomfield (1985)

(i) The five elements as they affect nature

Five Elements	*Wood*	*Fire*	*Earth*	*Metal*	*Water*
Natural development	birth	growth	transfor-mation	collection	storage
Colour	green	red	yellow	white	black
Taste	sour	bitter	sweet	metallic	salty
Season	spring	summer	late summer	autumn	winter
Climate	windy	hot	humid	dry	cold

(ii) The five elements as they affect man

Five Elements	*Wood*	*Fire*	*Earth*	*Metal*	*Water*
Yin organs	liver	heart	spleen	lungs	kidneys
Yang organs	gall bladder	small intestine	stomach	large intestine	bladder
Body tissues	tendon	blood vessels	muscle	skin-hair	bone
Sensory organs	eyes	tongue	mouth	nose	ears
Emotions	anger	joy, excitement	anxiety	grief	fear

In the Chinese astrology the Five Elements form a circle of one containing the other.

OVERLAPPING

Elements have both personal (material) and universal (spiritual) attributes. Water and Egg, which appeared in the beginning, have a fundamental feature of sacredness. The other primal Elements such as the Earth, Air, Fire, and Sky (with the sun, moon and stars) have also a similar indwelling sacred attributes. However, not all Elements are spiritually vibrant all the time and at all places; but they can be made so in a ritual way. The Elements exist in two spheres – material and spiritual – simultaneously with different ranges of time and space.

In tribal perception, the world is divided into two halves – the Sky and the Earth. There is a world beyond the Sky and another below the Earth. The Earth is a round-shaped flat surface; the Sky a hollow concave overarching the Earth. The structure of the universe is thus somewhat like a cone, similar to the structure of a tribal leaf-hut.[12]

The five Elements overlap in their formation and so also the world of the matter with the other worlds.[13] Life in this world is repeated in the other world in a similar order. Worlds are communicable in dreams and in trance.

TRANSCENDING

Cosmogonic myths describe how the limits of the natural state are transcended. The state of primordial solidarity was transcended as the Eggs broke open and the universe revealed. The natural order of self-origination was transcended by the origin of the male-female principle. The order of self-organisation was transcended by the interlocking of various Elements. The spatial order of the pluriverse was transcended by the overlapping of spheres in dreams and trance.

Life transcends the limits of the form. Death transcends all attributes of Elements, including the limits of the terrestrial time.

There is no intrinsic disorder in nature — dissolution is an integral aspect of the transcendent order of nature. Transcendence is the order of all orders. It is inviolable.

The Natural Order of Culture

THE ECOLOGICAL MAN

Tribal myths deny the uniqueness of man[14] insofar as his origin is concerned. Man is not unique even in the possession of knowledge. Primordial knowledge came to him from birds and animals. The priests of all creatures were born, ahead of human beings. Man is not the creator of knowledge. Cosmic Intelligence[15] is the self-existent source of all knowledge.

Man lives on the Earth in the company of animals and spirits. Natural Elements are under the control of spirits. The spirits are everywhere and in all things and beings. They are the invisible controller of human behaviour. They can be influenced only by the priest.

Not a single event takes place without any cause. As there is cause so there is an effect or *vice-versa*. Cause can be found, but not under ordinary condition. Following the ritual way one may return to the primordial conditions of life. Of the ritual objects, the Egg recalls the unmanifest state, the cowrie-shell symbolizes the primeval Water, the sacrificial bird typifies the Sky, and the rice represents the Earth. Rituals are performed in ecological space — the sacred grove, the source of water, hill tops and mountain caves — in ecological time determined by the Sky, seasons, lunar changes, day-and-night, moments of natural calamity, etc.

Ritual helps man experience the ecological rhythm of his life. The performer returns to a primordial state to reunite with the primal elements and to rejoice his earthly existence. There are rituals involving group pantomimes of rolling in dust, acrobating in water, walking on burning embers, and swinging upside down on burning ashes.[16] Such ritual acts affirm people's belief in the supernatural order.

As ecological being, man is fully conscious of his physical limitations. He is also aware of his innate quipment for safeguarding against the adversaries.

THE MAKING OF PERSONS

Elements of nature have a veritable role in the making of persons.

Biologically man is made up of the Earth, Water, Fire, etc. Pigmentation, formation and function of the body tissues, sense-organs, etc. are associated with the Five Elements. Psychologically also man is conditioned by the attributes (*guna*) of Elements.

Human personality type is determined by biological time, beginning from the birth. The twelve signs of the zodiac that form the body of **Kalapurusa** (Time Person) affect man's future, the rhythm of life.[17] The Chinese doctors classify people first by the body type and then by *yin* and *yang*.[18] According to *Jyotisa*, man's activities are guided by the position of the planets. The planets have distinctive spheres – some are benefic, others melefic. Their disposition and relational values affect human life. Rituals, ceremonies, daily life, economic activities, etc. are observed in due consideration of the propitious time.

The Man of matter (Elements) moves upward through a ritual process of socialization at different stages in life. Though sacerdotal in form and theme, ritual establishes the importance of this earthly life and help organize a distinctive and coherent cultural pattern.

In Indian astrology there is a belief that impurity (*mala*) clings to birth and the removal of it is the primary concern of man. The ritual process by which the body is cleansed is called *samskara*.[19] From securing the conception to the last rite of cremation a number of *samskara* rites are required to be observed. Only then one becomes a full member of the society and a cultùral being. Purification of body is obligatory for all kinds of worship and ceremonies. One such ritual is called *bhutasuddhi*,[20] the purification of the different layers of elements in the body (*bhutasarira*) of the worshipper.

To make the physical man capable of transforming into a cultural person correlations are established between the natural and the supernatural orders at all levels of human existence. A bio-spiritual principle operates.[21] Cultural activities are determined by the body, mind and spirit. Satisfaction of the body needs is a critical factor in the survival of man. The mind responds to the physical needs – it creates the urge to satisfy these needs. The spirit, which transcends both the body and the mind, mediates between and allows the satisfaction of the needs to such an extent that the world order is not disturbed.

All traditional societies are structured on a fourfold control system that orders human life, his subsistence, distinctions and desires. Life is ordered into four successive stages (*asrama*) from learning and performing to gradual indifference and final withdrawal. The ordering of subsistence ensures harmony, peace and purity in economic and social life. The ordering of distinctions on the basis of time, place, ethnic groups and aesthetic considerations allows the formation of distinctive lifestyles. The ordering of desires completes the cosmic rhythm of life. Human desires are fourfold: the desire to uphold the natural moral order (*dharma*), desire connected with wealth and power (*artha*), the desire for pleasure or procreation (*kama*), the desire for freedom from all desires (*moksa*). Although seemingly opposed in character, these primal desires stand in an organic and interactive relationship to one another. This fourfold ordering of life is called *purusartha*, that is, the making of a cultural person (*samskritika purusa*). At a higher level of consciousness, the cultural person is transformed into a cosmic person (*Purusa*).

From another angle, man is not the measure of all that exists. He can neither create nor destroy nature. He is a creator of culture only in a limited sense, because cultural forms are prone to the fivefold order of transcendence. Human culture is unique only in that it allows humans to satisfy their impulses in a far more complex manner than do animals. Another peculiarity which distinguishes man from animals is his innate capacity and will to transcend even the physical needs. This he often does for spiritual gains and emotional satisfaction. The urge for transcendence is attributed to the complex structuring of the sense-organs, and all that is known as *tattva.*

The Integral Vision

We see now how the polaristic position in the anthropological theory of nature and culture is nullified by the traditional vision.

Nature in its essence is not a machine. Living matter exists only by the order of the transcendent life, the one which is formless, invisible, but knowable through its effect. Nature constitutes a set of self-originating, self-organizing and self-sustaining forms. Life renders matter the binding abilities, interlocking powers, overlapping characters, and a transcendent state. The transcendent order of nature is that (*Prakrti*) which natures nature.

Elements of nature, in their living state, may appropriately be described as process. They are set into a technical order that causes bio-social types. Like natural forms, the forms of culture are also subject to the fivefold order: origination, binding, interlocking, overlapping and transcending.

Man of matter is culturally processed (*purusartha*). He is transformed into a moral person (*naitika purusa*). The gross body undergoes through a transcendental superpsychic process of cultivation (*samskara*) and purification (*bhutasuddhi*). Man discovers major points of power in his subtle body that functions as an instrument (*yantra*) for the inner meditative experience.[22] He invokes the spirit or deity to possess his body. In that state of possession, or meditation, the cultural man is transformed into a cosmic person, an archetype of *Purusa*, the source of everything, the supreme principle and all that we call divine. Man enshrines Cosmic Form (*Visvarupa*) in his body; God contains it in his mouth.[23]

The concept of *purusa* is central to the Indian thought and culture. Its echoes are obvious both in cosmology and in sociology. Ordinarily, the term *purusa* means male person. Originally it meant Cosmic Person, the unique one, as described in the Rgvedic hymns *Purusa-sukta*. Its divine connotation has been constantly sustained in the sacred texts referring to *Kalapurusa* in astrology, *Vastupurusa* in architecture, *Sangeetapurusa* in music, *Vriksapurusa* in botany, *Pitrapurusa* in genetics, and so on. There are other related terms of cosmic significance used in human context such as *purusartha*, the fourfold cultural process (*dharma*, *artha*, *kama*, *moksa*); *purusottama*, best among men; Prajapati, creator of heaven and earth, epithetically used for potter; *Visvakarma*, the celestial architect of the universe, used for the smith.

This vision of culture and cosmology is a challenge to anthropology. Anthropologists have discussed the Indian concept of person in terms of the level of the genealogical construction of the universe of kin and caste, ordered along a continuum of purity-impurity.[24] The emphasis is given on the form of the transmission of blood purity from parent to child in a purely clinical sense of biology and psychology. Obviously, the Western anthropological view of person is wholly incompatible with the Indian concept of *purusa* that combines caste, culture and cosmology in assimilable portions. The theory of *purusartha* presents an integral vision of the nature-man-culture continuum.

To understand and deepen the traditional vision of man, nature and culture, it is important to clear up the distinctions between the oral and the textual perceptions.

As indicated before, in the oral tradition the ecological man looks upon nature as the self-existing reality of which he is an inseparable part at all levels. This view of nature differs from the philosophers', or physicists' cosmology in which man takes a characteristic attitude towards nature. Here man is the knower and nature is the object known, or to be known. In all reflective thinking there is an implicit assumption that the forms of thought are different from the things to be lived with and that the existing reality is different from the conceptual reality. In the tribal oral tradition experience and expressions are kept together. In other words, there is no gap between knowledge and existence. Generalization in the tribal world-view is primarily cosmocentric. The textual tradition, on the other hand, is homocentric in the sense that all its paradigms come, essentially, from within man, crystallised in such concepts as *pancabhuta*, *pancakosa*, *purusa* and so on. Nevertheless, both these traditions are grounded in the same cosmology and shared faith in man's ontological communion with nature. Their 'ecocentric' view of culture is, of course, totally opposed to the 'modern', 'technocentric' view of man and the universe.

Indeed, the current generation of ecologists have begun to realize that 'ecocentric' culture has an innate (natural) equipment for prolonged survival, while 'technocentric' culture is doomed to extinction.

To sum up in the words of one of our greatest interpreters of the Indian vision.[25]

> Man is related to nature, the elements and animal and plant life. The environment in which he lives is not an alien environment. He always considers it his own, where he is like all other breathing, but endowed with the special faculty of self-reflection and speech, thus of *vak*. Indeed, man is constantly seen as an embodiment of the elements and forces of nature and in relationship to animal and plant life. This gives the world a different character from what is implied in the modern idea of progressive evolution. Man is not the best because he overpowers and conquers nature and is thus the fittest to survive, but he is one amongst the many with the capacity for 'consciousness' and self-reflection and transcendence from his pure physicality, through psychical discipline.

Notes

1. Culturalists take the same position on this point as the biologists with respect to the origin of life. The dictum in the biological issue is that "all life comes from the living". The problem is similar to the biological issue of biogenesis *versus* abiogenesis. Modern biology now comes to consider that such factors as enzymes may serve as a bridge between the quick and the dead.
2. Indian philosophical traditions such as Buddhist, Jain, Nyaya-Vaisesika, and Samkhya Schools differ on the enumeration of *tattvas* but they generally agree with respect to the Five Elements or matter (*skandha*, *pudgala*, *bhuta*, or *dravya*, *tanmatra*): Earth, Water, Fire, Air and Sky. In classical Chinese the Five Elements referred to are Wood, Fire, Earth, Metal and Water.
3. See Saraswati (1991). According to Chinese tradition, Water was created in the eleventh month, Fire in the sixth month, Wood in the first, Metal in the eighth and, Earth in the third month (Chung 1992).
4. See Prasad (1992).
5. See Saraswati (1992b).
6. See Mital (1992).
7. See Janaki (1988).

8. See Brouwer (1992).
9. Cf. Filippi (1992).
10. See Saraswati (1992a). In tribal cosmogony, Air, colour, and directions are linked up: From all the four quarters, the Wind brought colours – the east Wind blew white, the west Wind yellow, the south Wind red, and the north Wind black. In Chinese cosmology (see Chung 1992) west is associated with white, south with red, north with black and east with green. For the Chinese theory of the Five Elements and their chain of reaction, see Butt and Bloomfield (1985) and also Chung (1992).
11. See Table B, also Chung (1992).
12. See Adhikary (1992).
13. See Saraswati (1992b).
14. See Saraswati (1992a).
15. *Ibid.*
16. See Citaristi (1992).
17. See Saraswati (1990).
18. See Butt and Bloomfield (1985).
19. See Saraswati (1977).
20. See Janaki (1988).
21. See Saraswati (1989).
22. See Khanna (1979).
23. As in the *Mahabharata* war, Lord Krsna opened his mouth to demonstrate *Visvarupa* before Arjuna.
24. See Ostor, *et. al.* (1982).
25. With reference to the *Taittiriya* Upanisadic discussion on *pancakosa*, Vatsyayan (1983: 10-11) dwells on how man's nature is delineated from the most physical to the psychical and finally the spiritual. In the *pancakosa*, (fivefold constitution of man) each order is called a *kosa*, sheath or envelope: *Anandamaya* (beatific), *Vigyanmaya* (intellectual), *Manomaya* (mental), *Pranamaya* (vital) and *Annamaya* (vegetative) *kosa*. These are hierarchically organized. The Indian vision of man can be understood by reading the theories of both *pancabhuta* and *pancakosa* together.

References

Adhikary, A.K., 1992. "The Birhors and their universe". Seminar Paper. New Delhi: Indira Gandhi National Centre for the Arts.

Butt, Gary and Frena Bloomfield, 1985. *Harmony rules*. London: Arrow Books.

Chung, Tan, 1992. "Man-nature syntheses in Chinese tradition". Seminar Paper. New Delhi: Indira Gandhi National Centre for the Arts.

Citaristi, Ileana 1992. "The Five Elements in the '*Danda*' Rituals". Seminar Paper. New Delhi: Indira Gandhi National Centre for the Arts.

Filippi, Gian Giuseppe, 1992. "The Secret of the Embryo according to the *Garbha Upanisad*", In *Annali Di Ca' Foscari*, Estratto XXXI, 3.

Janaki, S.S., 1988. *Dhvaja-stambha (critical account of its structural and ritualistic details)*. Madras: The

Kuppuswami Shastri Research Institute.

Khanna, Madhu, 1979. *Yantra: the tantric symbol of cosmic unity*. London.

Mital, Kanak, 1992. "Lifestyle Study of the Santhals: a Thesaurus perception through Water". Seminar Paper. New Delhi: Indira Gandhi National Centre for the Arts.

Ostor, Akos, Lina Fruzzetti and Steve Barnett (eds.), 1982. *Concept Person-kinship, caste and marriage in India*. Cambridge: Harvard University of Press.

Prasad, Onkar, 1992. "Perceptions of *Bhutas* (Elements) in Oral Tradition: a Case of Santhal Musical Texts". Seminar Paper. New Delhi: Indira Gandhi National Centre for the Arts.

Saraswati, Baidyanath, 1977. *Brahmanic Ritual Traditions: in the crucible of time*. Simla: Indian Institute of Advanced Study.

——, 1989. "Lifestyles in traditional cultures: a conceptual framework". Seminar Paper. New Delhi: Indira Gandhi National Centre for the Arts.

——, 1990. "Ritual time: an exegesis of time and great time". Seminar Paper: New Delhi: Indira Gandhi National Centre for the Arts.

——, 1991. "Tribal Cosmogony: Primal Vision of Man and Cosmos", In Baidyanath Saraswati (ed.), *Tribal thought and culture: essays in honour of Shri Surajit Chandra Sinha*. New Delhi: Concept Publishing Company.

——, 1992a. "Cosmogonic Myths and the Forces of Nature". Seminar Paper. New Delhi: Indira Gandhi National Centre for the Arts.

——, 1992b. "Forms of Life in the World of Matter – Reflections on Tribal Cosmology". Seminar Paper. Pune: Inter-University Centre for Astronomy and Astrophysics.

Sharma, P.V., 1976. *Introduction to Dravyaguna* (*Indian Pharmacology*). Varanasi: Chaukhambha Orientalia.

Vatsyayan, Kapila, 1983. *The Square and the Circle of the Indian Arts*. New Delhi: Roli Books International.

11

The Zuni View of Nature[1]

Triloki Nath Pandey

I

I am a social anthropologist devoted to the study of the 'tribal' people of India and of the United States of America. Since I was introduced to the Tharus of the Himalayan terai exactly three decades ago, I have lived for five years among the Zuni, the Hopi, and the Navajo of the American Southwest. And during the past five years I have spent 15 months in India, visiting the 'tribal' communities in its northern, central, southern, and north-eastern regions. This has given me wonderful opportunities to learn first-hand about what the organizers of this symposium call "traditional visions of nature and culture". Relying on this field experience, I am going to reflect on the perspective of one such culture, the Zuni of New Mexico.

The Zuni occupy a unique place in the history of both America and American anthropology. The first mention of the tribe is found in the chronicles of the Narvavez expedition (1528-37). Eighty years before the landing of the pilgrims, the Spanish conquistadors were in the search of their fabled "Seven Cities of Cibola" Cabeza de Vaca and Estevan guided Fray Marcos de Niza north in search of these 'cities'. Fray Marcos found Hawikuh, one of the Zuni villages, in May 1539, and took possession of the province in the name of the King of Spain.[2] He reported a large population and vast wealth. As a result, an expedition organized and led by Francisco Coronado to investigate, conquer, and claim the new land arrived at Hawikuh on July 7, 1540. The people of Hawikuh were conquered after some resistance, but the area was found devoid of the anticipated wealth.[3] Coronado found Zunis living in six flourishing terraced villages (Spaniards called them 'Pueblos') for protection. Sheep, cows, pigs, and horses were introduced by the Spaniards, changing the agrarian economy of the Zuni people. The Zuni also borrowed wheat from the Spanish visitors, the cultivation of which involved hand irrigation in favoured localities.

The Zuni remained under Spanish control until 1821 when Mexico became independent. Mexican rule lasted for twenty-seven years when in 1848, the Zuni region was ceded to the United States. I have described elsewhere the major consequences of Spanish, Mexican, and American domination of Zuni (see Pandey, 1977 and 1983 for details). Here I would like to repeat just two things: (1) The consolidation of the population living in six villages into one village, which the Spanish named Zuni, and (2) the Zunis becoming very secretive about their religious beliefs and practices in order to protect them since religion is constitutive of Zuni society and continues to be the principal marker of their personal and collective identity.

Since Jesse Green, in his recent book *Cushing at Zuri* (1990), has given an account of the beginning of American anthropology, I need not go into that here. Suffice to state that since that beginning a century ago in Cushing's impressive studies of Zuni creation myths and folk-tales, about a thousand bibliographic references are available to document various aspects of Zuni culture and history. Since Zuni is one of the best known 'traditional' cultures in anthropology, and the organizers of this seminar hope to address "the traditional socio-centric and cosmo-centric vision", let me present my own reading of the Zuni viewpoint and sense of reality.

II

It has been emphasized by all observers that religion plays a central role in Zuni life. Ruth Benedict, whose *Patterns of Culture* is largely responsible for making Zuni so famous, says that "The Zuni are a ceremonious people, a people who value sobriety and inoffensiveness above all other virtues. Their interest is centred upon their rich and complex ceremonial life . . . and no field of activity competes with ritual for foremost place in their attention" (1934: 60). Ruth Bunzel, who worked in Zuni with Benedict, adds: "All of Zuni life is oriented about religious observance and ritual has become the formal expression of Zuni civilization" (1932: 509). The foundation of Zuni ceremonialism is the cult of the ancestors (*alacinawe*). Everybody participates in their worship, and they are involved in almost every ceremony. They guide, protect, and nourish human life. While priests and medicine men pray to special groups of ancestors, the ordinary Zuni prays to ancestors in general. In Zuni belief, ancestors are supposed to serve as mediators between the mortals and the gods. On this foundation a large number of esoteric cults have developed, each devoted to the worship of special supernaturals or groups of supernaturals, and each having a priesthood, a body of secret ritual, permanent possessions of fetishistic power, special places of worship, and a calendric cycle of ceremonies. Bunzel distinguishes six major types of cults: (1) the cult of the sun, (2) the cult of the rain-makers (*Uwanami*), (3) the cult of the Kachinas, (4) the cult of the priests of the Kachinas, (5) the cult of the War

Gods, and (6) the cult of the Beast Gods. The functions, activities, and personnel of these groups overlap and interweave in a bewildering intricacy that baffles analysis (see Pandey, 1977).

I believe that the Zuni rituals and ceremonies are not only an affirmation of their cultural values, but they are also means of shaping the processes of the natural world, particularly those having to do with rain and moisture.[4] The Zunis deal directly with the complex of cosmic forces that determines the weather, regulates the health of humans and insures the fertility of the people. The Zuni are interested not so much in the isolated manifestations of natural processes as they are in basic harmony and congruence. By approaching the super-natural, conceived always as a collective, a multiple manifestation of the divine essence, by the collective force of the people in a series of great public and esoteric rituals, the Zuni bend the processes of nature into a shape suitable both to their survival and cosmic well-being. An intensity of thought locked in a rigidity of pattern is, for the Zuni, a major weapon in their struggle for existence in the harsh social and natural environment of the American Southwest.

During the course of my research for the Zuni land claim case, I learned that a Zuni does not see himself set apart from the world so much as he sees himself a part of it: he sees himself not against but in nature (Pandey, 1981). According to Bunzel:

> The world, then, is as it is, and man's place in it is what it is. Day follows night and the cycles of the years complete themselves. In the spring the corn is planted, and if all goes well the young stalks grow to maturity and fulfil themselves. They are cut down to serve man for food, but their seeds remain against another planting. So man, too, has his days and his destined place in life. His road may be long or short, but in time it is fulfilled and he passes on to fill another role in the cosmic scheme. He, too, leaves his seed behind him. Man dies but mankind remains. This is the way of life; the whole literature of prayer shows no questioning of these fundamental premises. This is not resignation, the subordination of desire to a stronger force, but the sense of man's oneness with the universe. (Bunzel, 1932: 486)

Thus, it seems that the Zuni fuse man and nature into one more or less harmonious medium. It also shows that stability in human life is derived from the continuity of natural rhythms. Rhythm is implicit in nature, made explicit by the regular performance of rituals and the annual production of crops. It is symbolized by the Zuni calendar, determined and maintained by the Sun Priest and his associates, according to which agricultural and ceremonial activities are performed, year after year in unchanging sequence.

The 'sameness' of yearly activities contributes to a special sense of time. It is simply duration, continuation of past ways in an uninterrupted repeating cycle. The Zunis believe that everything should be as it was when their ancestors emerged into this world from the underworld, when they were given crops and a way of life, a culture. With faith in his own power, coupled with that of hundreds of others exactly like him, the Zuni dances his ritual dances, he fasts, he retreats, he chants, and through the sheer force of the persistent and unrelenting effort of his group he expects to restore the harmony to the world that makes his life livable.

It was the dominant role of religion in Zuni life that prompted anthropologists and casual visitors alike to cite Zuni as an example of a theocracy ruled by a council of priests. Thus, a German anthropologist, Richard Thurnwald, describes Zuni "as the extreme example of a sacred state, a theocracy ruled by priests who are heads of certain preferred or aristocratic families and who govern through civil authorities appointed by them". (Quoted in Pauker, 1966:196).

There are different types of priests in Zuni society (see Culin, 1907: 304). The Sun Priest, "who holds his power directly from the Sun Father, is the most revered and the most holy man in Zuni" (Bunzel, 1932: 512). Next to him are the priests of the four principal directions (the cardinal points), and they are regarded as his younger brothers and spokesmen. The Sun Priest is held responsible for the welfare of the pueblo, and he along with the other priests, performs proper rituals and ceremonies in order to maintain the socio-religious order. It seems that the priests are a distinct social group, and they function mainly in the area of sacred concerns. They are thought to be too sacred to be concerned with the secular problems of the pueblo. The sacred body appoints a different group of priests – the Bow Priests – who look after the secular problems and execute the decisions of the various priests. The Bow Priests are the earthly representatives of the mythical twin War Gods (the Ahayuta), and this obligates them to protect the pueblo from enemies, external and internal, and supernatural. In the past they led war parties in order to resist external aggression, and the enforcement of internal law and order was also in their hands. Thus, in such matters as settlement of disputes, raids, witchcraft accusations, and at certain ceremonies (communal hunts, scalp dances, etc.) absolute authority was accorded to the Bow Priests; otherwise they acted as an executive arm of the sacred body of priests and carried out their decisions.

On the recommendation of the Bow Priests, intelligent and enterprising members of the society were appointed as governor and other civil officers (see Pandey, in press). The governor is essentially a secular leader, and his primary function is to deal with outsiders as well as to attend to the general needs of his fellow tribesmen. Even in these activities he was assisted by the Bow Priests, and they were regarded as "brothers to one another", as Cushing observed (1882: 188).

While the Sun Priest and the Rain Priests are primarily concerned with securing rain, and the Bow Priests with providing protection, the Kachina Priests bestow fecundity. The Kachina Priests are the priestly hierarchy that rules the mythic Kachina village, Kolhuwala:wa, at the junction of the Little Colorado and Zuni Rivers, which Mrs. Matilda Coxe Stevenson visited and reported on (Stevenson 1904: 21, Ferguson and Hart 1985: 125). They are impersonated by men chosen by the priests, generally in terms of clan and kiva affiliation. They visit Zuni on Shalako, at New Year, and on other special occasions. The masks of the impersonators of the Kachina Priests are tribal property though kept in specific households and handed down from one generation to another. The *Koyemshi*, or sacred clowns, also belong to this group. According to the origin myth, they are the fruit of an incestuous union between brother and sister, and they are present in all masked dances and play an important part in public rituals, as Levi-Strauss (1963) pointed out in his analysis of Zuni myths and rituals.

Besides the Bow Priesthood mentioned earlier, there are also other religious organizations related to crises of war, sickness, and aggression. There are a dozen such organizations described in the literature on Zuni. There used to be a warrior society, Koshikwe, or Cactus People, which became extinct with the death of its last member in 1966. Its members were highly regarded as healers of wounds, and a man who killed but failed to scalp an enemy was expected to join the Cactus Society. Scalpers joined the Bow Priesthood.

There is a hunters' society (Saniakyakwe, nicknamed Suskikwe, or Coyote Society) which spiritually fosters the hunting interests of the tribe and supervises the rabbit hunts. This society used to hold four such hunts each summer, and this was a conspicuous feature of the Kachina worship in Zuni. There were ten other medicine societies of which only eight are active today.

All the thirteen societies are organized almost on the same pattern, with membership by initiation, secret meetings, and sacred rites. Only men can join the Bow Priesthood, and Cactus and Hunters' societies. All the other societies are open to men and women alike. The usual way of joining a society (except those open to men only) is by vow upon being cured of illness, but membership by trespass also takes place. Each society practices general medicine but also specialises in certain diseases or afflictions. While members of the Bow Priesthood worship the War Gods, the cult of the Beast Gods is in the hands of the remaining twelve societies. The most powerful of these gods is Bear (Anshe) who is impersonated in the curing societies. All medical practice, except for midwifery, is in the hands of these societies.

Let me recapitulate the main points I have made about Zuni tradition and values. The fundamental idea underlying Zuni cosmology, their assumptions about the universe, their obligations as Zuni, and what they perceive as threats to their personal and collective lives, is that everything is predestined. What was determined by the twin War Gods in the beginning at the time of emergence from the underworld is still the basis of their social order. In Zuni ritual poetry, in songs, in the worship of the Kachinas, in advice given by ceremonial fathers to their 'sons' at initiations, the same images are evoked and the same words and phrases are repeated. Thus, the repetition of endless orderly rituals, multiplied by the concentrated participation of the Zuni people, combines with religious and cosmic penetration to work together to instill harmony, balance, and peace in Zuni life.

III

So far I have been concerned with presenting a picture of Zuni society and culture derived from survey of anthropological and historical sources as well as from my own fieldwork. In doing that my emphasis has been on what Kroeber (1952) called 'value culture', and Dumont (1970) calls 'thought of order', or ideology. I would like to give a few more details on the Zuni sense of reality, popularly called 'world-view' by anthropologists.

Dennis Tedlock, in his paper, "Zuni Religion and World View", says that:

> There are six points of orientation in the Zuni world, each with its own colour and its own hierarchical position: the yellow north, the blue west, the red south, the white east, the multi-coloured zenith, and the black nadir. Toward the nadir are a black mountain and the four underworlds: on the fourth storey down is the Sulphur Room, totally dark, where the ponderosa pine, tree of the north, first grew; on the third is the Soot or Moss Room, with the Douglas fir of the west; on the second is the Gray or Mud Room, with the aspen of the south; and on the storey just beneath our own world is the Wing (sunray) Room, with the cotton wood of the east . . . Toward the zenith, beyond the inverted stone bowl of the sky, are a multi-coloured mountain and the four upper worlds, the first the home of crows, the second of Cooper's hawks, the third of nighthawks, and the fourth of eagles . . . In all, then, there are nine storeys, with the familiar world in the middle.
>
> Toward the north, west, south and east are the Oceans, which together bound the earth with a circular coastline . . . In the oceans are four mountains, each with the colour of its direction . . . The oceans are connected by underground passages with all the seas, springs, ponds and caves of the earth to form single water system; the Zunis compare this system with the hidden roots and runners that connect willow shoots into a single plant . . . At the water outlets and on mountain-

> tops are the Lelassina'we 'sacred old places', or shrines, of the world.
> (1979: 499)

In Zuni belief, the people who inhabit the world are of two kinds: 'raw people' and 'cooked people' or 'daylight people'. The earth, *awitelin citta* 'Earth Mother' the sun, *Yatokka tachu*, 'Sun Father'; his wife, the Moon Mother; and his sister 'Old Lady Salt' who lives in a lake to the south of Zuni are among the prominent raw beings. The cooked or daylight people — the humans — depend on cooked food, while the raw people eat food that is either raw or has been sacrificed to them by daylight people (See Bunzel, 1932: 498). Raw people can change their forms; they are 'people' in the sense that one of their potential forms is anthropomorphic, and in the sense that they and daylight people — the humans — should behave as kinsmen toward one another.

This view of nature and man's orientation to it as a kinsman was not only recorded in Zuni myths and folk-tales, but it was expressed by one person after another during my fieldwork at Zuni. The Zuni recognise that there is a symbiotic relationship between man and nature and they believe that in utilizing the natural resources — animals, land, plants and water — to sustain human life, reverence and respect should be expressed for the spiritual powers inherent in them. In their belief, the use of land for subsistence such as hunting, gathering, agriculture, and raising cattle and sheep is directly connected to the Zuni religious system.

During my research for the Zuni land-claim case, I discovered that the Zuni view their land as a 'church'. One of the Zuni leaders told the historian Richard Hart, "The whole land is our church, and you should visualise it that way. The shrines and religious spots are like altars in your churches. So all of the land is sacred to us."[6]

This view of land is elegantly presented by a Zuni scholar, who narrated episodes from Zuni history in a recent PBS film, "Surviving Columbus" shown on the television on October 12, 1992, the controversial Columbus quincentenary. Edmund Ladd reports that:

> The Zuni view their universe as a single complete whole. All parts are equally important. Metaphorically this include 'The four oceans, the moss covered mountains, the lakes that surround the land . . .' the total landscape is their religious universe. To put it another way: 'The world is their church.' The entire world is sacred, but certain portions, certain places are especially sacred. This concept and the relationship of the people to their environment permeate the religious life and use of the land. It is important to maintain an equilibrium with nature in all its part. (1980:6)

Thus, a Zuni believe that he exists in a special relationship with the land. He is dependent on it and it is dependent on him.

IV

Clearly, this view of nature and man's orientation to it as a kinsman is so powerful that it is easy to understand why it would be so appealing to Euro-American ecologists and 'New Age' groups. An American ecologist, J. Donald Hughes, asks:

> Shall we continue to move toward ever more destructive use of natural resources, thus making necessary a harsh reckoning with nature and unwelcome constraints on our ways of life? Or shall we direct change as much as possible in the direction of harmony between human beings and the natural environment; toward a state in which we can both use and save, in which we will act with forbearance and nature will provide a sustained yield of renewable and recyclable resources? If we choose the second alternative, we can gain much by studying our American Indian heritage and seeking modern applications of the wisdom we find there. (1983: 139)

This wisdom, considered by Durkheim and Mauss, in their book *Primitive classification* "a first philosophy of nature" (1963: 81), entails an integral view of man, nature, and Universe, governed by Awonawillona, the Zuni keeper of our roads of life. This sense of reality, this vision of life has guided the Zuni people for a very long time, but these days the elders worry that some of their young people are drifting away from this by the glitter of modern consumer culture. Elsewhere I have described some of the social strain and disorder which have afflicted Zuni as a result (see Pandey, 1987). But I believe that as long as the old rituals and ceremonies are held in the kivas and plaza of Zuni, the currents of secularization and modernity will stir only the surface of the Zuni world. No matter how strong, those currents have not touched the depths of the Zuni self, still constructed around ideas of permanence and perpetration. We can learn from this basic sense of reality.

Table: Zuni Correspondences*

Region	*Clans*	*Colour*	*Regions of*	*Prey animal*	*Seasons*	*Elements*
North	Crane, or pelican grouse or sagecock yellow wood, or evergreen oak (clan almost extinct)	Yellow	force and destruction war	mountain lion	winter	wind, breeze or air
West	bear, coyote spring-herb	blue	peace ('war cure') hunting	bear	spring and its damp breezes	water
South	tobacco, maize badger	red	heat, agriculture, medicine	badger	summer	fire
East	deer, antelope turkey	white	sun, magic and religion	white wolf	end of the year	earth, seeds frosts which bring the seeds to maturity
Zenith	sun (extinct) eagle, sky	'streaked with colour like the play of light among, the clouds	diverse combinations of these functions	eagle		
Nadir	frog or toad rattlesnake water	black			prey mole	
Centre	macaw, the clan of the perfect centre	'all colours simultaneously'				

* Jack Goody, The *Domestication of the Savage Mind,* Cambridge University Press, 1977, p. 56.

Notes

1. I have benefited in clarifying some of the points made here from consulting Stewart Culin's unpublished field notes and papers in the Brooklyn Museum, Brooklyn, New York. A National Endowment for the Humanities travel to collections grant and financial support from the research committee of the Division of Social Sciences, University of California, Santa

Cruz made this archival research possible. Grateful acknowledgement is made to them for their generous support.

2. See Adolph Bandelier 1892 for details.
3. See George Winship 1896 for details on Coronado's expedition and its findings.
4. There seems to be a similarity between my view of the role of rituals and ceremonies in Zuni life and what Jeanine Miller (1984) and Raimundo Panikkar (1977) have said about Vedic *rta*.
5. I believe that is precisely what the Zuni do when they perform their buffalo dance, corn dance, basket dance, butterfly dance or when they go on pilgrimage to various springs, to the Salt Lake, to Kolhuwala: Wa, to mountain peaks and caves in the south-west. Hunting ritual also took them to various places in the south-west.
6. See unpublished letter of E. Richard Hart to Stephen G. Boyden, February 11, 1980. On file in the Zuni Tribal Building, Zuni, New Mexico.

References

Bandelier, Adolph F., 1892. 'An Outline of the Documentary History of the Zuni Tribe', *A Journal of American Ethnology and Archaeology*, No. 3, pp. 1-115.

Benedict, Ruth, 1934. *Patterns of Culture*. Boston: Houghton Mifflin Company.

Bunzel, Ruth V., 1932. *Introduction to Zuni Ceremonialism. Annual Reports of the Bureau of American Ethnology*, No. 47, Washington D.C., pp. 467-544.

Culin, Stewart, 1907. 'Zuni Notes', Vol. 2. The Brooklyn Museum Archives. Unpublished Expedition Report for 1907.

Cushing, Frank Hamilton, 1882. 'The Zuni Social, Mythic, and Religious Systems', In *Popular Science Monthly*, Vol. 21 pp. 186-92.

Dumont, Louis, 1970. *Homo Hierarchicus: The Caste System and Its Implications*. London: Weidenfield and Nicolson.

Durkheim, E. and Mauss, M., 1963. *Primitive Classification*. Translated and Edited by Rodney Needham, Chicago: University of Chicago Press.

Ferguson, T.J. and Hart, E. Richard, 1985. *A Zuni Atlas*. Norman: University of Oklohoma Press.

Goody, Jack, 1977. *The Domestication of the Savage Mind*. Cambridge: Cambridge University Press.

Green Jesse, (Ed.), 1990. *Cushing at Zuni: The Correspondence and Journals of F.H. Cushing, 1879-1884*, Albuquerque: University of New Mexico Press.

Hughes, J. Donald, 1983. *American Indian Ecology*. El Paso, Texas: Texas Western Press.

Kroeber, A.L., 1952. *The Nature of Culture*. Chicago: The University of Chicago Press.

Ladd, Edmund J., 1980. 'Pueblo Uses of High Altitude Areas: Emphasis on the A. Shiwi-Zuni'. Paper presented at the School of American Research Symposium on High Altitude Archaeology, October.

Levi-Strauss, C., 1963. *Structural Anthropology*. New York: Basic Books.

Miller, Jeanine, 1984. *The Vision of Cosmic Order in the Vedas*. London: Routledge and Kegan Paul.

Pandey, Triloki Nath, 1977. 'Some reflections on Zuni Religion', In *The Religious Character of Native American Humanities,* ed. by Samgill, Tempe: Avirona State University, pp. 184-207.

——, 1977. 'Images of Power in a Southwestern Pueblo'. In *The Anthropology of Power*, ed. by Ramond

D. Fogelson and Richard N. Adams. New York: Academic Press, pp. 195-215.

——, 1981. 'Some reflections on Aboriginal Land Use of the Zuni Indian Tribe'. In *U.S. Court of claims proceedings. Zuni Indian Tribe of New Mexico Vs. United States.* Docket 161-79 Washington D.C., pp. 1-55.

——, 1983. 'Zuni Oral Tradition and History'. In *Zuni History*, Institute of the American Southwest. Sun Valley, pp. 9-11.

——, 1987. 'The Impact of Literacy on Traditional Cultures', In *Proceedings of the 15th International Symposium on Life Science and Progress of Society*, Korean Academy of Sciences, Seoul, Republic of Korea, pp. 1-12.

——, (In press) 'Patterns of leadership in the Western Pueblo Society', In *Essays in Memory of Fred Eggan*, ed. by Raymod DeMallie and Alfonso Ortiz, Norman: University of Oklohoma Press.

Panikar, Raimundo, 1977. *The Vedic Experience: Mantramanjari.* Berkeley: University of California Press.

Pauker, Guy J., 1966. 'Political Structure', In *People of Rimrock*, ed. by Evon Z. Vogt and Ethel M. Albert. Harvard University Press pp. 191-226.

Stevenson, Matilda C., 1904. 'The Zuni Indians: Their Mythology, Esoteric Fraternities and Ceremonies'. In *Twenty-third Annual Report of the Bureau of American Ethnology*, 1901-1902. Washingon: Government Printing Office.

Tedlock, Dennis, 1979. 'Zuni religion and world view', In *Handbook of North American Indians*, Vol. 9, *The Southwest*, ed. by Alfonso Ortiz. Washington: Smithsonian Institution.

Winship, George P., 1896. 'The Coronado Expedition, 1540-1542', In *Bureau of American Ethnology, 14th Report, 1892-1893, 1:329-613.* Washington: Government Printing Office.

12

Fire and Sun, The Positive Energy of the Cosmos in Mesoamerican Cosmovision

Yólotl González Torres

When one talks about Mesoamerican cosmovision, in a no mesoamericanist context, it is unavoidable to make a brief introduction about the sources where our data come from. The loss of the ancient Mesoamerican religion and everything related to it was almost total, as the Spanish held as one of their main excuses for the conquest the 'evil' rituals and practices the Indians had. Therefore one of their most important tasks was to destroy and persecute whatever had anything to do with the ancient religion.

The sources we have to study the Mexican ancient culture are the archaeological findings, the very few codexes or books written before the conquest which were not destroyed and which are mostly augural, the chronicles of the conquerors, and the writings, specially of priests, about the costumes of the mesoamericans; among these there is one book which was written by Friar Bernardino de Sahagun at the end of the sixteenth century which is a treasure of information specially about the Mexica. It is interesting to point out that Sahagun gathered around him many noblemen or children of noblemen, who were aquainted with the ancient costumes and registered all the answers in nahuatl, their language. Based on this material, he wrote several books which were published during many decades after his death. The information given to him by the Indians has been also published in nahuatl with its translation into Spanish and into English. There is another source of information, and that is the ethnographical material, registered by anthropologists because, in spite of the fact that the State religion was destroyed, part of the folk religion remained more or less intact in the far off places which were not touched or were partially touched by the catholic missionary zeal.

There are some other points to clarify: we don't have any corpus of knowledge like the *Vedas* or the Epics or the *Puranas* in India. There is a Mayan myth called the Popol Vuh, which is supposed to be very old and few legends from other places which were recorded in different manners. Most of the data we have belong to the Mexica, the people who were ruling most of the present Mexico during the sixteenth century when the Spanish came and which is placed chronologically in the late Postclassic period (900-1521). We know very little of the people who lived in the Classic period (200-900) in the cities like Teotihuacan, Tajin, (which has just been excavated and shows an incredible splendour), or the Mayans, about which there is still a controversy whether their writing has been partially or 80 per cent deciphered. In any case what was written by these people in the codexes and in the stones show a great knowledge of astronomy and a very careful recording of time, which goes back to many thousands of years ago; the date of the beginning of their era is 3113 BC which is very close to the date of the beginning of the *Kali Yuga* in 3102.

Having mentioned all these facts we can now talk a little about the Mexica who were the inheritors of other people who had lived in the high semidesertic plateau of Mexico. They had very recently arrived in the Valley of Mexico, their capital city, Tenochtitlan, which surprised the Spanish by its splendour, was founded as a small gathering of huts only in 1321, and from that humble origin they started growing till they became the rulers of almost all of what is today Mexico. Their city was founded on a lake, and even if they were agriculturists with maize as their main crop, the recollection of the products of the lake: plants as well as animals and insects played an important part in their diet. Two cactus plants of their semidesertic habitat also played an important role in their economy and in their cosmovision: the *nopal* and the *maguey*. The first one whose leaves and fruits are edible was the most important symbolic plant in the foundation of the city as after a long pilgrimage, travelling from a mythic place called Aztlan, their patron God told them that the place where they could establish themselves would be signalled by an eagle eating a serpent and standing on a *nopal*. The fruit of this plant – which in some species has dark red – had also the esoteric meaning of the heart of the captive which was offered to the sun.

In the same manner the maguey, which was a very useful plant, was also the source of an alcoholic drink which was used in many rituals. The Mexicas also gave a high symbolic meaning to animals specially to the snake, the jaguar and the eagle, the first two being associated to earth and water and the last to the sky and the sun.

In the cosmogonic myths of the Mexica there is a concept of a distant dual God called Ometeotl, 2 sacred, which became a feminine and a masculine God who created four masculine gods who were the real creators of the rest of the universe of the gods and of humankind. I have pointed out in other articles, the absence of feminine deities or powers in the process of creation. We can say that the Mexica believed in two opposite and complementary forces of the universe which had to be in harmony in order that everything in the world would function properly. The concept of opposite forces is practically universal, and it is characterized in China by the *yin* and the *yang*, the hot and the cold, the humid and the dry, the obscurity and the light, the earth and the sky and so on. In ancient Mexico this hot energy was known under the name of *tona*, and the sun, *Tonatiuh* was its maximum source, it was distributed throughout the universe in different quantities and probably in different qualities according to a very complicated combination of forces which included the ritual cycle of 260 days which received the name of *tonalpohualli*, the "count of the tona" or the "count of destinies" which was recorded in special books called *tonalamatl* which were interpreted by specialists called *tonalpouhque*. These books are some of the codexes I mentioned before and of which a certain number survived. The cycle of 260 day was formed by the combination of 20 signs: alligator (or *makara*), wind, house, lizard, snake, death, deer, rabbit, water, dog, monkey, weed, cane, jaguar, eagle, zopilote, ollin, or movement, flint knife, rain, flower and 13 numerals. Four of these signs: cane, flint knife, house and rabbit were also used to name the years, the four quadrants of the universe and the four elements. This cycle of 260 days which was repeated eternally, plus the combination of 9 figures of gods called the nine lords of the night, plus thirteen figures of different gods and different birds, and taking into consideration that each one of the 20 signs was ruled over each group of thirteen days, the amount and quality of *tona* energy which each person, kingdom, type of year, and so on had, and which decided their destiny, was very precisely measured and accordingly diagnosed, forecasted and if necessary remedied.

This cycle of 260 days which was also combined with a solar cycle of 360 plus five days, was prevalent all through the cultural area of Mesoamerica and it is one of the traits which characterizes it, along with other things like a particular type of ball game which also had a cosmic meaning.

I had mentioned long ago, that this hot vital energy or *tona* should have its equivalent and counterpart in a cold and humid energy, much in the same manner as there were specialists who cured the loss of *tona* energy, which was believed to be located at the top of the head, in such a way that sometimes in order to take the strength of a person, specially one with strong energy like the witches, the hair of the crown of their head was cut. But there were also shamans who cured diseases caused by the loss of the cold energy, probably related to the loss of the shadow, and they were also rain makers. Signorini and Luppo (1989) have found that in the nahuatl speaking village of Santiago Yancuictlalpan in Puebla there is a belief in the *ecahuil* or shadow, and they think that this is the counterpart of the *tona*.

At present in many of the communities which still believe in the *tona*, this concept has got a different connotation, and it is more related to the soul energy which is connected with a certain animal or animals, and which becomes a sort of soul animal of the person, in such a way that whatever happens to one happens to the other, if the animal or the person, becomes ill or dies, the counterpart animal or person suffers the same fate. This animal alter ego is also called a *nahual.*

While some of the energetic characteristics of the *tona* in Santiago may lead to the idea that they are the opposite concept of the *ecahuil*, the shadow, whose existence depends on the sun, on the light, but on the other hand is very close to the earth, it is the dark part of an individual, and it even has his form: "*ecahuil* constitutes the axis of the belief which links the individual with the animal *alter ego*, the *tona* . . . The coessence with the tonal is insoluble as long as both poles of relation are alive and thus sets a remedy to the lack of vital energy of man. The companion animal comes to be it's strongest link with the surrounding nature, a sort of insurance against the insufficient human forces to face the 'envies' of that natural world over which men becoming a 'cultural animal', has risen, but in which in spite of everything it continues to live and to act."

"The *ecahuil* which has it's seat in man but derives its strength from the tonal and ceases to insuflate the vital energy, which at its turn takes from the tonal, leading to disease and death. It should not surprise us that in this village the *tona* and the *ecahuil* are frequently mistaken . . . When there is fright, the *ecahuil* flies away from man." (Signorini and Luppo, 57)

Fire and sun have a strong link – both share the hot positive energy, that is why lightning can also be a very strong *tonal* or *nahual* of a person. Fire has a quadruple aspect, as it can be the fire of the sky, the fire of the earth – specially in a volcanic country like Mexico – and as such is the old God Huehueteotl; the fire of water, which is the thunder, and the fire of the wood, the fire which lives through the friction of two pieces of wood. It also has a feminine aspect, the Goddess of the domestic earth, which may be connected with the earth mother, for that is why when a child was born he was offered to the water and passed over the fire for purification and probably to strengthen his own energy. Fire had to be kept burning for forty days after the mother had given birth.

Fire, as well as water, could be benefic and malefic, as it was benefic for warming up men and cooking their food, and it was malefic as a destroyer, but this destruction brought purification and new life. (Most dead people were incinerated and only a few, the ones who were buried and had died in any way related to water or to diseases which they considered watery or to the gods of water.)

The four eras of the universe which had been ruled by four different gods of the elements came to an end when they were destroyed by water, fire, wind and earthquakes. But fire played an important part in the creation of the sun and the moon, and so the myth says that when there was total darkness, the gods decided to create the sun and they built a great fire in the ancient city of Teotihuacan and they chose two of them as victims to be transformed into the luminaries, one of them was rich and handsome and the other poor, ugly and full of diseases. When they were about to jump into the fire the rich and the handsome hesitated while the other had no fear, the sick one became the sun and the other the moon. The last one was deprived of its shining strength because the fire was not strong enough when he jumped into it or, after another version, because a rabbit was thrown to his face.

In one of the legends of the creation of the sun and the moon, it is said that the sun did not want to move and the gods became worried because the earth might become too hot, so one of them tried to shoot an arrow at him, but the sun was quicker and sent the arrow back and killed the god and, not content with this action, he asked for the lives of the rest of the gods and only then he would continue his way through the sky. This was the beginning of a new time, as with the killing and posterior resurrection of the gods, through fire, which was the destroyer and the creator, time was also created.

There was another case of purification and rebirth through fire, and that was when the culture hero Quetzalcoatl, "the feathered serpent", was made to abandon his city Tula, and headed towards the eastern sea, there in a place called the land of red and black, he incinerated himself and became the planet Venus, which is a very important star in Mesoamerica, and is very frequently depicted in the codexes, in the murals and in many inscriptions, specially of the augural type, as a man shooting an arrow which was believed to cause many evils. Venus seemed to have a most powerful energy which may very well have been part of the *tona*. Quetzalcoatl was also a very complex God, as we mentioned he was a cultural hero, the God of Venus, one of the four sons of the creator gods, he played an active part in creating the universe, he created a new humankind mixing the blood of his penis with a powder made of the bones of the ancestors, he helped in discovering the maize seeds, and he was the patron of knowledge and of the highest priests. During his life-time as ruler of the mythic Tula, he lead a life of prayer and ascetism. He was also the God of wind.

The myth of death and resurrection in the form of a star, specially the sun, is found all over what we call present Mesoamerica and it survives with different variants for instance among the Totonacs of Veracruz and the Huicholes of Nayarit and Jalisco.

The Mexicas, besides their ideological manipulation, which no doubt existed, believed that the hot vivifying energy acted as a reciprocally feeding stream: the sun which was it's maximum generator distributed it to the universe, but it had to be refueled as a cosmic dynamo, and this was done first, through the offer of the lives of the gods and then of the hearts and blood of the brave warriors, men who were in their full vigour.

Fire was one of the oldest gods, Huehueteotl, some of the oldest images found in the Mexican plateau depict this god with a wrinkled face and a bent back holding a fire container on his shoulders; he was also *Xiuhtecuhtli*, the Lord of the year, therefore he was also the Lord of time and the calendar. The God of fire presided the central direction, the navel of the world, which he shared with *Mictlantecuhtli* the Lord of death. He had images, representations, maybe shadows, of four colours, the colours of the four quadrants of the universe, and every four years a special celebration took place in the last month of the year, in which captives were offered to him.

There was also a very important fire ritual in the month of *Teotleco*, which corresponds to October, just after the hiemal equinox had passed, when a repetition of the sacrifice by fire of the sick God who became the Sun, and of the resurrection of the gods took place.

Fire and sun shared more closely their life and energy every 52 years, when the cycles of 365 and of 260 days coincided: the ancient Mexicans thought that a great danger threatened the world and that it could be destroyed, if the sun failed to appear. Then the greatest ritual, first of expectation, and then of celebration took place: all fires on the land were put off, were killed; a great ceremony took place in a hill near the city, where all the living images of the gods, who were high priests dressed in their costumes were present, then the heart of a very special chosen captive was taken out and in that hole, full of energy, a new fire was made alive through the rubbing of a vertical stick on a horizontal one: then the forces of *yin* and *yang* sprang again anew, creating fire, the sun and time. The first fire was fed with the heart of the warrior, and this fire was then distributed throughout the empire.

The daily appearance and disappearance of the sun in the firmament, was assumed as his daily death and rebirth, and it's annual movement to the north and south of the horizon which produced the seasons, and became compass and calendar, was thought as a pulsating increase and decrease of it's heat, *tona*, which had to be combined with the adequate humid energy to produce life, above all through maize, the plant which was the subsistence base of Mesoamerican man. Therefore one can very clearly see in all the festivals that were celebrated throughout the year in which the sowing and harvesting of maize played such an important role and how there were always the rituals which combined a propitiation to the God of the sun and the gods of water, as if precisely the maize, the sacred plant, were a synthesis of both.

In the same manner that the sun needed human energy through the life of the warriors who died in battle or were offered in sacrifice, the *yin* forces of the universe, specially — the gods of water also associated to mountains and caves — needed special victims who were mostly children.

As the Mexica was an eminently warlike and masculine society, the gods who incarnated the humid and dark forces were also masculine, as in the case of Tlaloc,

God of water and the moon, and the earth Himself, though it is sometimes pictured as feminine, it is more often taken as an androginous being which had the form of a crocodile or a frog, and even the name of the God of earth is Tlaltecuhtli, the Lord of the earth. This God is always depicted in the underside of the eagle vessel, while inside, there is the symbol of the sun; this vessel was used to contain the hearts of the sacrificed human victims.

We don't known exactly when the Mexica year started, even if all the evidences led to February, but one can clearly see how the festivals and the rituals which were celebrated along the year coincided with the days which become longer or shorter, with the sun reaching a solsticial, equinoxial, or zenithal point and it's relation with the rains, which in Central Mexico start usually in May, which makes a humid summer and autumn and a dry winter and spring. The vernal and hiemal equinoxes, spring and autumn and the birth and the decay of nature were celebrated with similar rituals, which included the flaying of the bodies of human victims who had been sacrificed by the usual method of taking out the heart, and their skins were worn in a terrible act of fusion of energies. The skins were worn by different people who were prepared for that discharge of energy; they were persons who had made a vow, or were ill, or were priests.

In the case of the vernal equinox, when the sun was on his way to reach its highest strength, the main actors of the ritual were the warriors of the community and war prisoners. The most important part of the ceremony, was a sacral performance in which the best captive warriors, fought an unequal battle against four Mexica warriors of the orders of the eagle and the jaguar who had been specially selected for the occasion, they were different from the men who had taken the captives, and who had offered them for this special sacrifice. When the captive was touched by the obsidian sword of one of his opponents, a special priest came and took his heart out and immediately offered it to the sun on the high, and then it was thrown into the 'eagle vessel'. The captive himself was called the 'eagle warrior'. In the festival which took place in the hiemal equinox, the sacrificial victim was a middle aged woman, who had been consecrated as the Goddess Toci 'our mother'. She was offered by the guild of healers and midwives, and later Her skin was worn by a priest, while in the following ceremonies and dances the warriors also played a role, but it was less important than during the vernal equinox, as this time the feminine, dark forces were specially propitiated.

There is no doubt that the sun was the maximum deity of the Mexica pantheon, even if it seemed to be shadowed by the God Huitzilopochtli who had been the guide of these people on a long pilgrimage from Aztlan to the valley of Mexico. He was a sort of an important ancestor and cultural hero, who dictated the rules of behaviour of His people, among which their obligation to nourish and worship the sun was of the utmost importance, and therefore Huitzilopochtli became also the God of war. It has generally been said that this God was the sun, but I insist on my idea that He was only a patron God who had risen to power and, of course, as a war and sky God, had solar characteristics but was not the sun. There was a special God of the sun whose name was Tonatiuh, represented as a young man with red hair, wearing a head-dress of feathers probably of eagle, with the head of a small bird in the front, as an ornament, and this bird is usually associated with *yang* deities. He had a red facial painting, a nose and ear ornament made of jade, and on his breast a round golden plate symbol of the sun. He wore a loin cloth with its end embroidered with feathers, and his sandals were called solar sandals. He had his own temple where, most probably, there was a great image in stone, very similar to the one in the 'Aztec calendar' which has the carved frontal face of the sun surrounded by rays, and the four calendrical signs meaning the four quadrants of the world and around the 20 calendrical signs of the count of *tona*. The sun God had His own rituals and the bravest warriors were dedicated to Him; they had a special festival and ritual in the day with 4 *ollin* four movement, when the "warrior of the sun", a human messenger, was sent to Him. It was believed that the men who died in the war or in the sacrificial stone went to join the sun in His paradise in the sky and so did the women who died in their first childbirth and were considered female warriors who had taken a prisoner. The sun in his daily trip was received in the sky by the souls of the dead brave warriors and was taken in a palanquin to the zenith, where the brave women received Him and took him to the west, to start his trip through the underworld. In Maya cosmology the underworld sun is usually depicted as a jaguar, the Maya also had different legends of the creation of the sun and the moon which had as its ingredients a sort of shamanic trip to the underworld, a mystic death to be reborn again. In this case the sun and the moon are also male and brothers, though the Mayans do have a Goddess of the moon which is very important.

I have mentioned the importance of the element water along with fire, and how in ancient Mexico, the God of this element was one of the most important, as most of the rituals which took place along the year were dedicated to Him. This God also had helpers or manifestations which were placed into the four quadrants of the universe. There was also a Goddess of running water which was called the "skirt of jewels".

From what I have mentioned we can see the great importance specially of the sun in the cosmovision of the ancient Mexicans and its relation to fire as the generator and creator of this important concentration of hot energy in the universe, and how the personal energy of all the human beings had to be in a constant feeding back to this cosmic energy, which the Mesoamericans translated into a need of the human heart and blood to keep the world going.

Plate 12.1 Tonatiulu : The Sun Codex

Plate 12.2 Xiulu Tecutilli : The God of Fire and Time

Plate 12.3 Fire and Sun

References

Gonzalez Torres, Yolotl, 1975. *El culto a los astros entre los mexicas.* Sepsetentas 217. Mexico.

——, 1979. "El panteon mexica", In *Antropologia e Historia* 25 Epoca III. Num. 25. enero-marzo. Mexico.

Lopez Austin, Alfredo, 1980. *Cuerpo humano e ideologia* UNAM. Mexico.

Sahagun, Fray Bernardino de, 1969. *Historia General de las Cosas de la Nueva Espana.* Ed Porrua. Mexico.

Signorini, Italo y Luppo, Alessandro, 1989. *Los tres ejes de la vida.* Xalapa.

13

Pre-Christian Eastern Slavic Reflections on Nature

Molly Kaushal

What follows is a simple account of how, in earlier times, the Eastern Slavs, particularly the pre-Christian Russians, interacted with nature. Pre-Christian slavic religion was mainly based on nature worship. Fire, Earth and Water figured prominently in its beliefs and ritual practices. The forces of nature were personified, feared, and revered, and the Slavs developed a whole pantheon of gods and goddesses. However, the three main gods of their pantheon were linked together not in a hierarchical way, but in a mutually complementary way, where each was incomplete without the other. A whole cycle of rituals revolved around various forces of nature and their personified images. The arrival of Christianity as the official religion and the establishment of the Russian Orthodox Church culminated in the banning of many folk ritual practices which were pre-Christian in origin, and in the persecution of those who practised them. Yet, a complete annihilation of earlier beliefs and practices could never be accomplished. Pre-Christian beliefs and gods exerted such a strong influence upon the Russian mind that the only way to come to terms with them was through incorporating them in the mainstream of the Christian order. Water, Fire, and the Mother Earth Goddess were, and have remained, the most powerful images of Russian religious beliefs and practices, and folk memory has remained loyal to the personified and non-personified images of these elements.

According to some scholars, Rusi, or Russians as we call them, have their origins in the word *Roce*. Although conjectural, this view is of a direct relevance to the paper, and I shall dwell upon it a little more. Roce was the name of an ancient river, a stream of the Dnieper, which flowed in the city called Rodnei. Rod or Svetovit was their clan god, and the bear their totem. Ancestor worship was common, and the dead were cremated. The central god — Svetovit or Belbog (the white god or the god of heavenly lights) later came to be represented by the thunder god Perun, the most revered god of the Eastern Slavs as late as the seventeenth century. If Belbog or Perun was the god of the heavenly lights, Chernobog – the black god – represented death. It has already been stated that the relations between these deities were not hierarchical; these three deities formed, as it were, the triangle of the slavic religion.

The richest temples belonged to the Svetovit. Perun was worshipped outdoors in a grove, where stood an oak tree. Perun represented justice and order. He was the purifier, as well as the devil's principal adversary. His actions were manifested in lightning and thunder; and ancient men heard his voice in thunder, and believed it drove away the devil and other evil forces. Many scholars see the origin of music, use of musical instruments and bells, and the beating of drums as attempts to imitate the voice of Perun, and part of the magical efforts to protect the world from the evil forces and spirits. The sacred animals of Perun are the bull and the he goat, his birds the dove and the cuckoo, his weapons the axe and the arrow. His influence on the Eastern Slavic people was so strong that the Church had to come up with another image – Ilya the prophet – to combat the worship of Perun. Ilya was different only in name. His actions, roles, and attributes were identical to those of Perun. The bull, which was earlier sacrificed to propitiate Perun, was now offered to Ilya. Perun was in the image of a man with a wooden body, silver head, and a gold moustache. The Perun cult, as stated earlier, is considered to be associated with the initial god of the slaves Rod or Svetobog. This cult is also associated with phallus worship. Scholars see in Perun, a god of common Indo-European heritage, and liken him to Indra. Perun represented the *arbor mundi* and the *axis mundi* in the slavic religion.

Frequently, the image of Perun overlaps with that of the sun-god (Dashbog), and he is often represented as the youthful sun-god. The personified sun (Dashbog) appears throughout slavic folklore. Each morning he rides out from his golden palace in the east in a two-wheeled horse-drawn chariot, beginning each day as a young man, and dying each night as an old one. The sun god is attended by two lovely virgins (the morning and the evening stars), seven judges (the planets), and the comets. As a year god, or the god of the seasons, he ages with each season, and the burning of the birch tree symbolizes his death.

The cult of the dawn was common among all slaves. According to some scholars, the slavic deity – Zaria, or the heavenly bride – has its origins in what is known to us as *Usas*. The primary female figures in slavic religion are the goddesses of fate, death, Baba Yaga, and the moist mother earth. In the Kievian pantheon they are represented in the image of a female deity Mokosh. She has a large head and long arms. At night she spins flax and shears sheep. She is associated with spring and the wet soil. She spins the threads of life and death, and is the dispenser of the water of life. Mokosh was later transformed into the eastern slavic deity Paraskova Pyanitsa, associated with spinning, water, fertility, health, and marriage. Like Perun, Mokosh is also seen as a goddess of water, fecundity, fire, and thunder. Mat sera Zimlia, or moist mother earth, is pure, powerful, and pregnant. The earth was believed to be in confinement until the 25th of March each year; it was a sin to strike the earth, and ploughing and digging were forbidden before that date.

Mother earth, as the corn goddess, made crops grow. At harvest, she was present in the last stalk of the grain left standing in the field. In some areas the mother goddess in the form of a doll (made of straw) or a wreath was symbolically drenched in water and kept till the next spring season, when some of its grains from the previous season's last stalk were mixed with new seeds at the time of planting.

Apart from these gods and goddesses of the main pantheon, there existed a number of spirits associated with rivers, forests, houses, hearth, air, etc. However, as stated earlier, Perun remained the central god. As the thunder god, he enters into an union with the mother earth (or sometimes creates it), and impregnates it through rain water, thus forcing her to yield and generate life. Thunder is his voice, and the winds and the tempests his breath. Water represents Perun's blood or tears. The sun and the moon are his eyes. Man receives his flesh from the fire that comes out of his eyes, and his soul from his breath.

One of Perun's main roles is to restore the earth's productive powers after the multi-headed snake demon steals the holy waters, takes away the earth's moisture, and renders her infertile. After killing the demon, Perun releases the holy waters which come pouring down to restore the earth's fertility. Closely associated with this is the belief that the rains, especially, of the spring season bless all those, who bathe in its waters, with strength, health, beauty, and fertility. These waters are also a protection against evil forces and spirits. The sun, which is referred to as the divine eye, also ages with the seasons, bathes in these pure waters and becomes healthy and youthful again. These waters are believed to cure human blindness, and there are a number of tales and legends in which the hero regains his sight after washing his eyes in the holy water collected at the crack of dawn before the "crow has bathed her children" from the seven springs or wells.

Rain is a happy omen and, falling before a new endeavour is commenced, guarantees its success. The sick are given rain water, or water collected from the seven springs to drink. Rain water, or the water of life, as it is called in Russian, heals wounds, makes mutilated parts of the body grow, rejuvenates the old, and resurrects the dead.

Russian folklore has two distinct variants of these life generating waters: live water, and dead water. Contrary to its name, however, the latter does know bring death; rather, it makes mutilated bodies whole, and heals wounds. But unlike live water, it does not possess the power of resurrection. Folktales are replete with motifs of dead and live water. Like the spring rains which first melt the earth, purify her, make her whole, while the following rains resurrect her, the dead hero too is first sprinkled with dead water, and then with live water, before he comes to life again. And like Perun, the hero in the Russian folktales drinks large quantities of holy/live water (or beer or wine, both of which appear as metaphors for live water) before the final battle, gaining strength with every sip till he becomes the strongest among the strong, and lifts the heaviest swords (the lightning is seen as Perun's sword), and like Perun, strikes the enemy dead with one blow.

What is the source of these waters? This brings us to the *arbor mundi*, the world tree. There, in the centre of the universe stands the oak tree, on its top sits the bird of paradise, the eagle, under its roots lies the snake demon. Two springs flow out from under the tree — one of live water, and the other of dead water. Near the springs sit three women, the fortune tellers. One knows the past, the other the future, and the third, the present. They decide what should be and what should not be, and the fate of every being. They bring death or life, and continuously work over the creation of the world (Here I may add that one of the magical values of live water is that it imparts wisdom and power to tell the future).

The *arbor mundi* is seen as a mediator between the world of the dead and the world of the living. The fight between the eagle and the snake demon is eternal, and represents the cycle of life and death, and of the seasons. The defeat of the demon results in the release of live waters. Death in slavic folklore is seen as a temporary state, a state of sleep. Nothing dies till the end. Every spring the sun comes out of the clutches of the forces of darkness; every spring Perun overpowers the snake demon, and life returns to the earth. *Arbor mundi*, associated with the theme of the constant revival and renewal, is seen as one of the attributes of Perun.

After Perun and the *arbor mundi*, I now come to the role of the stone in slavic folklore and mythology. The sun in Russian folklore is metaphorically called Ognioni kamen, or Bel goruch kamen — the white hot stone. Perun either holds the fire-stone — the fireball — in his hands, or his thick eyelashes hide the fire underneath them or, at times, he himself represents the sun. On the one hand, the sun the fire-stone dies every winter or, having become weak, is overpowered by his adversary the dark forces of winter and revives every spring after having bathed in the pure waters released by Perun. On the other hand, Perun has himself to drink first the living fluids of the celestial wells before he is able to kill the snake demon, and send life generating rains down to earth. The sun as the eye of god Perun or, as the fire hidden in the eyes of god, can burn and destroy everything when they are open but, soaked in holy waters, it generates life-giving forces. These attributes of the sun and Perun are transferred on the earth to stones.

Stone, like the oak tree, is seen as a mediator between the two worlds. The grave stone represents death. Like the oceans, it also separates the worlds of the dead and the living. The stone appears as a frequent symbol of death in folktales. The death of the hero is represented by his turning into stone. But since death is not absolute, the hero, like the earth in general, is brought back to life after he is sprinkled with live water, after which he invariably asks, "Oh, did I sleep too long?"

A dry stone represents death; soaked in water, it represents life. Perun is himself incapable of impregnating the earth without having first drunk the fluids of life from the celestial springs. The sun gets his strength and energy back only by bathing in the pure spring rains. The sun and fire are attributes of Perun. Fire is masculine in slavic religion, and water feminine. Both are seen as good phenomenon; neither can tolerate any impurity. One burns, and the other washes away or drowns all impurities. The pigeon (blue) book refers to fire as king, and water as queen. They are husband and wife. Through their union, procreation takes place. It is of interest to point out here some laments of orphans in Russian folklore:

(1) Oh, what a bitter orphan I am
as if born from stone

(2) I, it seems, was planted by stone

(3) I was born from the dry earth
from father, all from stone.

Perun, the sun, and stone are thus dry seeds unless soaked in female waters. In many places, Perun is said to be married to the celestial water maiden. He places stones in the wombs of women, thus blessing them with children.

In the Pigeon (blue) book we read the following verse:

White Latir stone is father to all stones.
Why is he father to all stones?
From under the stone, from under the white stone, flows the
river, the fast flowing river. This flows on earth, in the whole
of the universe, so as to heal the world, so as to feed the world.

These are the same celestial springs which spring out of the roots of the *arbor mundi* — the world tree.

It is not accidental then that in birth rituals, stone, water, and fire play important roles. The woman in confinement is brought to a preheated bath house (*banya*) for delivery. The bath-house is on the periphery of the house. Its specific association with water and fire made it the most important part of the various rituals related to the life-cycle. Three stones or burning coals are brought to the bath house and placed in the water tub. The mother and the child are given bath in this water; the mother and the mid-wife also drink this water, which is also sprinkled on the guests who come to see the child. The hot bath-house with water and stone stand, on the one hand, for the continuity of life, or represent life itself. On the other, it also plays a magical role in the preservation of life. The second dimension of this agent lies in its purificatory, evil-warding powers.

In birth rituals, water represents continuity, and the preservation of life. In death rituals, it is predominantly purificatory. In the marriage rituals, its role is associated with fecundity.

The bride to be becomes an absolute stranger, and is not allowed to perform any household chores. She does not come out of the house, and covers her face in a black scarf which is similar to a death mask. On the day of the marriage, before going to church she is given the ritual bath, and the groom's clothes are also sprinkled with holy water. The bride also gives the groom water to drink. He drinks some of it and sprinkles the rest on those standing beside him. After marriage, in some versions of the ritual, the mother welcomes the groom with a bucketful of water, and gives his horse water to drink. In some other versions marriages are solemnized by the bride and the groom going round a water source thrice, and the bride is blessed so that she may be "healthy like water".

The ritual food also includes the three elements, except that stone is replaced by grain (barley in the birth rituals, and rice and raisins in the death rituals). Hot porridge is made in an earthen pot which is decorated with flowers and ribbons, brought to the table and broken. The porridge is then distributed to the guests. The symbolic value of this food is the same as that of water, stone, and fire in the bath-house.

Honey and wine are very often used as metaphors for live water. In many regions the bride's hair was rubbed with honey. It was because of their metaphorical significance that it was a common practice to pour honey and wine on the graves of relatives at the beginning of the spring season.

Fire, water, and grain are important not only in life-cycle rituals, but they also play an important role in agrarian rituals and festivals. It is not possible to discuss these at any meaningful length in so short a paper. But it may be noted that lighting a fire, dips in ice-holes or river waters, shooting of fire arrows, worshipping the corn mother in the form of a virgin dressed up in green leaves and wearing on her head a wreath made from straw are some of the prominent images of Eastern slavic agrarian festivals.

In the beginning I had mentioned that Belbog, Chernobog, and Perun formed the fundamental axes of the Eastern Slavic religion. I end by saying that fire, water, and earth are the fundamental axes of their pantheon. The relationship between the three can never be hierarchical, as life can be generated only when the three come together. The male fire, or the male dry seed/sun/fire, soaked in the female waters enters the womb of the mother earth (again female) and keeps the eternal rhythm of life going.

I would like to sum up this presentation with the following lines from a folk tale:

> On the wall hung a sword and flask with live water. When sprinkled with this water the dry wooden stump will yield young offshoots and get covered by winter leaves; only then will arrive the moment of deliverance.

14

The Cosmic Nature of Bushman Law

A. J. G. M. Sanders

When some 4000 years ago, nomads, calling themselves Khoi-Khoi, came into contact with the much longer established hunter-gatherers of Southern Africa, they called them 'San', meaning food-gatherers. The seventeenth century Dutch colonists of the Cape of Good Hope called the hunter-gatherers who lived on the savannah or 'boschveld' of the Cape Interior, 'Boschjesmannen'.

Currently in vogue among those who dedicate themselves to the study of the hunter-gatherers of Southern Africa, is the Khoi-Khoi appellation of 'San'. It is felt that the term 'Bushman' has acquired too much of a pejorative connotation. However, the same holds true, albeit not perhaps among academics, of the term 'San' and its Bantu derivative 'Sarwa'. Unfortunately, a derogatory connotation is the fate of any appellation of a marginal group, even when in its original form the appellation was merely descriptive and meant no harm.

In this paper the hunter-gatherers of Southern Africa will be referred to as 'Bushmen', as this term need not carry a connotation of contemptuousness, and despite academic attempts to popularize the word 'San', has remained the term most widely used. The theme of this paper is Bushman law, as an expression of Bushman cosmic intelligence.

When I refer to 'law', I do not have some or other 'scientific' definition of law in mind, such as 'law is the command of the sovereign', but rather the description of law which is employed by legal comparatists, namely 'those norms for external conduct which are accepted by a community as obligatory'.

A complicating factor is that the Bushmen have never articulated their world-view. They would, no doubt, be bewildered by expressions such as 'religion', 'constitutional law', 'family law', 'contract law', 'property law' and 'succession law'. Hence, when in this paper I make use of these concepts, I do so for your and my convenience only!

The World of the Bushmen

The Bushmen are the longest-term inhabitants of Southern Africa. They are the last survivors of a Stone Age people who were once scattered all over Eastern, Central and Southern Africa. According to archaeological data, they were for at least 30,000 years the sole inhabitants of the Southern African region. Their history, style of living, language and physical appearance distinguish the Bushmen sufficiently, in the minds of others as well as in their own minds, as a recognizable ethnic group. However, subsequent to Khoi-Khoi, Bantu and European invasions, the bulk of what is left of traditional Bushman society in Southern Africa is now confined to the most arid part of the Kalahari Desert which falls within the boundaries of the present-day Republic of Botswana. Needless to say, that we are referring here to a small number of people.

Archaeological and linguistic evidence indicates that today's Kalahari Bushmen are the descendants of local Bushmen rather than of Bushmen refugees driven from other parts of Southern Africa into the Kalahari by African tribes and Europeans. It is therefore possible to speak of an aboriginal Kalahari Bushman culture; and it is on this culture that I will concentrate in this paper.

The Kalahari Bushmen are present-oriented people who, in their quest for survival as hunter-gatherers, live a thoroughly pragmatic, yet simultaneously religious life.

According to Bushman belief, man constitutes the beginning and end, or rather the cycle of life. Man is the immediate carrier of life but over and above man stand the planets, and then there are the rain clouds, water wells, trees, plants and animals, all of which are considered to be pre-deceased and transformed Bushmen. According to oral tradition, these Bushmen are endowed with extraordinary or magic powers of generosity as well as punishment. Hence, it is advisable to be on good terms with them.

The focus of religious contact among the Bushmen is the trance dance. It is seldom a pre-arranged event. Rather, some children initiate some rhythmic game around the evening fire, and adult men may join them. Some of the men may begin to leap and dance around the fire. The children will gradually retire to join their mothers who are now sitting in a circle around the fire, clapping and singing. As the dance reaches a peak of excitement, one or more of the men work themselves into a state where they transcend themselves and enter the realm of the magic to plead for the health of individuals and the community. The trance dance, which may last for hours on end, constitutes the Bushmen's major ritual and involves the entire band community.

Bushman Law

The world-view of the Bushmen as outlined above, is reflected in the law of the

Bushmen. However, just as there is in Bushman society a minimum of 'religion', as developed cultures know it, so there is a minimum of 'law'.

CONSTITUTIONAL LAW

Subsistence hunting and gathering requires group formation. In a habitat as barren as the central Kalahari Desert, the groups or 'bands', as they are known in the literature, are per force small in size and highly mobile. In fact, a central Kalahari Bushman band seldom numbers more than fifty members.

Bushman society is therefore band society. The Bushman band does, however, constitute an early form of political society with an elementary legal order.

Each band is composed of several families. Whereas the band constitutes the largest social unit, the family constitutes the most cohesive and enduring one. The family is also the basic unit of interband migration and the formation of new bands.

The formation of a new band is a comparatively rare event, but interband migration is a common occurrence. No band therefore forms a closed community. In fact, the average band is a rather fluid group which fragments and realigns continuously, and it is often difficult to distinguish between migrants and visitors. Major factors inducing migration or protracted visits are food supply, marriage, and the alleviation of tense social relationships.

Notwithstanding the frequency of social interaction between individual members and households of the various central Kalahari band societies, and the total absence of interband warfare, no society of bands exists. The separate bands do not interact, in any organized way, in ritual, economic or other social activities. Each band considers itself to be complete in itself and autonomous in respect of other bands.

The band has no chief or leader. Kalahari Bushman society simply does not lend itself to a centralized, hierarchical structure with specialized personnel. Decisions affecting the social life of the band are arrived at through discussions in which all adult and near-adult members of the band, irrespective of whether they are male or female, are welcome to participate. Discussion is informal, is not conducted in any special place, and seldom takes the form of a single, set-piece debate.

For outsiders, the egalitarian nature of Bushman political society must be rather striking.

FAMILY LAW

Girls and boys are equally welcome in a Bushman family. They will begin to share in family and band responsibilities when they are seven or eight years of age. The boys will join the men in their hunting and the girls will help their mothers with the gathering of vegetable-type foods.

Their parents, too, are of equal status, for the simple reason that the hunter-husband could impossibly do without the help of his gathering wife who, in fact, provides the family with the bulk of its day-to-day sustenance.

Marriages are arranged by the couples themselves, but in respect of the young, parental approval is required. No matrimonial property settlements are entered into. One may marry either within or outside of the band, but because of strict incest taboos, marriage partners will often be selected from outside. Polygamy occurs, but is not common. Divorce is accomplished by the unilateral decision of either spouse or by mutual consent. They only semblance of formality is the act of parting. Incompatibility and adultery are the main causes of marital break-up. After divorce, the father takes custody of the children, but as long as a child is still at the breast stage, it will remain with the mother. The band regrets divorces but adds no social stigma or legal impediments to them. Divorces are not uncommon among young couples, but overall there is a notable stability in marriages.

The only family relationship, and indeed the only relationship in wider Bushman society, in which authority is inherent, is the parent-child relationship. Significantly, however, parental duties are considered to be more important than parental rights. In addition, a nuclear family's duties may well extend beyond the immediate, parental sphere and include a duty of support to grandparents, siblings and other close relatives. Accordingly, should a family decide to migrate, they will take with them those relatives who need or want to accompany them. Thus, whole segments of a band may join another band.

CONTRACT LAW

In the absence of a 'social' contract, there would of course be no band society. Less apparent is the need for private contracts, this is to say contracts between individual band members. Certain forms of contract are definitely frowned upon, notably commercial contracts, as bargaining is seen as likely to create social tension. Rather the Bushmen engage in giving and receiving, borrowing and lending. Sharing possessions strengthens of course the fellowship, but it also promotes the mobility of the band.

PROPERTY LAW

The Bushmen have few personal belongings. These are largely made up of the shelter, hunting and gathering tools, culinary utensils, clothing, ornaments and musical instruments. They belong to either men or women, as the concept of matrimonial property is unknown to the Bushmen.

Personal belongings being so few, Bushman property law really revolves around the use of the common wealth. With the band operating within an ill-defined area within which it moves from place to place, it is not the area itself but rather its resources which are thought of as the common wealth. These resources, namely rain and ground water, the waterholes, the wild plant food and animals, are there for equal use by all of the band members. For people from neighbouring bands to hunt and gather in the band area or draw water from it, they will need permission. Usually, permission will have to be obtained from the founder-members of the band, their eldest descendants or long-standing band members who act as spokesmen of the band.

Rain and ground water belongs to no one, but the permanent and semi-permanent waterholes are band property.

The wild plant foods, which constitute between sixty and eighty per cent of the Kalahari Bushmen's subsistence base, are also band property but once collected belong to the woman who collected them. With her daily gathering the woman will feed her own family and visitors.

The game animals belong to no one until they are killed. Small animals become the property of the person who kills them, and are consumed within his own family. To catch the larger animals requires of course a hunting party. The composition of the hunting party, which is seldom larger than four or five adult or near-adult men, is not a matter of convention, and no one is formally in command. Once an animal has been arrowed, the hunters may follow it into neighbouring band territory, and should neighbours cross the hunters' track, they will be given a present of meat, but no tribute is obligatory. Already the animal belongs to the owner of the first arrow to have been effectively lodged into it so that it penetrated enough for its poison to work. However, the meat of large animals has to be shared with everyone in the band, visitors included, according to definite rules. It is upon the owner of the first arrow to make the initial distribution of the meat, and who receives from him, will give again, and so on.

What strikes one, is the communitarian nature of Bushman property law. The emphasis is clearly on sharing. Of course, this makes practical sense, for in a community as small as a band society, to look after the health of each and every band member, is to look after the health of the community. However, there is a much deeper, indeed religious meaning of Bushman property law, in terms of which the common wealth is a gift to the band from above.

SUCCESSION LAW

Birth and death among the Bushmen are treated in a 'casual' fashion, which is to say that there are no rituals attached to them. This merely confirms that the Bushmen have a vision which transcends an earthly existence.

Personal property being so scarce in Bushman society, and being neither of great nor lasting value, it is only the succession to a deceased person's interests in gift-giving partnerships which is an important matter to be settled. In order to assure the continuation of major partnerships, older Bushmen, on becoming less mobile and less productive, will gradually pass their partnerships on to their children or younger siblings. In respect of partnerships which have not been disposed of by the deceased, the deceased's children or siblings may ask the remaining partners to continue to relationship by offering them the deceased's possessions.

SOCIAL WRONG-DOING

The small face-to-face and, indeed, 'footprint-to-footprint' community of the Kalahari Bushman band is generally at peace, there being little scope and inclination to act anti-socially. Of the wrong-doings, the ones which are feared most, occur least, namely physical violence, the breaking of the incest taboos, flagrant adultery and theft. Most transgressions relate to the use and distribution of the natural resources.

A transgressor of the communal law is seldom considered to be a bad person, but is rather treated as someone who erred to the detriment of the communal, including his or her own interests.

THE SETTLEMENT OF TRANSGRESSIONS AND DISPUTES

Transgressions of the communal law and disputes among individual members of the band are judged by band opinion, and controlled by band action, rather than self-help. As violence is greatly feared because it would be destructive of band society, every effort will be made by the band to prevent self-help, and try to resolve a conflict through talking, which in appropriate cases may take the form of public shaming and ridicule. If a conflict cannot be resolved this way and the offender is not willing to leave the band of his or her own volition, he or she will be 'eased out' of it. However, an offender's departure could prove to be of greater harm to the band than was his or her original wrong-doing. Hence, every effort is made in band society to prevent or else channel conflict.

Conclusion

The law of the Bushmen cannot be separated from the Bushmen's religious orientation or world-view. They are interwoven in a peculiar, indeed practical fashion, for both are man-centred. By using the term 'man-centred' I do not wish to imply that in Bushman society there exists a confrontation between man and nature.

On the contrary, for according to Bushman cosmic feeling, nature is man: it is the community of 'transformed' and 'living' Bushmen. Hence, the environment is revered, and utilized and shared with great care.

As matters stand now, what is left of traditional Bushman society is under enormous pressure from outside modernist forces, and all we can really hope for is that some elements of the Bushmen's cosmic intelligence, such as environmental care, communal care and the art of dialogue, will be taken with us into the future.

References

Barnard, A., 1992. *Hunters and Herders of Southern Africa*, Cambridge University Press.

Roberts, S., 1979. *Order and Dispute. An Introduction to Legal Anthropology*, Penguin Books.

Sanders, A.J.G.M., 1989. "The Bushmen of Botswana – from desert dwellers to world citizens", In *Law and Anthropology* 4, 107-22.

Schott, R., 1959. "Die eigentumsrechte der Bushmanner in Sudafrika", In *Zeitschrift fur vergleichende Rechtswissenschaft*, 101-223.

Silberbauer, G.B., 1981. *Hunter and Habitat in the Central Kalahari Desert*, Cambridge University Press.

Tanaka, J., 1980. *The San Hunter-Gatherers of the Kalahari*, University of Tokyo Press.

Tobias, P.V. (ed.), 1978. *The Bushmen. San Hunters and Herders of Southern Africa, Human and Rousseau, South Africa.*

Van Der Post, L. and Taylor, J., 1985. *Testament to the Bushmen*, Penguin Books.

15

Nature and Human Development Among the Baka Pygmies

Concepts and Perceptions

John Mope Simo
Paul Nkwi Nchoji

Every human being, male or female, has some genetic endowment which is complemented by the environment in which he/she is born and/or bred. By the concept of environment here we mean the culture and the natural milieu in which it develops (cf. Nkwi, 1992). Both factors have great implications for the development, life-support system and socialibility of any person. In societies studied by anthropologists in Africa it can be deduced from the indigenous perceptions that there is still an integrating relationship between man and nature, the cosmos. In every culture this exterior universe which comprises essentially of the five primordial elements of water, fire, air, earth and the sun or sky are complimentary to people's rituals, cognitive systems, religious beliefs and sacrificial practices. Historically speaking some of these elements have become for man sacred objects of his external world and symbols of both spiritual and secular power and authority.

Despite the impinging effects of the forces for change and especially Western science and ideology on tribal society, the Africans' integral vision of nature is characteristically constant yet dynamic. In other words, although the natural and human surroundings are rapidly changing, man from time immemorial has successfully used both components to satisfy his/her material, spiritual and ritual needs and conditions. For instance, with regard to the sociological, psychological and environmental functions of ritual Roy Rappaport argues that "it produces a practical result on the world external not only to the social unit composed of those who participate together in ritual performances but also to the larger unit composed of those who entertain similar beliefs concerning the universe". (1988: 390)

Hence, from cradle to grave this man/nature relationship is maintained more or less in day-to-day encounters. Perhaps it can be argued that the interface between man and nature is prolonged to the world beyond for persons who die having regenerated themselves through procreation. They can be considered by their family or community as ancestors/ancestresses. This does not imply that the people worship their departed relatives as some observers have claimed (cf. Mbiti, 1975: 161). Nonetheless, in African society the dead are perceived as continuing to show interest in the affairs of the living or surviving relatives. The dead are part of the living continuum.

The primary goal of this discussion is to highlight the concept of man and nature in a given African culture. We also want to show how a culture shapes the lives of people into which they are born and grow up in a given environment, free from the constraints of other cultures. The main argument here is that African people live in perpetual communion with nature. Thus their human and cultural development are so much dependent on their external world that their survival would be unthinkable otherwise.

The focus will be on a descriptive analysis of the indigenous people's concept and perceptions of their environmental-ecological niche, using the example of the Baka pygmies of south-eastern Cameroon. We want to emphasize the extraordinary knowledge the Baka have of nature and the sophistication of their adaptation to it. We shall endeavour to analyze various Baka modes of social treatment of nature, selected for the purpose of demonstrating those processes of personal and community fulfilment that result from the interrelations of people with the external world – the tropical rain-forest.

The encompassing and explicit religious, cosmological, material and other kinds of relationships highlight the specific and general vision of nature within the Baka culture. The impact of the relationship between man and nature shows an interface between social life and nature.

The Baka

The Baka are a sub-set of the Pygmy polity in the equatorial Africa. They are found in Cameroon, Congo, Gabon and Zaire (cf. Silcock, 1988: 25). Like other pygmies the Baka are culturally, linguistically and physically different from their Bantu neighbours. The linguistic and cultural dissimilarities seem to be a result of the influence of the various non-pygmy cultures with whom they interact and socialize within the same social oecumene. As Lisa Silcock points out: "even so there is no common consensus among anthropologists as to whether they originally formed a single group". (1988: 24).

One of the most important differences between the Baka pygmies and their Bantu associates is the fact that they owe their total existence to the countless natural resources which nature has endowed on their habitat, the rain forest. The Baka have an estimated population between 20,000 to 35,000 (Silcock, 1988: 24). There are many reasons that account for the uncertainty of the population size. The most important is that as a semi-nomadic group, they roam the rain-forest taking up temporal residence in specific areas that offers rich games and natural resources.

The Baka occupy a forest ecology and they exploit skilfully the gifts of nature or the ecosystem. Over the years important exchange relations have developed between the essentially hunter-gatherer Baka and the Bantu cultivators. However, the relation has been at best one of tolerance, at worse characterized by hostility. This difficult situation has been caused by the condescending attitude and derogatory connotations with which the Bantu describe their Pygmy neighbours.

All the time, the Baka have been quite open to change and have been very flexible to external world stimuli. Acculturation process has permitted them to borrow and integrate into their culture foreign cultural values. At the same time they have successfully maintained their identity and independence. With regard to their positive reactions to change while maintaining an impervious attachment to their natural environment, Silcock succinctly argues that:

> Change has not always been thrust upon the Baka and they are naturally attracted by much of what the outside world can offer. But throughout all change and adaptation they have always had access to the forest, a world which is completely their own. Their culture is robust enough to survive as long as the forest remains: but without it, this same culture will be meaningless. It is their lifeblood, without it their culture would collapse. (1988:27).

The above citation explicitly summarizes the interface between Baka people (that is a specific culture) and nature and their mastery over it. We shall elaborate this salient point in the next section with emphasis on Baka pygmies' traditional knowledge system and how this relates to nature.

Baka Culture and the Tropical Rain-Forest

The natural heritage of Baka pygmies is the tropical rain-forest. The Baka have adapted to this ecosystem and their social ecology is entirely enhanced by the forest ecosystem. This natural world has enabled them to develop their defences against it, their specific culture and strategies for human development are largely determined by this environment.

As mentioned earlier, the external world of the Baka forms part of the green centre of Africa which nineteenth century travellers referred to as the Dark Continent (see Matthews, 1990:48). The African rain-forest is made up of six layers, each with its characteristic flora, fauna and micro-climate. Descending from the top are: the emergent layer open to the sky; the canopy, often of interlocking tree, crowns, lower the upper part of the complex understory; shrub layer, with mature, woody plants and young canopy trees; and at the floor, a base layer of dead or decomposing vegetation (*Ibid.*, 50).

Animals are few and far between, while those not easily visible in the forest's dense vegetation use it at night for feeding purposes. At the same time this habitat is riddled with poisonous or inedible compounds of one sort or another. According to Silcock "The paradox of tropical forest is that while it is biologically and botanically the richest place on earth, it is also the hardest in which to subsist". (1988: 7)

Over the centuries Baka man like other humans has been able to master what may appear to be an insurmountable difficulty and how his/her culture has evolved. Again Silcock puts the point nicely in her remark that "The sophistication with which these people exploit their environment is equal only to the sophistication of the forest". (*Ibid.*, 8) The pygmies will not be pygmies without the forest. The forest ecology is the lifewire and basis of their culture.

The Baka consciousness of their forest environment and the ways they have developed skills to exploit it represent a rich wealth of knowledge. This knowledge has been embedded into their culture during the course of centuries of living as hunter-gatherers and handed down by elders to the younger generations through word of mouth. As a matter of fact, the Baka so much depend on the forest resources: for medicines (they know plants in the forest can provide curative ingredients; building materials especially for their huts or mongulus; subsistence products other than the cultivated produce they receive from their non-pygmy neighbours; for ritual purposes, as well as for their means of socialization). For example, apart from skills learned in the domestic sphere, children acquire knowledge of gaming through play with traps for catching small rodents and birds for food. Basically, children absorb most of their knowledge simply by watching and listening to their elders. As in the case of adults, there is a strong association between these activities for the social reproduction of the households and the music and/or the rituals that go with them, and so by extension the forest (see Silcock, 1988: 22-23).

In addition to what has been said, the Baka know the variety of forest foods and animals and the specific seasons when these subsistence products can be easily found. Of the different seasons which these pygmy people experience each year, the three-month period of prolonged heavy rain is the most important. During this period when the forest is in its abundance the Baka leave their permanent villages for the deep forest, and for several months roam the forest. The women carry their few possessions in baskets and follow their husbands. The sexual division of labour in this society, impose on the women building of camps composed of huts (*mongulus*) as they go from one place to another. They rarely stay in one place for more than a week. Meanwhile, the men perform the more prestigious but undoubtedly more hazardous job of supplying meat for the group through hunting and trapping.

Animals are easier to track in the wet ground during this long rainy season, because their feeding sites are more predictable as they flock to fruiting trees. Although the Baka have no specific marriage ceremonies, there is evidence that men usually contract their marriages during this crucial season. The reason is because a man is able to prove his hunting ability by the number and quality of the game he brings home to the father/mother of his future wife.

The Baka depend on the forest ecology during the heavy rains for their food sufficiency. This pygmy group like the many others who live in the Central and Equatorial African region have developed skills in identifying many edible roots and yams (see Silcock, 1988: 25). Usually this is by spotting a thin stem above the ground and digging several feet to get at the yams. Another example of this adaptability process to nature is how to obtain the fruit of the wild mango or *peke*. The search for this fruit is the principal reason for the Baka's long trips into the forest during the rainy season (Silcock, 1988:11). The kernels of this fruit are processed to produce a delicious oil paste which is scarce in other forest foods and highly valued in the people's diet.

Finally, as the forest cycle continues the Baka follow it by switching from the collection of one major food source to another. The honey or foki season is partly induced by the rain as they end, and the rain forest trees flower. At this time there is an excess of nectar and pollen available to the African Honeybee. Silcock describes the process very vividly:

> To collect honey, the Baka climb 120 foot trees to reach the nest in the canopy. A liana belt goes around the trunk and the climber, who cuts footholes with his axe as he ascends, places himself against the trunk and hoists himself up another foot using the belt. (1988:130)

This is a prized Baka food. The search for bees' nests and the dripping golden combs are not so important.

Admittedly, there are specific seasons for the collection of numerous other foods which are common place in Baka households. For instance, caterpillars, different species of mushrooms and edible beetle larvae in the forest are collected to improve the protein content of their diet. On the other hand, the approaching dry season brings its rewards too, when the forest streams drop in level. This is the best time when women demonstrate their adaptability to the environment as many of them do dam fishing. In normal circumstances the streams are blocked at an arrow point so that below the barrier the water drops to just a few inches. This permits the stranded small fish, crabs and shrimps to be caught.

Whatever the season, the Baka are often ready to turn any opportunity to their advantage. Almost anything can provide them with the due they need to find food and many non-material means of satisfaction in their forest environment. This point logically leads to an examination of how the Baka relate other aspects of their social life — music, dance, ritual practices, religious beliefs, and so on — to their external world.

It must be said that like in other African cultures there is no dividing line in Baka life between the physical and the spiritual. For example, as in the well-known case of the Azande described by Evans-Pritchard, when a Baka man falls ill, it is attributed witchcraft by an ill-wisher. In cases like this Silcock argues that ". . . the ritual dance which heals with fire — the *nganga* — may be performed, to counteract the magic and to persuade the sick person to fight for his life". (1988:30)

Although the Baka do not actively worship or pray, they adore Komba, their supreme god, who is the creator of all things. However, unlike most other religious belief systems described by John Mbiti (1975), Komba is somewhat distant from the day-to-day life of the Baka. According to Silcock, ". . . he exists as an explanation for the Baka's presence in the forest and for the order of the world around them". (1988: 20)

Unlike Komba, Jengi, the spirit of the forest, has a very direct influence over the lives of the Baka through a particular important ritual observance. **Jengi's** presence is called upon once every few years. The decision is taken during the concentration of male elders when a number of young boys are judged ready for initiation into manhood. As a matter of fact, the Jengi ritual reinforces Baka cosmology and society as a whole. Those people who are initiated on a particular occasion have the protection of Jengi, and through him, the forest. These men in turn protect the women. By and large, **Jengi**'s presence reminds the people of their debt to the forest as their source of life. On the other hand, it does not only symbolize the unification of men and women but also reconfirm their disparate roles in the community (cf. Rappaport, 1988).

The point should be made here that the Baka do not only use the forest's chemistry in the acquisition of the variety of foods. They exploit the very chemicals evolved by plants to defend themselves against predators. Some plant compounds are used as sources of fishing and hunting poisons. For example, a Milletia vine (called *mongombo* by the Baka) is macerated and the pulp rinsed into the water, which has the effect of making the fish float to the surface where they are easily caught. Similarly in hunting the Baka use the vine strophanthus gratus (*nea*). Their seeds are combined with other plant extracts to form a deadly poison which hunters use on the tip of their arrows for hunting. According to Silcock "The active ingredient in this case is strophanthine – a potent cardiac poison which is used in Western medicine as a heart relaxant". (1988:14)

Evidently, much value should be attached on the rich traditional knowledge of the Baka about their external world and how this accounts for the unique features of their cultural heritage. Despite the rapid changes that are taken place around them, this indigenous knowledge system still has a vital role to play in the development of this pygmy group and the modern Cameroonian society as a whole.

Conclusion

Available evidence shows that the relationship between the Baka and their environment (land, the forest and its many resources, streams, etc.) is not problematic. Rather is can be said that man and his/her external world are intricately and inexorably dovetailed. Moreover, Baka mythologies, ritual techniques, social organization and systems of value significantly testify that the focus of their knowledge is upon the opportunities and limitations of their ecosystem and how they socialize in it. For example, Bakan ritual practices for hunting, food gathering and harvesting are sociologically complex and form an integral part of their cosmologies and their spiritual links with **Komba**. Their metaphysical importance are demonstrated by the psychological and philosophical value of the practices to the people.

Over and above all aspects of nature which surrounds the Baka pygmies, they perceive the tropical rain forest as the most valuable force with which they interact. Perhaps they will refuse to be resettled in the other natural environments where their Bantu neighbours have found life and the process of socialization both geographically and culturally more rewarding. Put another way, the Baka value their forests and the ritual practice and mythologies associated with them as much and, it may be suggested, often more than their fellow human beings. Thus their whole life is occupied with the welfare of their forests and *vice versa*.

There is a rich wealth of traditional knowledge that links Baka culture and other African cultures to their nature which, if properly understood and used by outsiders as the insiders have done, could provide a solid basis for the challenges of the future. But what could happen if the rapid rate of ecological destruction and especially deforestation which is taking place in other tropical forest areas of Cameroon (see Mope Simo, 1992: 5-15) eventually affect the Baka natural world too? Surely they will not only experience a 'divorce' with their forest and all that it means for their material, spiritual and symbolic well-being, but also cease to exist on the face of the earth.

References

Matthews, R.O., 1988. *The Atlas of Natural Wonders*, London, Guild Publishing.

Mbiti, J.S., 1975. *An Introduction to African Religion*, London, Heinemann.

Mope Simo, J.A., 1992. *Agricultural Expansion and Tropical Deforestation: A Case Study of Cameroon UNRISD Discussion Paper.*

Nkwi, Paul Nchoji, 1992. "Social Anthropological Framework of Environment Management in Cameroon", In *FAO/UNDP Report.*

Onwerejeogwu, M.A., 1975. *The Social Anthropology of Africa: An Introduction,* London, Heinemann.

Rappaport, R.A., 1988. "Ritual Regulation of Environmental Relations Among a New Guinea People", In J.B. Cole, (ed.) *Anthropology for the Nineties: Introductory Readings*, New York, The Free Press., pp. 389-411.

Silcock, L., 1988. *Baka: People of the Rainforest.*

16

Pancatattva in Artistic Manifestations
A Case Study of Tribal Gujarat

Haku Shah

In a primary school of tribal children they made their own song and were singing:

dilli jatra jahva bhoja
dilli jatra jahva na
paklo ambo khahva bhoja
paklo ambo khahva na

Come *bhoja* (brother's wife) we will go to Delhi for a pilgrimage and there we will eat ripe mango fruit.

Each creative act of a tribe comes from direct contact with *prakrti*, the elements: the earth, the wind, the fire, the space and the water. They are too near him. The creative act is a ritual too, far from him – known and unknown; so he wants to fathom them through the arts that grow out of his own self.

He has a past, also the future. Present is very much lived by him through this creative act. He is very much a man amongst men, but then he is a man himself – anonymous.

In his art he respects all known and unknown forces.

He respects nature – *Prakrti,* and uses it discriminately to its minimum and maximum.

He knows how to use it; so there is a purity about it and the truth behind it. While pursuing it, he then transfers his creativity through different material into form, performance and transformation.

This paper deals with three aspects of the artistic manifestations:

Perception of Creativity

The theme of the tribal creative expression mostly deals with 'Life' – known and unknown forces. It is always guided by tradition, but that does not negate the individual expression.

'Form' evolves automatically through intuition. There is no dry logical exercise involved.

A small element in nature, which is lived through life like a 'grain', is celebrated as a dot, or a grass blade, as a line in innumerable ways with interesting forms.

The tools made by the tribes guide the technique as well as the final expression.

Out of their own perception certain modules are created which passes through a process to get to the final results. This then certainly manifests in their own vocabulary of the creative act. Thus modules give discipline, but they do take risks also to overrule it for getting better results. The vitality in the creative act comes through their intense participation in life.

Styles differ enormously from tribe to tribe because of their socio-economic and environmental differences; and this guides the perception too.

The language of the artistic manifestation evolves through the visual and audio perception and objects and from the moment which is the basis to all creativity.

Celebration of Nature-Environment

In their celebration of nature they deal with a wide range of the known and unknown forces. It can start just with a particle of Mother Earth, a drop of water, or a spark of fire, or a breez of wind, and include anything and everything which they see, they dream, and they or their forefathers thought or felt.

Almost all their creative manifestations evolve out of their own environment. This becomes their material wealth, the 'tool' bank.

They in their creative expression use this to its maximum and minimum.

In celebrating this a tribal man has behind him the tradition and his finest sensibility.

Even the smallest sprout in nature becomes his greatest joy as he puts it into his creative act.

In celebrating nature there is nothing like a waste. In fact, the 'waste' becomes a marvellous material wealth for the tribes.

The material then automatically leads to the technique and a piece is formed

Plate 16.1 Panchmahal, Gujarat. Bhil making of a jar

Plate 16.2 Lambadia, Gujarat. kiln for preparing terracotta hourses

Plate 16.3 Dahnu, Maharashtra.
making of a Varli painting

Plate 16.4 Dahnu, Maharashtra.
Varli marriage painting

which is then celebrated with all the interdisciplinary arts. This piece does have the reality which is real like a votive terracotta figure, or a painting of a god.

The tribal mind takes a material, finds one and many usages and also the resources by moulding it with his own creative genius. There is no set values attached to nature. Like night and day, both have their own intrinsic values. So, nights are celebrated through their various creative manifestations by calling all the forces of the universe.

Response to Nature-Life lived

1. In any art piece it is the wholeness – totality that counts, as the different art forms mingle to create one in its totality.

2. Creative act is a ritual which in itself is a search of one's own being.

3. Their vocabulary of art is direct, intuitive and simple. Form performance and transformation are the integral parts of their art.

4. For them the basic elements of nature are too near them, i.e., known to them, but so unknown, far from them as well.

5. The tribal expression of art means to fathom the known and the unknown and to link oneself with those elements of nature.

Their respect for *Prakrti* is like a part of their own selves; so the skill, the creativity, the love and, that way, also the truth is being felt in the manifestations of their art forms.

Thus art form becomes a living entity, a part of the tribal self, family, village and, that way, the universe – cosmos.

17

Nature, Man and Art
An Irano-Islamic Perspective

Amir H. Zekrgoo

An exploration of any subject must begin, as a matter of logical progression, with a definition of that subject. And so it is with Art.

Many thinkers believe that art cannot really be defined. As a consequence they shy away from definitions in the usual scientific and operational sense. There are others, however, who do not feel comfortable about art having no clear, accurate definition. An exact definition convinces the scholar that all is known; all elements have been observed and understood. Hence, definitions are attempted and art is duly analyzed. The *Encyclopaedia Britannica* has this to say concerning the definition of art, "In any attempt to arrive at a clear and comprehensive definition of the meaning of art, it is necessary to disregard all philological and etymological derivations which, in the past have led to much confusion of thought and to an expansion of the human activities embraced by this term, which oversteers the limitation imposed upon it by the modern conception of its meaning."

The Modern View of Art

Scholars of art are agreed that art cannot be understood in isolation from that which has created it; a concept stated quite simply by Kandinsky in the words, "Every work of art is the child of its age". While it is well accepted that any definition or description of art must take into account the period and the culture within which it came into being, most academic conceptualisations of art have tended to be Western in character. Conceptualisations that encompass both the Western and the Eastern quintessence of art are few, if any. Furthermore, the view of art today, perhaps reflected a fast-changing world-view, is becoming increasingly superficial. There is an inclination to regard altogether the complexity and ambiguity inherent in art, thereby diluting its essence and significance. Ultimately, then, this view is more of an exercise in aesthetics, taking no account at all of the basic philosophy and ethics of art.

The modern view of art is moulded by man's view of nature. It has become the habit of science and modern thinking to view nature as an adversary, as a dimension to be conquered. Man, in the course of his progress and civilization, has ravaged nature to such an extent, that he can no longer consider himself one with it. In many ways, man has violated nature and its laws. He has taken from it, more than enough to meet his needs and has given nothing back. This alienation from nature is reflected in the view of art today. Whereas art once represented nature, purity and harmony, it now reflects agitation, restlessness and the frenzied pace of modern living.

Art is an inseparable part of being human. Not only is art almost as old as man himself, it has travelled with him the misty paths of pre-history, through centuries and civilizations, to remain until the present time. Contemporary thought that overlooks the fact that art springs from nature, tradition and spirituality cannot but be cursory.

Modern thought focuses on a concept of beauty based only on aesthetics, forgetting that there is an ambiguity and complexity inherent in beauty as well. Replacing one concept that is as yet poorly understood, by another, which is equally, if not more poorly understood, serves little purpose. In the words of Ananda K. Coomaraswamy, "Aesthetic pathology is an excrescence upon a genuine interest in art which seems to be peculiar to civilised people". Margaret Mead puts the same idea forward in a more harsh manner, "The concept of the artist and the related concept of fine arts are both specially bad accidents of the local European tradition."

The modern view of art also spotlights the new. Whatever is 'new' is valued *per se*. Novelty has in itself become a value held more sacred than cultural heritage, tradition and the spiritual. Beauty, nature, ultimate truth, and purity of thought and spirit bear no relevance to this modern view.

The Traditional View of Art

The oldest examples of art are the ancient cave paintings. Art historians have discovered that primitive man painted pictures deep in the hidden recesses of his cave dwellings. This meant that he did not paint only to decorate or satisfy his aesthetic sensibilities or even to record events. Caveman used drawings to rehearse the events of a hunt. Drawing wild beasts, the caveman used them as targets to practice his hunting skills. However, this alone does not explain the beauty of these paintings nor why they were hidden in the deepest parts of the caves. It is obvious that simpler geometrical forms would have served the same purpose. While there is ample evidence that primitive man used his paintings to practice hunting events, the truth is that he believed that the soul of the creature he painted was captured within the paintings. With the cardinal spirit of the creature in his power, the creature would become weakened and would be easily destroyed. Despite the functional aspect of the ancient paintings, one cannot ignore the relation between man and the spiritual element inherent in these paintings. In truth, man's urge to paint is born from a communication with a greater and unseen power.

The traditional view of art shares little with its modern counterpart. The Islamic view of art is diametrically opposed to the modern view. Central to the Islamic and traditional view is a belief in the oneness of nature and man. Nature and man are of the same origin, and like man, nature is alive and intelligent. According to Islam, nature is beautiful because it is infused with the light of the Almighty. The idea of conquering nature is entirely blasphemous and comprehensible. A view of the close relationship of nature and man is found in the East, particularly in the Islamic tradition and is reflected well in the words of Rumi:

جمله اعضای عالم در نهان   باتو میکویند روزان وشبان

ماسمیعیم وبصیریم وهشیم   باشمانا محرمان ماخامشیم

Every small bit of the world tells you secretly, day and night
We listen, we see, and we are conscious. But, to you Na-Mahams
(strangers to the secret of existence) we are silent.

According to this view every atom in nature is believed to be living and conscious. Man may commune with nature through this consciousness and share its secrets. Man and nature, being of one origin, can interface in spirit. Separation from nature is again, reflected in Rumi's words:

جون شماسوی جمادی میروید   همدم جان جمادان کی شوید

از جمادی در جهان جان شوید   غلغل اعضای عالم بشنوید

As you drift towards soullessness, how may you become intimate
with the soul of the inanimate?
Enter from the intimate (state) into the world of the soul. Only
then, may you hear the whisper of the parts of this world.

Ancient civilisations and religions have evolved from the conviction that nature has consciousness and power. In India, the Vedic gods, *Surya*, *Vayu*, *Agni*, and so on represented forces of nature; forces that were elevated to the status of divinity because of the reverence accorded to them. This reverence for nature was by no means confined to Eastern thought. The ancient Greeks too deified the forces of nature. The Vedic god Mitra is also the Avestic god Mithr or the Persian god Mehr. In the *Avesta* of pre-Islamic Persia, one may find the characteristic of Indra, the all powerful god of Vedic India.

It is a veneration of nature that has led to these divine forces assuming shapes of beauty in paintings and sculpture.

Historically, the view of art has been influenced by religious belief. With the advent of Islam the polythesian view gave way to the monastic view and the worship of idols was condemned. This, however, did not diminish reverence for nature. In the Islamic tradition, nature is a creation of *Allah* and the *Quran* devotes chapters pledging an oath to nature. Some of these chapters are even titled after natural forces, such as *Shams* (Sun), *Qamar* (Moon) and *Ra'd* (Thunder). Such is the Islamic veneration of nature that it is believed that:

برگِ درختان سبز در نظر هوشیار

هر ورقش دفتری است معرفت کردکار

> A single leaf of a green tree is in itself a complete book of the wisdom of the Creator.

It is an interesting fact, that one of the many names of *Allah* is 'Musawwer' or, 'The Artist'. Further, man is considered the greatest work of art created by *Allah*. In Islamic art, representing the complete human form is frowned upon for it may lead to man becoming idolised and his evanescence being forgotten. Art, in the Islamic tradition, extends beyond nature, into the wisdom contained in its depths, depths which can only be reached by the pure in mind and spirit. In the Persian tradition, art or *Honar* is a holy act. The most exalted form of Islamic art is epitomised in calligraphy, particularly the transcription of the *Quran*, and Islamic architecture such as is embodied in mosques. For such magnificent beauty to be regarded as mere objectified aesthetic appreciation seems blasphemous for, surely, there is a more profound truth incarnate in such art, a truth unapproachable through analytical procedure and unexplained by mere appropriateness of form, line, shape and colour.

Today, the word *Honar* and the concept it represents has been adapted to the Western approach to art. *Honar* may connote art, but originally the meaning of the word extended beyond art to include insight, wisdom, grace, excellence and truth. An encyclopaedic definition of *Honar* describes it as being a degree of perfection great enough to embrace insight, knowledge and vigilance. Thus, the *Sahib-Honar* or artist, is no ordinary person, but an exalted being.

Persian literature contains many examples of the use of the word *Honar* in its classical sense. In the following lines, the word *Honar* may be replaced by art for a better understanding of the ideology of art,

در همه جیزی هنر وعیب هست   عیب محو تا هنر آری بدست

In everything there is *Honar* (art) and there is *Ai'b* (defect)
Do not be open to defect and *Honar* (art) will come to you.
(Nizami)

هست صد عیب طالعم رالیك   یك هنر دیده ام زطالع خویش

In my fate are a hundred flaws, but in my fate too, I see one *Honar* (art). (Khaqani)

ظرافت بسیار هنر ندیمان است وعیب حکیمان.

Naivete is a *Honar* (art) with an intimate friend but a fault in the prudent and wise. (*Qulistan-e-Sa'id*)

تکیه بر تقوی ودانش در طریقت کافری است
راهرو کر صد هنر دارد توکل بایدش

Relying on virtue, knowledge, and obedience in the path of perfection is out of infidelity. A traveller of this path may have a hundred *Honar* (art) but he must have trust and faith in god. (Hafiz)

In the above examples, *Honar* (art) is the antithesis of defect. *Honar* connotes perfection of form as well as moral and noble attributes.

It is interesting to note that the word *Honar* also means great danger, or an event of significance. Observe the following examples:

هنر بزرك آن است كه رود بزرك جيحون درميان است.

> No mistake can be made as the big *Honar* (art) is that this great river of Jaihum is on the way (Beihaqi)

هنر بزرك اين است كه در جهان ديكر روز قضا خواهد بود.

> The great Honar (art) is that there will be a day of judgement in the other world. (*Ibid.*)

In some instances, *Honar* is used to denote skilfullness of soul and body, worthiness and potential. The word is also used for industry, profession and vocation. In the modern sense, art is used similarly, to indicate skill or distinction in painting, sculpture, drawing, music, writing and so on. The artist is one who has achieved mastery in creative fields such as the ones mentioned above whereas in the classical connotation the artist is one who is perfect and able in the highest moral sense. Till the present-day, in Iran, the reverence and respect accorded to *Honar* is not lost. No painter, musician or writer would profess to being a *Honar-mand* (artist), for this would mean that he is claiming to be flawless in morality and ideals. Instead, they would call themselves *Naqqash* (painter), *Tarrah* (designer), or *Ahang-saz* (composer) and so on.

Art and Man's Values

It is clear from a comparison of the traditional view with the modern that the profundity of meaning and the exalted values associated with art have diminished over the years. This change began to take place as far back as the sixteenth-seventeenth century, with the advent of industrialization. The industrial progress of man brought him into direct conflict with nature, which he began relentlessly and greedily to destroy. The reverence accorded to nature, its beauty and its powerful forces shifted instead to an unquestioning worship of science. Entire value systems changed, ideals were replaced by hard facts, and intuitive knowledge was replaced by statistics. Gradually, science was believed to be the only medium through which the world could be understood. The philosopher August Comte declared that from then on, science would be the religion of the world.

Until the sixteenth century, the boundaries demarcating religion, art, spirituality and nature were nebulous. A work of art that was not founded in the spiritual and the natural was inconceivable. The catastrophe that is Modernism has meant man's estrangement from his basic origin, nature, and has resulted in all his values, moral, religious, ethical as well as artistic, being radically changed.

> We look back into the past and see art and religion emerging hand in hand from the recesses of pre-history. For many centuries they seem to remain indissolubly linked and then, in Europe, about five hundred years ago, the first signs of definite break appeared. It widens and with the high Renaissance we have an art essentially free and independent, individualistic in its origins and dimming to express nothing beyond the artist's own personality. The history of Western art since the Renaissance is chequered and distorted . . . and finally we begin to think that there can be no great art or great periods of art without an intimate link between art and religion. (Herbert Read)

Indeed, the history of art through the ages, is lamentable. Much like a tree that has been struck by lightning and has been burned and hollowed, but still is a little green and alive, art too has been impoverished of its beauty and basic meaning. Modern and post modern art have been likened to a powerful body with no soul. Perhaps this, more than anything else, describes accurately the condition of mankind today.

Art and Era

When Kandinsky stated that art was the child of its age, he was surely referring to more than just a chronological relationship. Children everywhere are heir to the characteristics, both psychological and physical, of their parents. Yet, there exists a difference between the old generation and the new. This difference is reflected in art. Studying the characteristics of each generation, can steer us towards a better comprehension of the art created in that generation.

The above analogy can be useful in understanding art from a socio-cultural perspective. We may examine a child by studying the process of birth, physical growth, and from the psychological and spiritual dimension.

The process of childbirth was once fraught with difficulties. Infant mortality was high because of unsophisticated methods, an ignorance of hygienic methods and because science and medicine were as yet undeveloped. Today, the process of childbirth is easier, less dangerous and babies survive to become adults. In much the same way, creating a work of art was once difficult because materials were not easily found or even known of, and when they were, not everyone could afford them. Methods of studying nature too were not known or accessible. It is possible that many a great work of art remained caged in the imagination of the artist, never reaching tangible fruition.

Earlier, the growth of children was as difficult as was their birth. Science had not as yet developed methods of enhancing growth and illness was not readily overcome.

Children today are growing better, more healthily and are stronger. Art too, grows faster in the present-day. It gains in popularity because of better communication methods, easier methods of display, etc. Techniques are aided by science and technology to make the production process swifter. The use of computers today, has opened up a new world altogether. While science has advanced enough to make accurate analysis possible and while all elements of art, such as line, form, composition and so on, can be closely studied, both artists and admirers of art have lost sight of the fact that excessive analysis destroys beauty. So closely are we able to examine the separate elements of art that the whole loses its identity and the essence fragments and the meaning is diluted. The closer the artist comes to each constituent of art, the further he moves away from its meaning. Again, this may well reflect man's relationship with the world today — the more closely and minutely he scrutinises the elements of the world, the less he understands it.

To return to the analogy of the child and art, it may be observed that the family unit and social support structures are tending to become less stable and secure. Close family ties have given way to marital discord and children today grow up with more psychological problems than they did earlier. In the same way, the student of art once had a strong relationship with his teacher. Master and disciple had a special relationship wherein the disciple was humble and entirely receptive to the teachings of his master. Learning to be an artist was not a mere matter of learning the techniques of sketching or painting, but learning a way of thinking and a way of life. It involved self-discipline, learning to be pure in spirit and to revere nature and the highest power. Because these values have changed today, the harmony and balance in art, the deeper significance and unity of the work has been diminished, if not lost.

Art and Humanism

Any major influence on man's thought has also been an influence on man's art. For many centuries, religion and spirituality have resulted in art being monopolised by those who wielded religious power. Gradually, humanistic values gained importance and the very subject-matter of art changed to include the human element. Paintings of the regal splendour of courts gave way to those of ordinary people and their lives. The depiction of pain, poverty and stark reality gained acceptance. By portraying severity and deprivation, the artist tried to fulfil a social and moral duty. This is true of Vincent Van Gogh, who in his letters to his brother, said, "My only anxiety is how can I be of use in the world? Can't I serve some purpose and be of any good?" Van Gogh's painting, *The Potato Eaters*, is an example of a painting influenced by humanistic values. Regarding this work, the artist writes, "I have tried to emphasise that those people eating their potatoes in the lamplight have dug the earth with the very hands they put in the dish and so it speaks of manual labour and how they have honestly earned their food. I have wanted to give the impression of a way of life quite different from that of us civilised people. Therefore I am not at all anxious for anyone to like it or admire it at once . . . it might prove to be a real peasant picture, I know it. But he who prefers to see the peasants in their Sunday best may do as he likes. I personally am convinced I get better results by painting them in their roughness than in giving them a conventional charm."

This approach to the subject-matter of art soon gained wide recognition and became an ideology in itself, Socialism. Art reflected the ideology of 'Social Realism', particularly in Russia and the Soviet Union.

In a sense, the status of art regressed from being rooted in truth to being based on reality — not reality as a whole, but merely social reality. Works of art from this period show a muscular, aggressive man, struggling for existence in a universe of which he is the nucleus. Man, is shown as a working machine against the harsh backdrop of factories, tool in hand and resentment in his face. The finer qualities of grace, beauty and love, are absent.

Art: A Protest Against Alienation

One of the hallmarks of modern living is speed. There is perhaps no sphere of life today that remains untouched by the hunger for speed. It has become so crucial to move as fast as possible, man has forgotten where he is going.

Speed, today is an idealogy of civilised life and like all other ideologies that assume an importance for mankind, it has affected art. To begin with, the compulsion for speed has robbed man of his time for reflection and introspection. Nor has man left himself room for ease and rumination. So absorbed is man in the speed of his travel that he does not have time to enjoy the journey. For example, rarely does a person stop to enjoy the sights on his way to work, or revel in the nature that surrounds him. The faster a journey becomes, the less one is able to attend to the elements that one passes. It is a limiting of experience and of the essence of living. Man has forgotten that the journey is more important than the destination, just as living is more important than either birth or death.

When one considers that art is a kind of journey, a seeking of truth and beauty, one immediately realises that speed can serve as a destructive force.

In the Islamic tradition, spiritual travel with two stages, the first Sayr Ilallah, is a search for truth through an understanding of the self leading to enlightenment, and the second Sayr Fillah, (Sayyad Jafar Sajjadi, *Farhang-e Maaref-e Islami*) is oneness with the infinite vastness of the source of enlightenment, Truth. Since there is no concrete destination, the concept of speed is superfluous. In art which is after all, a spiritual journey, today the quest for speed has destroyed identity and has left in its place estrangement. Through the years art has lost its support in religion and spirituality, humanistic values have declined, and there no longer exists a principle for beauty. Instead, there is alienation.

Today, the artist protests against the alienation by protecting his world. He does this by turning inward. Seeking stability and credibility, he begins to rely exclusively on himself. Thus, he is often found to be a recluse or a rebel, unable to conform to the norms of society. Gaugin renounced the world he knew and retired to the island of Tahiti from where he wrote, "I want to forget all the misfortunes of the past. I want to be free to paint without any glory whatsoever, in the eyes of others and want to die there to be forgotten here". In a letter to his wife he writes, "May the day come, perhaps very soon, when I will bury myself in the woods of an ocean island to live on ecstasy, calmness and art. With a new family and far from the European struggle for money."

Post Modernism and Future Art

Alienation and the turning inwards to the self may have resulted in individuality in art. However, the artist, living in a society unable to cope with the stress and pace of modern life is uneasy and restless. This feeling has led to a new form of art known as Post Modern art. As yet vague and inexplicit, post modern art is thought to have freedom from restriction of form, colour, plane, volume, and content. One may well wonder whether this also means a freedom from meaning, for the artist expresses without responsibility for meaning. Devoid of form, content and meaning, post modern art is soon striving for a freedom from existence altogether. With this, the rift of man from nature is almost complete. It is a dead end.

It is interesting to note that the concept of Post Modern art is applied with some difficulty to architecture, since architecture must necessarily have form and content. The fact that traditional elements may be used along with modern style is perhaps a hopeful sign of recovery from the pseudo-freedom of post modernism. The words of Rumi represent this hope:

هر کسی کو دور ماند از اصل خویش

باز جوید روز کار وصل خویش

> Whoever has fallen apart from his origin will again find (search)
> the fortune of his unity.

Art is not a sum total of its period plus material needs. Art was born with man and is a part of his nature. Though art may be passing through a severe winter, the soil does not die, but awaits spring and rejuvenation. As for the future of art, time in nature and in art is not linear but cyclical. The signs that we may go full circle again are already evident. An Easternisation of the West is taking place and all over the world the synthesis between East and West, between one extreme and the other, and between spirit and matter is being sought.

Chapter 24, Verse 35 of the Holy *Quran* states:

> *Allah* is the light of heaven and earth . . . Neither Eastern nor Western . . . *Allah* guides through his light whom he pleases . . . and *Allah* is cognizant of all things.

Man seeks tranquillity and equilibrium and when he finds it, so will his art.

18

Five Elements of Ecology

Satish Kumar

Gaia, Deep Ecology, Permaculture, Bioregions and Creation Spirituality are five new ideas upon which we can build a more holist world-view.

The contemporary thinkers of the green movement are collectively developing an ecological world-view. It has five basic ingredients, or five key terms; they are: Gaia (James Lovelock), Deep Ecology (Arne Naess), Permaculture (Bill Mollison), Bioregionalism (Gary Snyder *et al.*) and Creation Spirituality (Matthew Fox). These five elements give us a structure for an integrated view of Nature.

Gaia is a scientific explanation for understanding the Earth. The majority of scientists do not see the whole Earth as one living organism, or as an interdependent and interconnected whole. But the Gaia hypothesis is changing that. For example, my body is one system. On the top of my head I have my hair which is totally connected with the toe-nail in my foot. Similarly the whole Earth is one body – Gaia.

The Earth as one system has been very graphically presented to us by the pictures of the Earth from space taken by astronauts. They saw, from space, this beautiful icon, looking like a great work of art, all of a piece; there is no division there; you don't see Africa or Europe, white or black, Muslims or Christians, Arabs or Jews, poor or rich, human or non-human, living or non-living – there is no division. You don't see the division between the rainforests, the oceans and the earth. All are part of one body – a planet home.

I experienced that the living Earth as one organism in my own way when I walked around the world. Going across the continents and the countries, across the religious boundaries and the language boundaries, across deserts and wilderness, mountains and valleys, across rivers and forests, was quite an experience, a similar kind of experience as if I had gone into space and seen the Earth from space, because I saw that all those boundaries were artificially created out of fear by the human language.

If we can transcend our perceptions and prejudices, we can see that the Earth is truly one.

The Sanskrit scholars of India believed that *vasudhaiva kutumbakam* which means "the whole Earth is one family". So a tree is not a utilitarian object to build a house with, or make furniture. A tree is a member of my family. Even a worm in the earth is not merely a creature to create nice soil for the food to grow. The worm is a member of my family. If we have this kind of thinking, we will not upset the balance of the Earth, we will not destroy the fabric of nature.

Gaia is an emotional experience as well as a scientific discovery. It is a poetic expression as well as an intellectual concept. Scientists and ordinary people can relate to Gaia equally. Everyone knows that we depend on each other; not only on human beings, but we depend on the worm. If worms were not in the soil working for us, we would not be alive, we would not be able to speak, we would not be able to stand. Whenever we eat our delicious meal we must thank the worms without which the food would not grow.

Once we have understood that the whole Earth is one interconnected entity, then Deep Ecology becomes the next step. The Gaia hypothesis will not be of much use without realizing that everything upon this Earth has intrinsic value — a tree, a worm, a river, all and everything are good in themselves. The tree is not good because it will make nice furniture, or a nice house, or nice firewood. Those are all useful but secondary aspects. The most important thing is that everything upon the Earth has a deep intrinsic value; all things maintain a deep intrinsic relationship to each other. They are good in themselves. We have no right to think that we human beings are more important than, say, rainforests.

There are seven elements, from which this whole universe is made: the earth, fire, water and air are recognized as basic elements by most people in Europe, but for the Indians and Chinese the fifth element is space. Without space we cannot exist. And the sixth one is time; not clock time, but eternal time. And the seventh element is consciousness. Without consciousness we would not be able to relate to anything. Here I will not ponder on the question, whether consciousness came first and then Gaia emerged out of it, or whether Gaia came first and produced consciousness. Perhaps it is truly the chicken and egg problem.

These seven elements are intrinsically and inherently good. Even an earthquake is good. It shows that in the short term it is very painful. But in the long term the Earth is managing, maintaining, correcting and balancing itself. Everything that naturally exists has its own natural balance and harmony; that is Deep Ecology.

Once we accept that Gaia is good, how do we interact with it? We human beings need food; we have to cultivate land; and we have to fulfil our vital needs. We have to collect some trees to build our house; we have to take water from the river; we have to make clothes; we have to make fire to keep warm; we have to breathe air, and we have to use animals. What is the guiding principle upon which our relationship with Gaia is determined? That principle is Permaculture — a culture of permanence, of sustainability.

When we are tilling the soil, or making a product, whether it is paper or shoes or clothes or furniture or electricity or whatever we are producing, we need to do it in a sustainable way. Whether we are in business or farming, in politics, or industry, Permaculture is applicable in every field. The idea of permanence is very much an old idea. The American Indians believed that whatever you do, remember how your action is going to affect the seventh generation. Permaculture helps us to think of posterity, of our children and grandchildren and great-great-great grandchildren, and how they are going to be affected by what we do today. So we cultivate the land, we produce goods, we run our economy, we run our business — we need to design all our activities in such a way that all designs for living contain the idea of permanence. In the back of our minds we need to keep the question, is it sustainable? Is it only for a short-term profit, or is it a long-term, continuous and durable design? The economics of permanence is Permaculture.

Now, once we accept that our relationship with the Earth should be based on the principle of permanence, we need to develop a sense of the place. The Earth is a large planet. Can we depend on butter from New Zealand, coffee from Kenya and tea from India? The Japanese cars are exported to Britain and the British cars are exported to Japan; is this sustainable? Here we have the idea of Bioregions. Mahatma Gandhi called it *swadesi*. Bioregionalism is a decentralized, locally-based economy.

Whatever things can be made locally and produced locally, we should use them first; and things which cannot be produced in our immediate locality should be imported from the nearer neighbourhoods and districts. If they are not available within that area and we still need some, and if it is a vital need, maybe we should get them from a national area. If we still need a few things — but only very, very few things — then we might get them from a continental area. But free World Trade is neither ecological nor sustainable — the amount of energy, the extent of bureaucracy, the amount of time, the degree of administration spent on import and export of goods is wasteful. We need to understand the carrying capacity of a local region, and maintain a stable population. We learn to celebrate the genius of a place. There are so many things growing without even cultivating, but we don't know them — because we think that an exotic thing is exotic only when we get it from Africa or China. But there are also exotic things under our noses.

We are always chasing the foreign market. Governments always say that the only way to develop and strengthen the economy is to find the export market — but what about the home market? They forget it, and they are chasing a competitive market abroad. A bioregional economy is a complementary to the concept of good and durable Gaia. Big institutions cannot be sustained in an ecological world. Bioregional Politics is also an important component. Present national boundaries are residues of past empires and military conquests. Gaian boundaries will be based on biological realities such as rivers, mountains, valleys, cultures and languages.

Gaia, Deep Ecology, Permaculture and Bioregions are practical ideas for an integrated view of nature. But the world cannot be sustained with practical ideas alone. It also needs the spirit. If we do not have a place for the spirit, we will lack meaning. Therefore Creation Spirituality which helps to develop a sense of the sacred is an essential part of an ecological world-view. What does Creation Spirituality mean? It is not a religion, it does not mean that you have to go to church or you have to read the Bible. It means that the human soul and the soil are imbued with the divine principle.

Creation Spirituality helps us to see nature and ourselves differently. The Earth is sacred, trees are sacred, rivers and mountains are sacred. In India people say, "This is the holy river of Ganges". The river of Ganges symbolizes all rivers of the world and they are all sacred. In India there are lots of tree shrines. We don't need to build temples, every tree is a shrine. Creation Spirituality develops a sense of reverence for all life, not just for human life but for all life. Most people accept that human life is sacred, but we cannot choose human life. We value a human being for what he or she is. We believe in the sanctity of human life; we have to extend it to all life. Within human relationships we accept help and service from others. On such occasions we say, "Thank you", and we express a sense of gratitude – that gratitude is Creation Spirituality.

In the same way, when we select a fruit from the tree, or a branch from the tree to make fire, we should say, "Thank you, tree". Even if we don't verbalize it, even if we don't articulate it, it doesn't matter. But deep in our heart if we have that sense of gratitude, then it is Creation Spirituality. If we have that sense because of our attitude of reverence, then we will never be able to pollute or destroy or deface nature. The modern industrial society doesn't have that sense of reverence for nature, and it results in the pollution and degradation of the Earth. The crisis of environment comes out of a utilitarian, materialistic, non-sacred, non-spiritual world-view – "the Earth is there for us to use, for our comfort, for our convenience." As a consequence we have taken from nature without knowing its limits. When we have a sense of reverence, we shall take from nature only what meets our vital needs. And when we take something, we thank, we show gratitude – like we take milk from the mother's breast; the mother is very happy to give her milk in the same way as the Earth is happy to give its fruits as long as we take only what we need. When the baby is full, he or she stops sucking and doesn't go on sucking. Well, unfortunately we humans go on sucking the Earth. Mahatma Gandhi said, "There is enough for everybody's need in this world, but not enough for anybody's greed." So need and greed have to be differentiated. How can you differentiate them? A government cannot legislate for it. A dictator cannot force it. It has to emerge out of our own individual heart, from a sense of beauty, a sense of the divine. When we have that, then we take things from the Earth and always replenish her for what we have taken.

In India every citizen was required to plant five trees and see them to maturity; take care of them, nurture them, look after them, and worship them. That was the *pancavati* of India. Those five trees were seen as a contribution every citizen was making as an act of replenishment, an act of *yajna.* They were for the children and grandchildren and great grandchildren, and for posterity. The earth provides enough essence for the humans, animals and birds to eat, but also enough to return to the earth; the peels, the straw, the pips, the skin, the fruits and vegetables have plenty of good for us to eat and plenty to put back into the compost which goes back into the earth. Thus the earth is replenished. A tree stands out naked, there all winter without leaves; the tree is now replenishing the earth with its leaves; all the leaves have gone back into the earth; they are rotting, making the soil fertile, so that the roots are nourished which in turn gives life to the leaves and to the fruits, a beautiful cycle of replenishment. Nature is our great teacher, and we can learn to replenish and not waste. There is no greater teacher than nature. Even the Buddha and the Christ learned wisdom from nature.

Creation Spirituality is not dependent on any organized religion. It is a sense in your heart that there is much more to life than meets the eye; there is a greater mystery than we can know or measure; and there is greater meaning behind the world of appearance. The light is burning inside us. We need to close our eyes and look within, not in a temple, or in a mosque, or in a synagogue, or somewhere else. The light is not outside. The spiritual light is inside our soul.

The world cannot be saved just by the technocrats, or by the shallow ecologists. They say, "We can manage the environment, we are clever people". But everyone knows that environment cannot be managed. We can only revere environment; we can only respect environment; and we can only see environment as part of us and us part of environment. This total unity can come only when you have a spiritual base and not just a utilitarian base.

19

Common Roots for Transfer of Culture

M. Vannucci

Dr. P. Banerjee said, during giving a lecture at IGNCA, October 27 1992, on "Arts of Central Asia: Chinese Turkistan", that "intuition is sometimes more valuable than knowledge." This never applies better than when we search into the human mind of centuries past and when we try to understand what were the roots of human habits and culture. The intuition of the scholar is akin to the revelation that a *rsi* or a saint may have had. The concept of the five 'elements', usually designated as "The Elements", is a concept that developed and evolved, independently or not, in most ancient cultures: how much was due to intuition and to the common nature of the mind of man and how much was due to direct transfer of knowledge and culture among different people, is a difficult proposition that has no general or sure answer.

Each one of the 'elements' is roughly comparable to the corresponding one of other cultures, however each one has its own characteristics in the context of each culture and each one is tinted by the peculiarities of the culture to which it belongs. Furthermore, in comparing the perception of the five elements by different people, it becomes clear that the relative importance given to each varies; the differences appear to be influenced by the type of environment and climate in which each culture developed.

It should be clarified that the "five basic elements" that are the subject of the present note, are not the same as the chemical, simple or compound 'elements' that are the units of which organic and inorganic matter is formed; the study of the structure and dynamics of chemical molecules and elements are the subject and object of chemistry and physico-chemistry while at that atomic and sub-atomic levels, they are the object of physico-chemistry and physics. At the environmental level they are ecological, cultural and philosophical 'elements', as for instance air, water, or the properties of mercury.

The "five basic elements" already recognized at the origin of most cultures can best be described in contemporary scientific terms, as the "basic environmental elements". It is precisely because they are environmental elements that they have been observed and considered of great importance by all men in all cultures in one form or another. Life and death are the main concerns of thinking man and one may venture to imagine what would the mind perceive as the basis of this unexplainable phenomenon that is life. Man would see:

EARTH

The solid matter from which comes all food directly or indirectly; all materials for shelter, clothing and utensils. Hence earth or soil and rocks are usually called Mother, or the one who feeds and carries her children before and after birth, while alive and after death.

WATER

The liquid matter for drinking, indispensable to preserve life but necessary also as a cleansing agent, for cooking and for extracting substances from solid matter. Earth and Water are closely related.

AIR

The gaseous matter necessary for respiration and combustion and for the production of light; earth, water, air are the indissoluble trio without which there is no life.

FIRE

The transformer of matter into non-matter, is the heat or energy that keeps everything, living and non-living always on the move.

ETHER or *AKASA*

Non-matter or void which is the imponderable, unexplainable, undescribable aspect of nature that pervades everything. Everything has an opposite and *akasa* is the opposite of matter. In a way *akasa* is similar to the magic or *asu* that endows the Great Asura Varuna with *maya* or magic power and that gives existence to the unreal, whatever it is that we call 'real'. The most ancient Aryan Gods, it would be recalled, are frequently invoked as *Asura* in the *Rgveda* (*RV*), because they are imbued with *asuryan* or '*asura*-hood' that gives them almost illimited and infinite power; consequently, therefore, they are endowed also with *asurasya* or lordly power, as Varuna himself has.

The five environmental elements were first conceived from the observation of nature and as natural elements they were born in the mind of man. In many cultures they have retained their original characteristics, as for instance in Vedism, Brahmanism, Hinduism, Buddhism and Jainism, while in other cultures they may have acquired different connotations, even those of what later came to be known as chemical elements. In ancient Greece, the original four elements were earth, water, air, fire and they were well defined and established by the fifth century BC. Aristotle (384-322 BC) superimposed on them four qualities: cold and dry (earth), cold and wet (water), hot and wet (air) and hot and dry (fire). Though this perspective is to some extent biologically and ecologically valid, the resulting rigidity of thought imposed by the great personality of "The Master" who always had the last word: "Magister dixit" or: "the master has said", lingered on and stiffled European scientific thought up to the fifteenth-sixteenth centuries and the Renaissance. The basic elements in Europe after Aristotle gradually became absorbed into alchemy, hence the use of the same noun: elements for the chemical as for the environmental ones.

But let alchemy go its own way and let it eventually develop into chemistry and let us return to our four or five environmental elements.

In contrast to the ancient Greek learning where the character of the original elements was changed early, in other cultures the four – or five – elements maintained their original characteristics and acquired a defined meaning as the basis of the body, intellect and spirit, and of the whole world we live in. Man tried to give concrete expression to his identification with nature and to his desire to participate in natural events. There is an ancient practice still widely used in Bali, to dress tree stumps with clothing and with a head gear, the colours of which are symbolic of the elements or of some of them, to give them a human semblance. The Indian folklore is rich in the personalization of plants and animal forms and species; thus the interaction between man and nature is intimate, constant and consciously kept alive.

Let us consider the importance of the five elements in the Indian cultural context. The most remarkable trait is that the concept of the elements remained unchanged over the ages and the respective rôle of each was preserved intact, which shows that the original perception of nature was rational and therefore valid. Stated briefly the reasons of this persistence and of the correct view of nature's functioning could be that man in India, pre-Aryan autochthonous people, the Vedic man and the following people who lived in geographically major India, have always lived in close symbiosis with nature and obedience to *Rta*, the natural law was a must and man had to learn his lesson well. Another reason could be that the sub-continent as a whole offers all types of ecosystems and therefore all environmental elements are represented, but they carry different weight and exercise a different impact on the daily life of mankind in different places, say the arid zone of Rajasthan, the high Himalayan mountains, the sub-tropical southern part of the peninsula or the humid forests of north-east India;

taken together the role that is recognized for each element is balanced in relation to the others. Finally, an added reason could be that Vedic man on reaching Saptasindhu, after migrating over many generations from Central Asia through different types of environments and climates, had the opportunity to observe the action, the effects and the relative importance of each of the five elements. The balanced role and mutual interaction of the five elements is a fundamental trait of Vedic philosophy.

The concept of basic elements is practically the same in the Asian tradition as it was in the Hellenic pre-historic or Mycenean age and the early historic period tradition. The main difference lies in that Indians did not expound precisely formulated theories that could be tested experimentally, while the philosophers of the Hellenic tradition in the Mediterranean world, did formulate scientific theories regarding the function of nature's elements, and these influenced decisively the evolution of the European thought. The establishment of fixed theories or rules, like the Aristotelian principles of unity of space, time and action or logic, were in practice a cause of stagnation rather than evolution of thought and the acquisition of new knowledge was starved at its roots. In contrast the fluidity of thought and the non-formulation of dogmatic laws about the universe of nature permitted an open-minded development and evolution of the thought of Indian philosophers. This in turn favoured the incorporation of the knowledge acquired into the corpus of Vedic lore. The formulation of the concept that everything changes and may evolve or involve uninterruptedly, left all entries open to further developments anchored, as it were, in the laws of *Rta* that govern the functioning of the cosmos, including Earth and all that is in and on it. The theories were not expounded as such, but the relations of cause and effect and the interrelation of natural elements and laws were and are well-known in practice. Practicalities of everyday life could be adapted to changed places and circumstances while at the same time the basic philosophic formulation of nature's laws could be retained, exactly because of its openness that always admits one more exception or one more "special case". Adaptations of plants and animals to the limits of their survival capacity can be observed everywhere in nature, but Aristotelism inevitably condemned the obvious evolution and constant change of everything in space and time. In contrast, in the Indian context, knowledge — or Truth — is not bound by rigid theories and would naturally accept the obvious fact of the evolution of all processes of matter and spirit. Consequently it is logical to admit that the five basic elements acquire different roles and weight under different conditions of geography, climate and ecological factors. This could be termed scientific alertness or constructive criticism; it is philosophically expressed as tolerance and open-mindedness.

In medieval Europe scientific endeavours and discoveries were suppressed and

Plate 19.1 A guardian at the enterence of the sacred enclosure, Bali

Plate 19.2 The violent volcanic environment of Bali

even as great a personality as Dante Alighieri only shily expresses natural laws in as disguised a manner as possible. For instance the law of the identity of the angles of the incident and reflected rays of light is clearly formulated in the Divina Commedia, but it is unobtrusively stated and it can easily remain unnoticed. In contrast the concept of *Rta* as the law and order of nature that varies in the space-time continuum promotes and favours the "unveiling of Truth" which is the same as favouring the continuous acquisition of knowledge through understanding. From this lack of rigidity the *Artha* are derived that in turn pave the way for further search of knowledge, for instance *Ayurveda* has not ceased to evolve and develop since its inception.

It may be interesting to note that the rural folk and the "home sciences" in Europe, themselves innocent of Aristotelian principles, developed their own empirical 'science', important among them the health sciences, the proper use of different foods at different times and seasons for different purposes, genders and ages of man and his domestic animals, according to the seasonal changes of earth, water, air, temperature and vitality of nature. This is vividly reflected in the title of a book in 543 pages on medicinal and other useful plants by Palaiseul (1972) that reads: "Nos grandmeres savaient . . ." or: "Our grand-mothers knew . . ."

In India the perception of the five elements is well balanced. Earth is solid matter, the substratum on which we walk, sleep and are — or where — entered, meaning buried; earth is the provider of foods and all sorts of useful materials. As the good provider, *Prthivi* is 'mother' and there would be no better epithet. Water as liquid is indispensable to sustain life in all biological systems, for drinking, for the metabolic functioning of the body and for cleansing body, shelter, domestic animals and to prepare food and medicines. Air as gas is the weightless vital breath without which life and fire, the universal energy, are suffocated. Agni, Fire, the primordial God, is the energy of the whole universe that expresses and manifests itself in an unlimited number of ways, fire is capable of interchanging matter and energy and its omnipresent. Finally *Akasa* or void, which is the undeterminable 'something' that reason indicates must exist to fill in the gaps between the element's particles and inside the elements themselves, throughout the cosmos. But none of this would ensure correct functioning of nature and the universe, if each did not "do its duty by observing *Rta*". The balanced and adequate action of each element is recognized as indispensable, the best example of this order is the disciplined movement of celestial bodies, considered to have a life of their own because they move, even if a peculiar type of life.

According to ancient thought the existence of the physical and the essential or spiritual worlds is due to the interaction of the basic environmental elements, therefore all natural things are sacred, specially the most mysterious of them all: life. As Quintus Curtius (1st century A.D.) remarks about Indians: "*Deos putant quid quid colere coeperunt, arbores maxima, quas violare capitule est*" (. . . they . . . consider as God all that they can collect or reap, specially trees, the falling of which is a capital offence) and in the *Divyavadana*, I, p. 1 it is said that there are *devata* for everything: gardens, forests and jungles, trees, river *sangams* and everything else; but the *deva's* main duty is to see that the laws of *Rta* are not broken.

Living a wholesome life close to nature ensures a rational view of the necessary interaction of the basic elements. However, climatic and local factors, as for instance the fierce sun — *Surya* — is inevitably considered to be the dominant element in water and vegetation-scarce desert areas. The greatest title given to Rajput kings was that of *Suryavamsa*. The high peaks are abodes of Gods for all people and the more inaccessible they are, the more sacred; wind is violent expression of air that may occasionally fall out of tune and cause avalanches, whirlwinds, dust or sand storms or other calamities. Coastal areas and riverine people have water as their main object of devotion and while ritual washing may be pardoned to water deprived dwellers of dry areas, it would be unforgivable for a coastal or riverine person to offer prayers without prior ablution with water, "the cleansing one". At Eleusis in Greece and at Rameswaram in India, both places near the sea shore, a sea water bath for purification of initiates, worshippers and sacrificial animals was — and is — obligatory or common practice. *Agni*, fire, the great purifier, is universally revered, honoured and invoked by all people from all culture since their origin; fire is the manifested or potential ubiquitous energy of "what moves not and moves".

Rgveda Mandala X.121, is a hymn dedicated to *Ka* or *Kah*: Who? Whom? We shall not discuss here whether this hymn is a "recent addition" or whether some of the stanzas are later interpolations; I shall abide by Max-Mueller's conclusion that it must be "previous not only to the *Brahmana* period but also to the *Mantra* period, or earlier than 1000 BC." According to scholars *Kah* is the interrogative pronoun "Who?" and authors have followed Max-Mueller in considering *Kah* "the unknown God". The refrain has been translated: "to what God shall we offer oblations?" (Max-Mueller) or "what God shall we adore with our oblation?" (Griffith) or "to what God may we pay worship with oblation?" (Whitney). It seems to me that it is more correct to regard *Kah* as the unnamed or nameless, but not the unknown God. *Kah* should be translated plainly as 'who' or 'it'. The Supreme Entity cannot be designated by name, out of respect its name should not be pronounced, it is awe-inspiring, it is the Supreme Entity. The South Siberian Turks say: "it is not permitted to call you by name". Hence the general use of the neutral as an uncompromising appellation of the unthinkable, undescribable, unimaginable, illimited in space and time, without beginning or end, present nowhere and everywhere, the self-existent. The same approach is expressed beautifully in the questions that Yudhishthira addressed to Bhishma. The replies given by Bhishma and the commentaries by Adi Shankara in his *Vishnu Sahasranama Bhasya*, all point clearly in the same direction: *Kah*, Who or Whom, is the Supreme Entity, perhaps mentally represented by *Akasa*.

The Sanskrit word *nama* is literally translated as name, though the original meaning would be rendered better by the word 'attributes': the nameless in fact has infinite attributes, as recited by Bhishma. The name of the hierophant, who was the chief priest of the temple of Demeter at Eleusis, could not be spoken because his sanctity was paramount. Hieronimy was the rule forbidding under severe penalty the calling or mentioning the hierophant by his personal name. The personal name was lost upon entering the sacred office, "the mystic law cast it away into the sea !" Much importance is given to the name and the reticence in pronouncing people's names as a mark of respect persists and persons are usually addressed by their title or family name or by their special designation rather than by their personal names. The South Siberian Turks are forbidden to pronounce the name of Amagan Calu Gadaci, the feminine spirit that lives on mountain Yalangjiy and who is extremely powerful; only the shaman can pronounce her name (Invocation to the spirit of Amagan Calu Gadaci). The habit has also been imposed by the Hebrew-Christian tradition as a binding law though in a different form: "Thou shalt not use the name of the Lord in vain", which is one of Moses' Ten Commandments.

Here rises another misleading factor that has negatively influenced Western scholars. Because of etymological reasons, the sanskrit *Deva*, *Devata* which is the same root as the Latin and neo-latin word *Deus* has been rendered into the English word God. As Max-Mueller has correctly pointed out (p. 3, *Notes to RV*, X.121): "to us (Europeans) the conception of one God pervades the whole of this hymn"... to *Kah*. In the *Sastra* however, the *Deva* are nowhere equalled to the Supreme and they are not exactly the same. Proves it the fact that the *Deva*, except for *Agni* are not indefinitely immortal and their life comes to an end at the end of each *kalpa*. The misconception that the Vedic, Hindu, Buddhist word 'God' is the same as the "one God" recognized by Max-Mueller in *RV*, X.121, has caused much confusion in the interpretation of the Sacred Texts. It can be concluded that *Kah* – Who? It? – is indeed *Isvara*, the Ultimate Reality, the *Brahmam* "who is the God to whom we shall offer sacrifices", and not the unknown, but the unnamed or nameless.

RV, X.121 is particularly interesting in the context of the present note since among others, it explicitly expresses the view that the four basic natural elements are the elements of which the universe is formed, plus *Kah* that is everywhere and always, that is unseen, unfelt, unheard, untasted, unsmelled and difficult to visualize mentally or even to understand. In this sense *Kah* is unknown, it is so great that it cannot be mentally apprehended; it is a fulfilment or added dimension to the concept of *Akasa*. In other words, the basic query of the hymn is a search for the ultimate cause of the existence of the universe. *Akasa* can be inferred in the text and the other four elements are clearly expressed.

In 121.1, "earth and sky are said to be fixed and held up by *Hiranyagarbha*, the golden embryo or golden germ or seed that marks the auspicious beginning of all that is, of all created beings: *bhuta*, which of course includes also living beings, infused with the life principle of golden *Savitur*. In fact, in 121.2, *Hiranyagrabha* is said to be the giver of breath, power and vigour "whose shadow is immortality or death". This can be interpreted thus: "the unnamed God, the initial seed gives protection and under its shadow life can be used well, giving immortality, or poorly spelling death. In fact 'he' (ish) became the ruler of living things, man and animals (121.3). Under 121.4 it is stated that mountains (solid matter) and water (liquids, sea, rivers) are "his arms", or parts of it's body. Under 121.5 'he' establishes the firmament and measures 'sky' or air. Finally the fourth element, the energy that animates the universe and transforms the material into immaterial and *vice versa, Agni* or Fire, is mentioned in 121.6 as expressed by *Surya*. Accordingly *Agni* is not only the energy principle that governs the struggle for life (121.5), as is also mentioned in other contexts in the *RV*, but also the energy of God himself and obviously of life that sustains the germ or seed that was carried by the mighty waters. The word great or mighty is also used to describe the mountains that are the source of water of the mighty rivers of Saptasindhu, sustainers of life. Further, 121.8 reminds us that the overlord, the God above all Gods is the one who surveyed the floods that held the power. Power here means energy, all forms of energy, including the life energy of golden *Savitur*. *Kah* the nameless God with infinite attributes is finally (121.10) invoked as the righteous, the one who beget the earth, water, air and light. In *RV*, X.121.10 the name of Prajapati is mentioned, but there is no reason to believe that *Kah* and Prajapati are one and the same, as some authors have done. On the contrary, what is most probably meant is that Prajapati as the lord of all creatures, as the elder of men is the one who can understand the meaning, since: "O Prajapati, thou alone comprehendest all these created things, and none other". It would also be recalled that this hymn is recited at several important occasions, even the *caturmasya* and *agnicayana* rituals, which proves its universal validity.

Most significantly, the refrain of the hymn to *Kah* is reflected in almost identical terms in the first four of the six questions that Yudhishtira addressed to Bhishma lying on the bed of arrows awaiting the beginning of the *uttarayana*, or the winter solstice. The first four questions can be rendered thus: "What is the one supreme Godhead?"; "What is the one supreme goal?"; "Praising which do we attain the goal?"; "Worshipping which do men gain good?". As a reply Bhishma first describes the nameless and states that the supreme goal is Reality or *Brahman*; then he recites the thousand names of God. Adi Shankara gave a well-known beautiful image saying: "As air that enters into material things takes many shapes according to the things it has entered into. So the One who is the internal *Atma* of all things is outwardly of many forms." The questions, answers and commentaries appear to be derived directly from *RV*, X.121.

Even this short analysis of *RV*, X.121 shows the balanced importance given to the five elements in the thought of Vedic Man. All elements are necessary and indispensable and the whole world or universe as seen with Vedic eyes would not function if the parts were not equilibrated in their mutual interaction; if the balance is broken, malformations, disease and death are the unavoidable consequences. This truth is universally valid.

Another important hymn reveals the clear understanding of nature that the *rsi* had, this is *RV*, VII.103, a Vasistha hymn, dedicated to the *mandukah*, the frogs. It reveals a mature concept of the five environmental elements, their mutual relationships and their interaction with other elements. Unfortunately Max-Mueller remarks (*Ancient Sanskrit Literature*, p. 494) that "the hymn . . . which is called a panegyric to the frogs is a clear satire of the priests". This misconception was repeated by many scholars after Max-Mueller, including Renou (1956, p. 45). The hymn far from being given in a light vein, reflects a good knowledge of nature and of the relationship between the environment and man as exemplified by a description of the behaviour and life cycle of frogs; it also mentions the relationship between rain and climate in general, soil, water and the elements among themselves, as expressed also in *Atharvaveda* (*AV*), IV.14. Frogs are symbol of fecundity in many cultures because their life-cycle can be completed only if there is water in the ponds, which in turn indicates that rains have been adequate to 'fertilize' the fields for agricultural activities and for pasture. Among the South Siberian Turks, frogs are also mentioned, together with others, as inhabiting the netherworld, perhaps because they must hide themselves in underground holes during the hot, dry season. In a curious parallel, Aristophanes in his comedy 'Frogs' that was undoubtedly known to Max-Mueller, was said to ridicule the cult to Demeter and the 'open' part of the mysteries of Eleusis because of the chanting of priests that was compared to that of the frogs.

Saraswati and Vidyalankar (1980, p.2799) have cleared the misconception concerning the hymn to the frogs and have explained it thus: ". . . the frogs . . . practice penance throughout the year like *Brahmanas* and utter prayers to clouds (1); they hybernate throughout the year and the moment clouds pour water, they wake up and croak (2); at the time of rains, one frog greets the other with croaking as inarticulate as a child (3); the speckled frog leaps up and greets the green one (4); they play in waters with their bodies fully developed (5); they are of a variety of colours and their voices different; some bellow like a cow and some bleat like a goat (6); like the Brahmana at the Soma and Atiratra rites these frogs croak around the lake replenished with water (7); they appear to be reciting perennial prayers, like the ministrant priests with their *gharma* offerings; and during the heat they hide in holes (8); they come out only when the rains return and attain freedom from their hiding places (9).

Two of the species described probably are *Rana tigrina* that is large, congregates in tanks and ponds at the breeding season and is a voracious feeder. The other could well be *Rana cyanophlyctes* that is very common, entirely acquatic and has the habit of skipping over the surface of the water over small distances. Frogs are very sensitive to environmental factors, specially temperature, humidity and atmospheric pressure; indeed they are almost like natural barometers and species are quickly decimated by the growing pollution throughout the world; their colour changes to match the colour of the background, they also become darker at night. Their behaviour, as any village child knows, such as feeding or not, burrowing or not, mating or not is indicative of environmental conditions. Most species are active after dusk and hide away during daytime when humidity drops below their limit of tolerance and there is the danger of drying out. *Rsi* Vasistha was a keen and accurate observer of nature.

In the *Nirukta* it is also said that Vasistha praised Parjaniya, the cloud, to propitiate rains and that the frogs applauded him so that the *rsi* in turn praised them. Whatever the mythology behind it, this loose rendering of the hymn (*RV*, VII.103) shows that it is zoologically and ecologically correct, though much more can be inferred from the text. For instance, frogs give many useful services, as adults they feed on insects, worms and other small animals some of which are noxious, like malaria vector mosquitoes; as tadpoles they clear the water from algal and weed growth. At present rearing of frogs has been practised to help combat malaria. I have shown elsewhere (Vannucci, under press) that the hymn implies several important details, such as the existence of frogs of different species each with its specific mating call; the metamorphosis from tadpole to adult, mentioned in (5) where it is mentioned "with their limbs (only the adult has limbs) fully extended or developed". Seasonal cycles are described, as well as the frog's reaction to climatic changes; details of the habits of different species, such as floating motionless with legs extended at the surface of the water, their reproductive cycle (6) and their posture. The overall life-giving aspect of rains is beautifully expressed and in the context of the present note, the hymn is interesting in that it shows perfect understanding of the relative roles and interrelations between earth, water, climate, seasonal cycles and of the dynamics of life, or life energy that is clearly expressed in (5): as they move and leap on the waters with limbs swelled with energy, or, as SS and SV write: "every limb throbs and swells" or "every limb seems to be growing larger" in Griffith's translation. To this day throughout India it is taken as natural to relate many frogs with good pastures and good crops, fat cows and goats; this in Vedic terms means that the frogs are granting us riches.

Frogs are bearers of good omen among the Central and northern South American ancient civilizations as well as in the Mediterranean folklores. In Italy it was common to see in the junior classes aquaria for rearing tadpoles to teach practically the details of the life-cycle and metamorphosis from tadpole to fully formed four legged adults, and after metamorphosis, frogs and tadpoles were let loose in the fields.

The parallel that *rsi* Vasistha draws between the frogs and the *Brahmanas*, far from being derogatory expresses the meaningfulness of everything and the wonders and sacredness of all nature. The *Atiratra* ritual mentioned in (7) is held at night and lasts the night long as also the song of the frogs that marks the mating season and the renewal of life. Frogs in fact link earth, water, air and fire as energy and if there is not a good balance in time and quantity of these four elements, frogs cannot complete their life-cycle. The presence of frogs is indeed an auspicious sign.

Among the South Siberian Turks, frogs are spirits of sacred terrestrial place, including, as mentioned, the underworld. In the invocation to the spirits of the Earth it is said: "rich six-legged frog". Six-legged camels and six-eyed tigers are mentioned as auspicious, however six-legged frogs could also refer to the mating posture when the male's front legs are hidden under the female while he holds her firmly in the amplexus; the pairs of frogs during the many hours of mating look like a single animal with six legs. The act of mating in general is taken as a good omen and one to be respected, as also the act of consuming the earth given food and water. The frog, as an auspicious animal is represented on the lower part of the shaman's ritualistic drum and accompanies him in the voyages that his spirit does while he is in trance. There are many common denominators between the myths and legends of the Mediterranean and the Asian Indo-European and other people of the same stock, but at this late stage of evolution, it is difficult to have a correct perspective of the exchanges that have taken place between different cultures.

To avoid lengthening unduly this discussion I will refrain from quoting the large number of places where the elements, their place in nature and their interdependence are mentioned in the *Veda*. I would rather draw only one more example: *RV*, X.168 is a hymn addressed to *Vayu* that shows how powerful the Wind is, it has the voice of thunder and reaches to heaven, it causes whirlwinds and dust storms over the earth while unremittingly he speeds forth in his car in middle air. But *Vayu* is also the friend of waters, he is the vital spirit of deities and there is no life without air and water.

Shamanism is an ideological system with a peculiar concept of the world's structure and function. It can be viewed as a complex of different techniques practised by the shaman with the purpose of establishing a direct relation between man and the supernatural world; it usually culminates with the trance of the shaman. In Asia, shamanism has its centre in Central Asia but is practised throughout the continent irrespective of the religion of the people, because shamanism is not a religion. Essentially most ancient Asian cultures have contributed to the techniques used and to the beliefs expressed by the shaman which he uses to achieve the contact desired. Shamanism incorporates certain aspects of ancient naturalistic religions, magic pictures and the concept of four or five environmental elements; in many ways it preserves the oral tradition that is incorporated in the shaman's words, functions and practices. Only since the middle of last century have the words of the shaman in trance been recorded in written form, they show clearly that the ancient roots of different people and traditions are alive and have become integrated to a greater or lesser degree into the cultures into which they have become assimilated in the course of time. As preservers of tradition the chants of the shamans are interesting in the present context of the perception of the five environmental elements by the different people. The largest amount of transcripts taken *ipsis litteris* comes from the lore of the South Siberian Turks who are of Indo-European stock; it is therefore not astonishing to find many similarities and parallelism between their culture and that of Rgvedic man. Two simple examples could be mentioned: "Let everything be transmitted (to the Gods) to and by fire" — "Let everything be transmitted to the Great Yayiq (flowing water)" and other expressions in a lengthy invocation to the spirit of the taiga, which is **the** earth for the people living there. Originally, as elsewhere, there were probably only 'white' or benevolent shamans, the development of harmful practices or "black magic" is a late development inexistent in the original shamanism and ancient traditions. Finally, the word 'shaman' is taken from the Tunguese language and it has been postulated that it is derived from the same roots as the Sanskrit *sraman* (Marazzi, 1984, p. 21).

The ideas and concepts of the oral tradition and early philosophies of life are incorporated in the present-day chants and texts recited by the shaman in trance, but they have been influenced over the ages, by different religions. Traditionally the shaman, both male and female, is saddled with the heavy burden of the power with which he or she is endowed not at his or her request. This power the shaman has the duty to use to obtain concrete benefits for humans, their domestic animals and fields. The texts that we have at present in direct transcript are the supreme word in the relations between the spirit of the shaman and the supernatural entities called spirits and rarely called by name, though they have one. A direct relationship is established between similar beings: the non-material spirit of the shaman and that of the non-material spirits invoked for a particular purpose; the spirit of the shaman leaves the body during the trance to contact the spirits that live in the void and who are believed to be capable of rendering the services requested by the shaman on behalf of the common human being who does not have the power as the shaman has. The shaman thus assumes the role otherwise performed by fire, they are both mediators respectively between God and man and between spirits and man.

In the context of the present note, I have not found in the large number of texts consulted any systematic treatment of the five elements in the shamanistic literature of Central Asia. Environmental elements, however, are frequently invoked in isolation or not and they are eulogized, their attributes and powers are recognized.

Fire, presumably taken since the origins as energy, or what would more naturally be called power, is invoked at all important rites and at all important homely rituals and actions, such as for instance putting the new-born baby into the cradle, or before invoking different divinities; no shaman would ever approach any spirit without the permission of "mother fire"; interestingly fire is invoked both in the feminine and in the masculine genders. Fire boils or roasts for human consumption the flesh of animals sacrificed during rites and fire is itself fed with butter: "May powerful fire transmit my requests". In the invocation to the spirits of the "Real Earth" of the South Siberian Turks fire is the most eulogized element because of its power, its omnipresence as heat and energy and its practical uses. Offerings to fire include horse fat, tea, an alcoholic drink made of fermented mare's milk, butter and more rarely also milk. Fire and iron are here as elsewhere closely associated and one is reminded of the three-ridged dagger if the Tibetan *lamas* that is used for killing the spirits and of the waving of iron objects to frighten them away in many other places.

In everyday life it is admitted that there is a spirit to everything, from the door of the yurta of the Turks, to the fermented mare's milk, tools, forests, people and animals, but the spirit of the yurta's hearth is the most powerful of all spirits. It is the spirit of fire that alone can transfer the spirits of the shaman from one sky to the next during its travels for pleading with the spirits to fulfil human desires and needs and for healing purposes.

The sky is often the object of important prayers and invocations; air is mentioned in the fumigation processes common to all rituals, it marks symbolically the link between fire and air, the sublimation of solids and liquids into nothingness and fumigation also has practical purposes of disinfection. Air is praised as the medium through which birds and spirits move, including the spirit of the shaman who also 'flies' and air is praised as sky or heaven. The cult of heaven or sky is very ancient and amongst others marks the link between air and water, it is invoked as giver of rain and as such it is related to earth, its mountains and rivers. The South Siberian Turks for instance, believe in the existence of three cosmic levels; sky or heaven, nether-world and earth in between; "venerable great earth, we beseech you . . ." as is a repeated invocation and earth is the praise of the fourth sky "with its handsome earth and its forests"; earth is invoked as the one on which and from which mankind lives. At the centre of the world is placed the mountain Aq Toson Altai Sini where resides Cari-Su, a name that literally means earth/water and that derives from a very ancient deity of the early Turks, called Yar Sub. Similarly the Lord-spirit of the Altai mountains is the one who nourishes everything while the spirit of the cold wind, Canagan Qam inhabits the glaciers. Mountains as earth, are object of veneration and at the centre of Mount Altai Sini is found the navel of the Earth. The tayga and vaste prairies and forests, as elements of earth, are also objects of devotion.

We could recall here that the classical Japanese flower arrangement or *Ikebana* has three levels: Heaven above, Earth the lowest and man in between.

Interestingly, among the Turks, water is usually thought of as rivers, lakes and only seldom as rains.This reflects the geography and climate of rain starved Central Asia that is however traversed by several important rivers and has many lakes. The Lord-spirit of water is present in every lake and has to be propitiated with food before fishing, probably a symbolic gesture related to recycling in nature: whatever one takes must be returned to nature in one form or another. The Lord-spirit of waters is requested to give healing power to springs in general and to warm water springs in particular; it obviously refers to the cleansing power of water and to the medicinal value of mineral waters. Medicinal waters are called *arsan* by the South Siberian Turks, a word that has been approximated to *rasayana* in Sanskrit. One is reminded of the hot water springs and the health value of the Kulu-Manali valleys and the "Vasistha baths" not far from the source of the Beas river.

All offerings made to the four elements include libations with fermented drinks, specially *araqi* that is distilled from fermented milk and *ayran* that is a special fermented milk. However, unlike other places, names and genders usually are not strictly determined. As mentioned, fire can be both masculine and feminine or even mentioned as "sweet mother of fire" and there are many names and different genders for spirits of the same elements; there are even several deities and spirits of fire of both genders, however the fire of the hearth is the most sacred.

This is not the time to go into details of the parallelisms between the shamanistic texts of different people of Central Asia and many aspects of the *Rgveda* or more so of the *Atharvaveda* suffices it to say that there are many and they are significant. One may wonder how much is due to common origin of Indo-European cultures, how much is due to the fact that human mind and people are basically the same everywhere, and how much is due to direct transfer of cultures. In comparing the relative importance given to the four — or five — elements in Central Asia, earth is mainly seen as mountains, forests and the wind-swept tayga; water is rarely mentioned as rain but rather as rivers, lakes or even glaciers; air is mainly feared as wind and is traversed by a host of spirits that animate and inhabit everything everywhere. Fire is of course ubiquitous and powerful. I could not perceive the concept of void, ether or *akasa* in the texts, unless we consider the immaterial ever-present spirits of good and bad to exist in void and use air as a mean to travel about, they have no material entity. The texts of the Yacut people recited during the travels of the spirit of the shaman at the most important and very ancient ritual called *Isiax* roughly follow the sequence "earth, water, air, fire" but the elements are neither treated individually as such nor is there a discussion or description of their attributes. The same could be said of the Yacut invocation to the Lord-spirit of the forest. One is thus led to believe that the long history of the evolution of the Central Asian cultures has abutted to rites and ceremonies that include ancient wisdom but the roots of the knowledge are lost in time. Knowledge has been crystallized into rituals and practices that may include ancient wisdom but the details of the original ideas and concepts have become blurred and are often unrecognizable.

Lievre and Loude (1990) produced a book dealing with the shamanism practised in the Hindukush-Karakorum range where live the Chitrals, the Kafirs, the Kalash and other people of Indo-European extraction. These people remember their ancient culture and frequently repeat: "In ancient times, when people were mixed . . . at the beginning, gods, spirits, humans, animals and plants lived together and spoke the same language." Among these mountain people the concept of the five environmental elements is not, at present, expressed as a well defined body of knowledge or description of the world is which they live; but the whole life of the individual, of the family and of the society revolves around the annual cycle of nature, marked by the observation of the solstices and equinoxes. While the major festivities occur at the winter solstice that usually marks the beginning of the year, the spring equinox is the most joyous one. A close analysis of the celebrations carried out at these occasions, the chants, dances, sacrifices, rites and rituals and ritualistic performances, the preparation and consummation of food and fermented drinks from grapes, the libation and the interventions of the shaman indicate an holistic appreciation of nature and respect for all the elements. They also show a strong will of man to fully participate in the natural phenomena of the universe of which he knows to be a part. Thus the four — or five — elements are, so to speak, merged into a single whole: NATURE, and in this capacity they are celebrated and venerated. The habits and culture of these people are not far removed from those of Vedic man and their main God is Indra, who may have slightly different names art different places, but who arrives figuratively at the festivals and celebrations on horseback, usually during the trance of the shaman.

Here too air and fumigation are an essential part of most home and community rites and of course Fire is always the most exalted and ever present entity without whose participation nothing spiritual, religious or practical can be transacted. Fire is also among these mountain people the messenger between man, Gods and the supernatural in general. Spirits and fairies are ubiquitous and participate in human affairs. Fire, juniper, blood are common denominators in the practices of communication between man and the supernatural powers throughout the Hindukush-Karakorum range.

In ancient Egypt, the rising of the star now called Sirius, which is the *alpha Canis majoris* or *Mrigavyadha,* in ancient Sanskrit terminology, marked the summer rise of the waters of the Nile. Of the five elements, water was specially important since the parched land would not produce unless watered and fertilized by the Nile floods. Hence the importance of the rising of Sirius. The Sun was object of very special adoration both by the priests of Ammon as by the heretic cult installed at Tell-el-Amarna by the pharaoh Amenophis IV or Akenaton who declared it to be the only God. The good earth provided the bitumen to give immortality to the mummies. The four elements were recognized in the annual cycle of nature and the Book of the Dead gives at places the idea of void, or ether. River water is otherwise the dominant element in the nature cult of ancient Egypt and is still one of the objects of major concern for modern Egyptians. Finally I would like to mention the curious coincidence that the soul of the deceased is called *Ka* and represented as a small bird sitting at the edge of the sarcophagus.

I would like to add a note about Demeter, her daughter Persephone and the ancient 'mysteries' at Eleusis, not far from Athens, in Attika. Demeter is an earth goddess, mother earth in its agricultural aspects, related to wheat and barley. Demeter lost her daughter Persephone to Pluto, the king of Hades, the nether world, who abducted her. Demeter desperately searched for her daughter until Zeus took pity on her and allowed his own daughter Persephone, to visit her mother Demeter once a year. The major ceremonies of the cult of Demeter were held annually at Eleusis, where she had built her temple and where she had instructed the first priests. Initiation took place there at different levels, from neophytes to the highest priests. What is interesting in the present context is the secrecy under which the ceremonies of initiation to the lower and to the higher mysteries were held. The climax of the lower mysteries for the initiation of the neophytes was reached when the *hiera*, which were the sacralia or sacred objects, were shown to them under solemn oath of secrecy. The secrets of the mysteries were so well guarded that to this day and probably forever after, it will not be known what the *hiera* were nor the details of the cult and of the initiation ceremonies. The great antiquity of the temple at Eleusis is proven by the fact that its origins are attributed to goddess Demeter herself who taught how to cultivate wheat and the related ceremonies when she arrived at Eleusis as a stranger from other lands desperately in search of her daughter. She probably arrived at Eleusis about the fifteenth century BC, perhaps between 1462-1423 BC during the reign of a man called Pandion, in the pre-historic Mycenean age that has left no written records; later writings at Crete, however, do not mention Demeter. Dyonisios probably arrived at about the same time or together with Demeter. The second millennium BC was a period of intensive evolution of cultures, travel, commercial and cultural interchanges among people of the old continents and not only in the Mediterranean world. The name of the place, Eleusis, itself could be one of the many pre-hellenic, non Indo-European names that are common in Attika. Attika was the first to produce wheat and barley and Demeter is normally represented bearing ears of wheat or barley on her head or on her head-gear. There are many similarities between the legend of the abduction of Persephone and that of Rama's Sita, except that it is the mother, not the husband who is desperate. It could be speculated that Demeter had to instruct the priests on agricultural practices, as tradition tells us, because she had lost her daughter who would otherwise have carried over the tradition had she been permanently on earth rather than hidden away in the dark netherworld. What greater tragedy for Mother Earth, the giver of plenty, to loose her only daughter to the Lord of Hell and Death? According to Mylonas (1961, p. 270) Demeter conferred upon the land of the Athenians a double gift, "which is the greatest ever given to mankind: the gift of the *telete* (mysteries) and the gift of the fruits . . . the produce of earth."

Demeter represents certain aspects of Earth, while other aspects of mother Earth are embodied in other goddesses of the Hellenic pantheon; undoubtedly ancient Greeks were concerned with earth as the basic natural element from which sustenance was to be had, with the participation of water, air and fire as vital energy. All had their role to play in the rites that Demeter herself dictated to the priests of Attika. While scholars have had to admit that the origin of Demeter is mysterious as well as her cult, it is clear that she represents a basic element of the Indo-European – and perhaps of all human traditions.

As mentioned, little is known about the mysteries, but according to Hippolytus in his Philosophoumena, at a certain stage of the initiation, the priests and initiates gazed up to heaven and cried aloud: 'rain', they gazed down upon earth and cried: 'conceive'; also the words 'rain' and 'conceive' are part of an inscription on a well in front of the Dipy on gate of Athens. Similarly to other parts of the world, the festivities marking the seasons and agricultural events were an important part of the 'open' rituals of the Eleusis mysteries; then included "that which is enacted" (*dromena*), or songs, dances, recitations and invocations; the showing of the sacralia, *hiera* to the initiates (*deiknymena*) and the "word spoken" (*legomena*). The latter, or the words spoken by the hierophant were so important that if they were not heard clearly by the initiate, he or she could not be considered initiated. The hierophant was the highest priest, interpreter of the unwritten, ancestral laws, the *patria*. Next to the hierophant in importance was the *dadouchos*, the barefoot torchbearer who had a knot of hair called *krokilos* on the nape of his neck and who nobody knew where he had come from. It is known that there were libations on the last day of the lower mysteries and the initiates poured the content in two vessels, one facing east and the other west, then they turned the vessels upside down as a libation to earth; a similar habit involving cups thrown on earth precedes some rites of the Siberian Turks.

The function of the *Dadouchos* was for life and it alternated between members of two traditional families. The name Dadouchos is suspiciously similar to Dadhicha, from the old form Dadhyac, who was a *rsi* son of Atharvan, regarded, together with his father, first founder of sacrifice. Dadhicha was later merged with the personality of Dadhikras.

These are only a few examples that indicate the recognition of earth, water and also air in addition to fire, as basic elements of concern of a developing agricultural society. They also suggest extensive cultural interchange among ancient people and the fundamental importance given to the word – *Vak* in the *RV* – the oral tradition that must have reached a very high level of development and maturity before the written word was invented. All the rituals express unequivocally though in a different manner, the sacrality of knowledge. Probably because of the attitude of respect for knowledge, secrecy was imposed and only the initiated and the priesthood would have access to the most fundamental knowledge. An attitude expressed also in the *Veda* and in most religions.

The importance of the cults to Earth, the performance of rituals and the initiation to 'mysteries' and imposition of secrecy that exist in all cultures and religions are related to the desire for immortality and the fear of death. Mother Earth or Demeter at Eleusis alleviate this fear, the earth does not only produce food and all materials necessary for physical life, but it also renews itself and regenerates what has perished of a natural death. For this reason the beginning of the year coincides with the winter solstice that is easy to determine exactly and marks the beginning of the season when nature takes rest and stores energy for the next solar year, it also marks the beginning of the period when the days grow longer, hence the importance of the *uttarayana*; alternately the beginning of the year coincides with the spring equinox that marks the awakening of nature after the winter stasis. Earth, particularly agriculture goddesses have the last word and the annual revival lessens the fear of death with the promise of a good future and of rebirth. Cicero himself said (De Legibus; 2,14, 36) that "Athens has given to the world nothing more excellent or divine than the Eleusian mysteries" and it would be recalled that the mysteries of Demeter were celebrated at Eleusis over a span of two thousand years.

I would finally like to recall the well-known letter sent in 1854 by Chief Seattle to Franklin Pierce, the then President of the United States of America, who had expressed the intention of buying land from the Indians. The letter begins with asking "how is it possible to buy or sell the sky or the warmth of the earth?. . . As we do not own the freshness of the air and the brightness of the water, how could they be bought? . . . Every little piece of land is sacred to my people . . ." The text of the letter is an enlightened hymn to earth, water, air, life energy and their products and interrelations. It is a masterpiece of understanding of nature and a lesson in ecology from the first to the last word. It is a hymn to the sacredness of the order and law of nature and of the sanctity of life. It is too well-known to be repeated here, but it is one to be kept always in mind, read and memorized, never to forget its content. The letter also has some prophetic sentences that are now becoming a sad reality: "your appetite will devour the land, leaving a desert behind it."

Chief Seattle has been proved right; man has dangerously drifted away from nature, the gap is widening and is filled with pollution of matter, mind and spirit, while deserts continue to expand.

I would like to close with two quotations from the Introduction by Seyyed Hossein Nasr to his book on *The Encounter of Man and Nature* (1967): "Few would be willing to admit that the acutest social and technical problem facing mankind today comes not from the so-called 'under-development' but from 'over-development' " . . . "To remedy this situation the metaphysical knowledge pertaining to nature must be revived and the sacred quality of nature given back to it once again".

References

Lievre, V. and J.Y. Loude, 1990. *Le Chamanisme des Kalash du Pakistan*, ed. Recherches sur les civilisations; Presses Universitaires de Lyon, 558 pp.

Marazzi, U., 1990. *Testi dello Sciamanesimo*, UTET/TEA, Torino, Italy, 610 pp.

Mylonas, G.E., 1961. *Eleusis and the Eleusinian Mysteries*, 87 t. Princeton University Press, 346 pp.

Nasr, S.H., 1968. *The Encounter of Man and Nature*, George Allen and Unwin Ltd. London, 151 pp.

Palaiseul, J., 1972. *Nos grand-meres savaient*, ed. Robert Laffont, Paris, 543 pp.

Renou, L., 1956. *Hymnes Speculatifs du Veda*, Gallimard, Paris, 276 pp.

Saraswati, S.P., and S. Vidyalankar, 1980. *Rigveda Samhita*, Vol. VIII, Veda Pratishthana, New Delhi, pp. ix-xiv + pp. 2339-2808.

20

Modernization as a Form of Cultural Adaptation to the Environment

Napoleon Wolanski

Each change can be progressive. This is rather a matter of public opinion, the evaluation of this fact. Progress can also be called modernization. It is not a biological matter, and only in part it is a social matter (judgement what is modern). First of all, it is a cultural matter (category).

Material culture has a practical beginning, as this was a production of the primitive tools. Early artistic activity also had a practical value because it was presumably magic in the intention of the artists. Material and non-material cultures became a unity. The genesis of culture was, thus, of adaptive value and at the same time it was conservative. Where biological mechanisms failed, culture determined survival.

It is not univocal which elements of culture are old-fashioned and which are modern, or which are regressive and which are progressive. Each time this requires a separate evaluation with respect to a certain criterion. This criterion can be adaptive value.

Nouveaux riches and parvenus take fashion for progress and modernization. Unfortunately, this seems to be also the case of the young generation. Thus, it can be stated ironically that the present modernization is worthless as, related to fashion, it typically neglects cultural traditions (often breaks them deliberately) and has no adaptive values.

Modernization in the contemporary European and North-American civilization is associated with the elements of urbanization and industrialization processes. It is thus worth considering the consequences and cost of modernization to the environs of humans. A question arises whether modernization always means progress.

Modernization should be associated with the comfort of life. But this is a controversial issue since for most people a comfortable life is associated with material goods, and the side-effects of their production, utilization, and disposal typically account for degradation of the environment and deterioration of well-being.

It is important not to oppose modernization to tradition. Modernization rooted in tradition should contain adaptive values, determining persistence and worthiness life.

Evolution and Civilization

According to the present state of knowledge the humanization processes occurred in savannas of southern Africa over millions of years ago. About 20-25 thousand generations of nomadic groups of humans extended their range over distinct climatic regions (*Fig*. 1). And man himself changed accordingly. Less than 10 thousand years ago (4000 generations) nomadic groups settled because they started to cultivate the land, and over the life span of 300 generations permanent human settlements had been developed. These settlements became the basis of the urban civilization, lasting for about 100-150 generations. Genetic adaptations occurred through changes between generations. Thus, a generation is the unit of biological evolution. The number of generations since the time of the colonization of cool regions and since the development of towns is too small for the evolution of biological adaptation (Wolanski, 1989).

The biological (genetic) adaptation thus replaced by the cultural protection of the organism adjustments became secondary in importance, relatively small and not inheritable (*Fig*. 2). Such a cultural protection can be called progressive from the perspective of time and environment.

Civilizations are typically defined as very advanced forms of the social existence, based on the written language, arts, belief (religions), and relatively high technology. They are cultural expressions of a specific form of socio-political organization adequate to the environment. Civilizations emerged, developed, and died, like species in nature. Similarly, in nature some common attributes of life evolved and consolidated, also a universal trait of human culture developed, which now-a-days predominate in all civilizations. A common property of life are the functions of proteins, (some authors define life as a spontaneous tendency to a permanent reduction of disorder or entropy). Similarly a universal trait of mankind, developed in the process of evolution, is culture as a non-biological form of satisfying the needs along with the preservation of the common interest. The essence of the biological existence lies in the struggle for existence between organisms, whereas the essence of the social existence of the humans lies in the altruism understood as humaneness.

The evolution of mankind followed biological, social, and cultural pathways, presumably just in this sequence. Many authors argue that the biological evolution of the humans is finished (Wolanski and Henneberg, 1990). It is a paradox that culture sustains (secondarily so to say) the 'animal' nature of the humans, as it protects the organism against the necessity of the biological changes. Culture thus counteracts the evolution of human organisms towards the forms progressively more distant from the animals. Thus, if it is true that the biological evolution of the humans has stopped, this is due to culture. In the 'animal' body a "creator of culture" evolves. Culture stabilizes the biological essence of the human beings. That is, culture, which is subjected to evolution, inhibited the biological evolution of the humans. In other words, developing the psyche, culture petrified some of the humans. I am not sure if this contradiction cannot lead to the destruction of *Homo sapiens.* When a 'climax' equilibrium is reached, the ecosystem does not evolve any more. If this is also true of a species, this would imply that culture, which is the second environment for the humans (E.B. Taylor), is leading to the state of an 'adjustment' of society to environment, that is, to a 'climax'. Further improvement of the species becomes impossible, and this seems really to be true with respect to the humans. Thus, does it imply a threat to the species?

A parallel problem, however, is the extent and rate of environmental changes brought about by over 5 billion brains of the humans living now-a-days. The mass of "thinking tissues" of the contemporary human beings is equal to the body mass of 100 million people living 3 thousand years ago (Wolanski, 1989). Minds (brains) of those 5 billion people conceive ideas and transform the world, whereas their bodies require food, clothes, apartments, and still need new products of civilization for a comfortable life.

Some social changes accounted for large cultural changes. For example, the dominance of ownership yielded a division of people, giving their needs a largely intimate character. In this case, progress means either increasing the sum and diversity of needs (demand) or more goods, especially new products (supply).

In the evolutionary sense life is maintained as a result of the genetic transmission of the structures determining the needs and functions, whereas humanity is maintained through the cultural heritage (transmission of verified experiences) deciding upon the existence of a society, in particular, under given conditions (to which it is not adapted biologically). Like the gene the pool of population can be modified from generation to generation, also, the cultural heritage (the contains of culture) is subject to changes. Just at this point we can speak of the genetic mutation as a new genetic information and of the innovation as a new element of culture. Mutations that are not eliminated are considered in biology as the so-called adequate as they have an adaptive value. Analogously, the innovations that have adaptive values within the scope of culture could be called modern, as they determine progress.

If a new civilization predominated even on the scale of a large part of the globe, it can dominate the world only for a while on the scale of the history of mankind. But it will also have its contribution to the formation of the human culture as a group experience. Factors integrating the world are permanently present in history. In biology, however, competition with other organisms to propagate their individual genes is the form of existence, whereas in culture the assurance of a common persistence seems to be the form of existence.

It is argued that more than 20 important civilizations developed in the history of mankind, of which at the most five survived (Toynbee, 1934-54). This might have happened because they had a stimulating contribution to the general culture of mankind. In my opinion, only civilizations beneficial to the mankind as a whole could persist, although they decided the existence of local societies.

Individual species represent specific systems of behaviour. These systems are directly (genetically) transmitted. When they become useless, the species either evolve or die. The humans adapt to the environment almost directly through their culture. There are, however, many ways of survival, depending on the conditions under which a given culture was formed. The extinction of some civilizations can be related to the extinction of the nations representing them. This happened when a given mode of life, called civilization in social sciences or an adaptive strategy in biological sciences, proved to be inefficient.

Culture, like genes, is subject to evolution which is of adaptive importance in the face of the new environmental conditions and has conservative importance to the species and social values of the earlier generations.

Modernization is a new kind of adaptation. A new culture represents a new kind of linkage with the environment. New civilizations are new adaptive systems, new homeostatic systems. Inter-civilizational transition can thus be the source of a break in the earlier relations to the environment, and can create new relationships.

Modernization is a cultural adequacy to the actual environmental conditions, including natural, social, and technical surroundings. Progress thus involves everything of positive value to mankind. Other changes cannot be called progress from the point of view of human evolution.

Consequences of Development

(a) IS CIVILIZATION PROGRESS A NECESSITY?

New needs cause actions forming new cultural environment. In the evolutionary perspective they lead to the transformation of civilization.

If the biological evolution of the humans is really ended, this will be the reason why the development of civilization cannot be stopped. The following attributes of human nature can corroborate this statement: the immanent tendency of the humans towards changes (E.B. Tylor), instinct of progress (A. Comte), primeval habit of making progress (E.A. Westermark), vanishing of the feeling of satisfaction with the existing conditions (the concept of the spiral of progress).

The spiral of progress works in the following way. Humans adjust to new conditions physiologically, and psychologically they are habituated to them soon. If these conditions are favourable, the satisfaction with them gradually disappears. A need for new conditions satisfying the requirements and aspirations develops, releasing the initiative of new changes. But in these new conditions, the feeling of satisfaction vanishes again with time, giving rise to new needs, aspirations, and so on. In this way, circles are made and never follow the same trajectory, and this is a sort of spiral (*Fig.* 3), because the earlier conditions are changed. Typically, we call progress the general direction of the development. However, as the intended favourable changes have different side effects and because of their high rate and large scale, one may ask if the total effects can be called progress. This is an important ecological problem.

(b) WHERE DOES THE CIVILIZATION PROGRESS GO?

An increase in the consumption of goods combined with an environmental pollution can have a deteriorating net effect on the quality of life. This happens because side-effects emerge with a delay, they are often difficult to predict, and not always impress the imagination. Attempts to stop the progress lead to frustration and degeneration, whereas activity can be switched in another direction (e.g. toward a useful action).

The sequence of events given above can be summarized as follows (*Fig.* 4). As a result of the specific character of human nature, a change of needs takes place at certain time intervals or permanently. This has an effect on the innovator activities and civilization progress. Modernization conceived in this way leads to hygienic activity, increased safety of life, easier or more efficient work. This change in the mode of life and living conditions accounts for a decline in mortality and longer life span, directly leading to a higher density of the population, and indirectly to a numerical increase in the needs. The last two factors enhance both consumption and production. When the production and consumption exceed a certain threshold, they account for the exhaustion of non-renewable resources, environmental pollution, and stress. These three evident factors deteriorate the living conditions, enhance civilization diseases, shorten the life span, etc.

Presumably, specific factors disturbing the health condition in the urban-industrial civilization include the excess of the stimuli overriding the capacity of the nervous systems of the humans (Spengler and Dunckan, 1956), the abundant new sub-threshold stimuli to which the organism was not adapted in the evolution, and the cumulative effects which cause changes in the organism, generally non-specific (Duda and Aleksandrowicz, 1990). This problem requires further epidemiological studies.

A cultural feedback of the described cycle of changes and their consequences (*Fig*. 4) is a new correction of the needs and the resulting activities which can be called modern.

Consequences of Cultural Maladjustment (Non-modernity)

The consequences of changes in the mode of life and the environment are most readily seen at the beginning and the end of life, that is, in the periods of the greatest order and the highest entropy in the human development respectively (Roszkiewicz, 1991). For this reason we will analyze the biological consequences of the social and cultural changes with respect to these periods of the individual development of the humans.

Infant mortality is considered as an index of the level of the health service and economic condition of the country. It seems, however, that it is also an important index of social tension and cultural values. Infant mortality in Poland dropped over the post-war period from a mean of about 120 to 16 per 1000 live born. Fluctuations of this index in the post-war Poland are closely related to the fluctuations in economy (*Fig*. 5), as indicated by the analysis of the changes in the annual national income. Any acute change in the economy was combined with an increased infant mortality, including an increase in the difference in the infant mortality between towns and villages to the disadvantages of the villages. Such periods were also the times of an increased social tension.

All these fluctuations, however, did not essentially change the position of Poland among other European countries (*Fig*. 6). It seems that this permanent position is primarily due to the health culture (health habits: diet, mode of life, hygiene, stresses, etc.). Culture in this sense is equally conservative in the society as genes are biologically. The position of Poland in terms of health does not seem to be determined by the economic position of Poland and even less by the organization and development of the health service, especially with respect to the infant mortality. Culture is responsible for the idea that Poland is on positions 4 to 7 among the countries with the highest infant mortality in Europe.

The virtue of poverty advocated by some ethical systems promotes neither the economic development nor the civilization progress. Cultures that adhered to the credo of asceticism and the virtue of poverty still remain in poorer sanitary conditions, and have higher infant mortality (e.g. in countries of Roman Catholic Church as Poland, Italy, Spain, Portugal) than the countries that reformed their ethical and cultural systems, and propagated the acceptance of wealth. Making wealth a virtue, culture was reformed in such countries as (protestant) Germany, Sweden and England, made economic progress, raised the level of education, reduced the infant mortality, and extended the life span.

Quite a different matter is the unbridled consumption related with wastefulness of goods, which now-a-days threatens in various forms of the pollution our planet and exhaustion of non-renewable resources. An example of this direction is the excessive production of goods and the philosophy of life in which "to be" is replaced by "to have". And here moderation should really be recommended.

An essential difference exists among moderation, controlled progress in the world economy and asceticism, which is worth emphasizing when considering civilization systems predominant in the contemporary Europe, and even in the contemporary industrial countries in Europe and North America.

Early in this century, the Jews in Poland had higher incomes, better apartments, and higher level of life in general, but their culture did not enhance their health because of the "rituals imposed by culture" (Miklaszewski, 1912). Among the people arriving to new industrial centres and towns in Siberia over the last four decades, the incidence of disease has been 10 times that of the Russians inhabiting these areas for several generations (Alexeeva, 1986). This has also been the case with the new harbour in Gdynia, constructed in the 1930s, and repopulated in the 1950s when Szczecin changed the state. Infant mortality there was one of the highest in the country during the period when the rate of immigration from other, mostly rural, areas was high (*Fig*. 7). Functioning of rural cultural patterns revealed a biological inadequacy of these families to the life in town. Culture developed under different climatic and social conditions, when indiscriminately transferred to distinct ecosystems, including socio-economic systems, combined with the maintenance of ethnic barriers to the residents, leads to cultural inadequacy. Using an ecological language, a niche formed under given conditions cannot function under different conditions.

Another example of the discussed relationships can be the mean life expectation of newborns in Polish villages and towns. On the world scale, the life span in individual countries increases when the urban population reaches 40-50 per cent of the total population. Above this threshold, no further increase in the life-time is observed, and even a decrease seems to occur. This pattern is apparent in Poland. The life-time is shorter in towns than in villages when the urban population is reaching 50 per cent for men (this happened in 1963) and when it is above 50 per cent for women (*Fig*. 8). This is also likely to be an environmental effect the contemporary towns are facing, a crisis and the degeneration of mankind.

Modernization is a new outlook on the world, where intelligence determines the ability to detect patterns and gumption defines as the ability to utilize these patterns. They are the different aspects of modernization: cognition and action. The value of these two aspects can be measured by the effectiveness of the adjustment to the environment.

Politicization and management are also innovatory activities. The activities of politicians and economists leave traces, sometimes wounds, in the biology of the nation. This can serve as a warning for hasty decisions that in my opinion predominate our social life. A transfer of models developed under distinct biological and socio-political conditions to a given country with different history and specific character can be deceptive and cause new wounds. Our results (Wolanski *et al.*, 1992 a, b, c) show that the optimum conditions for child development in Polish families (high education, high income, and small family) are not optimal in Japan. In Western societies, family is mostly based on the productive effort of one person (typically the father of the family), whereas in the Far East on the family as a social unit. Under those conditions, child development is optimal in large families with average education level and average income.

Differences between civilizations cannot be compared to differences between species, but they cannot be neglected, as they represent distinct features making mutual understanding difficult.

The values of modernization range from positive to negative, and real values of the same changes can be different, depending on the situation (e.g. environmental conditions and habits). They are typical of different civilizations.

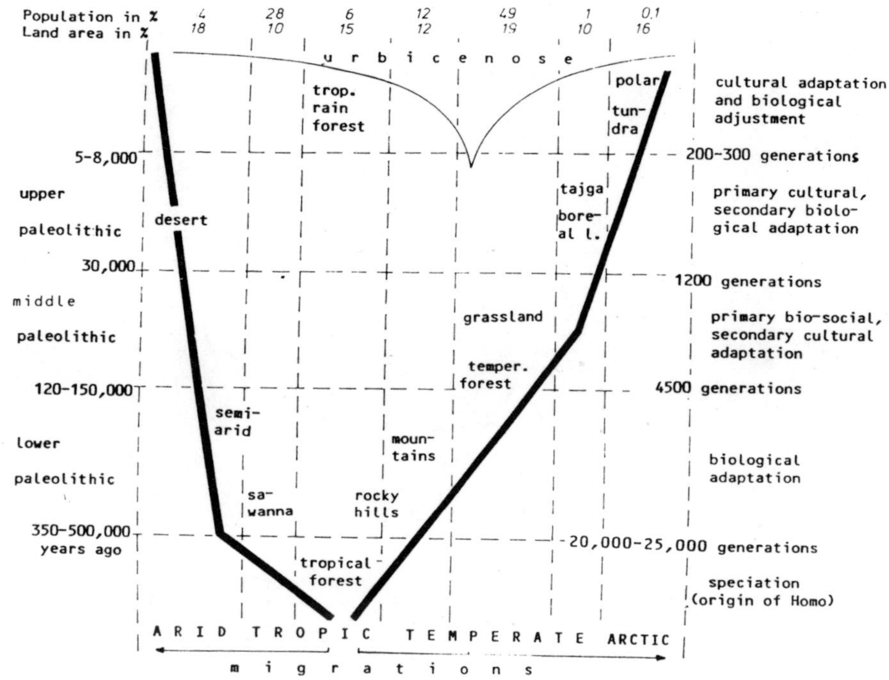

Fig. 20.1 : Proliferation of genus Homo to various ecosystems, including creation of urbicenoses. On the left — thousands of years of evolution, on the right — the number of past generations, and a form of adaptational changes. The generation is a unit of human evolutionary changes.

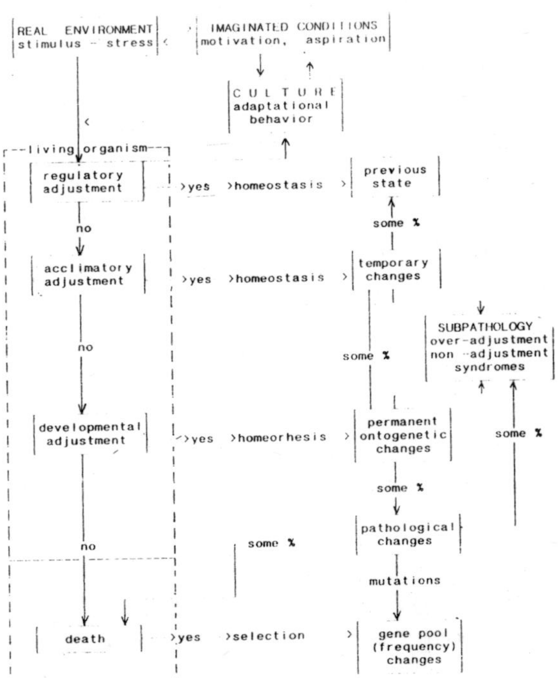

Fig. 20.2 : Model of biological adaptational changes in man to real and imagined environment, the role of culture, and results in structure of population.

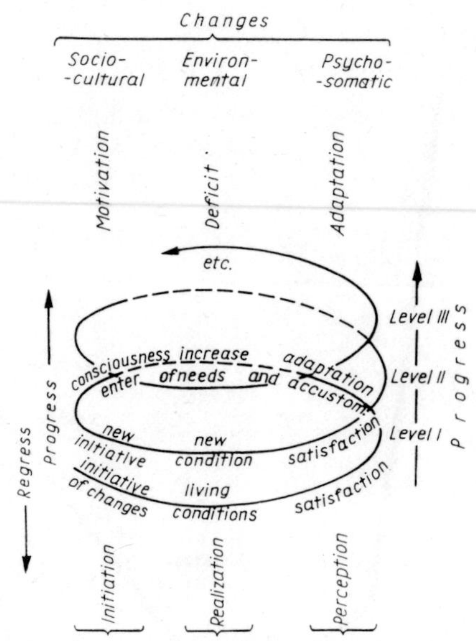

Fig. 20.3 : The spiral of changes, as the inevitable consequences of man's psychological and biological features. The cultural progress of man is an inherent nature of his species.

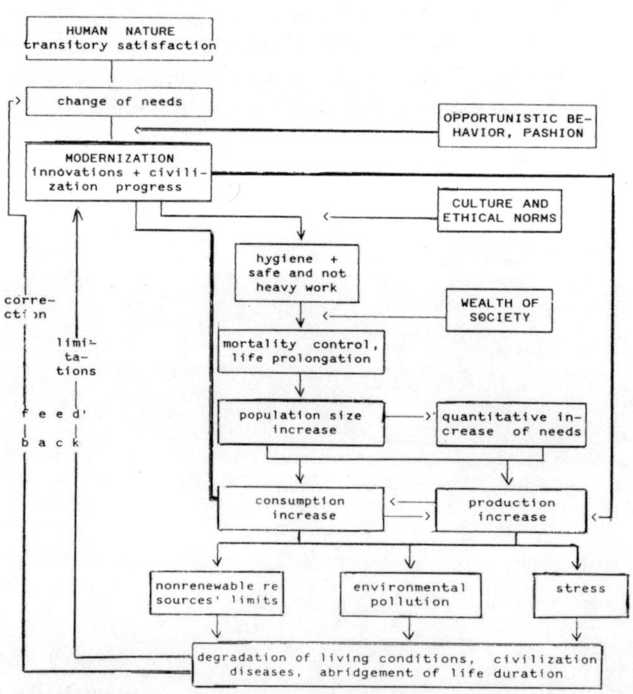

Fig. 20.4 : Expected and non-expected results of civilization 'progress'. Aside expected positive effects, are mostly negative influences, the last should be greater than positive. In this situation are observed some feed-back actions resulting in limitation or correction of initial changes.

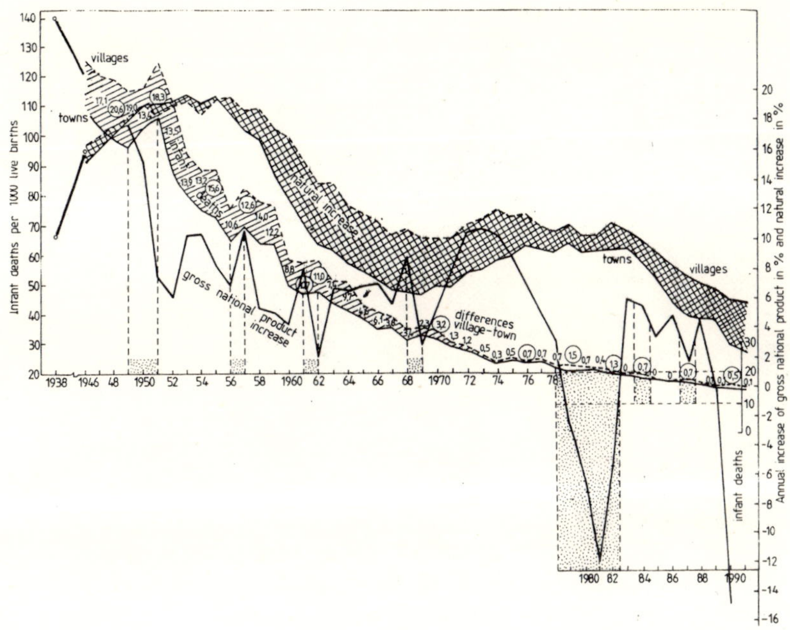

Fig. 20.5 : Infant mortality rate (per 1000 live births) in Poland in the post-war years against the background of annual national gross product (in percentage, in relation to its value of previous year) and the birth rate per 1000 persons. Numbers next to mortality curves show the differences between infant mortality in cities and in rural communities (in circles — increase of this difference in relation to previous year), shaded areas — critical period in history of Poland in 1946-91: economic drastic changes, social disturbances — increase of infant mortality rates and village-town differences.

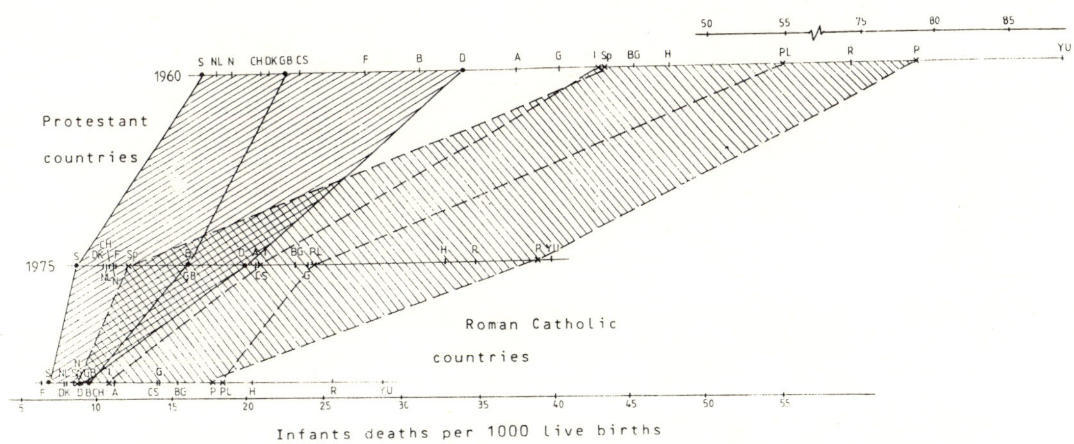

Fig. 20.6 : Infant mortality in European countries in 1960, 1975 and 1985. Trends of changes are marked in four most typical Roman Catholic countries (Portugal = P, Poland = PL, Spain = Sp and Italy = I), and in three typical Protestant countries (Germany = D, England = GB and Sweden = S). Italy in these years reduced distance, and Spain broke borders between the two groups of countries.

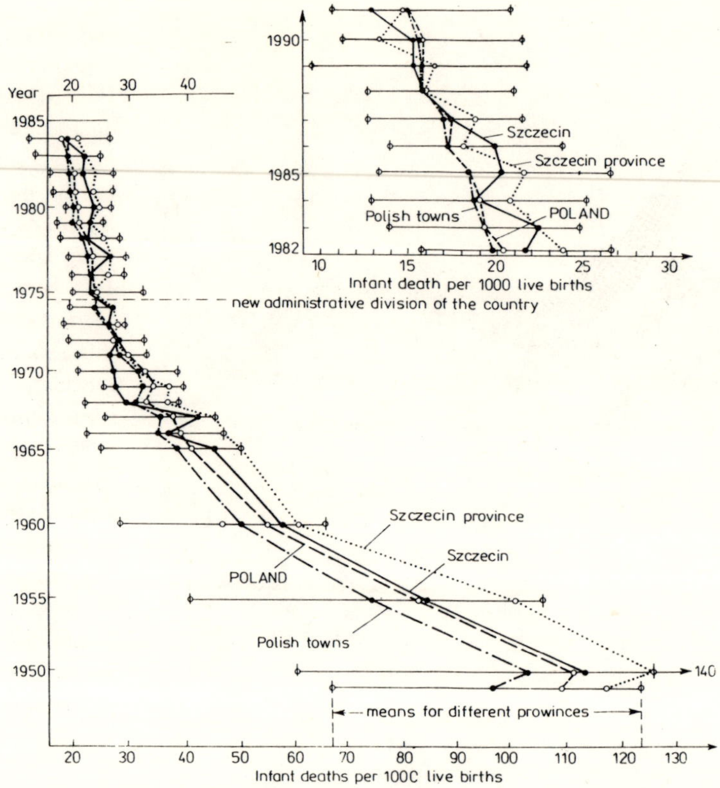

Fig. 20.7 : Changes in infant mortality rate for all over Poland, for Polish towns, for Szczecin city and region, and variation (horizontal lines) for Polish provinces in 1949-91.

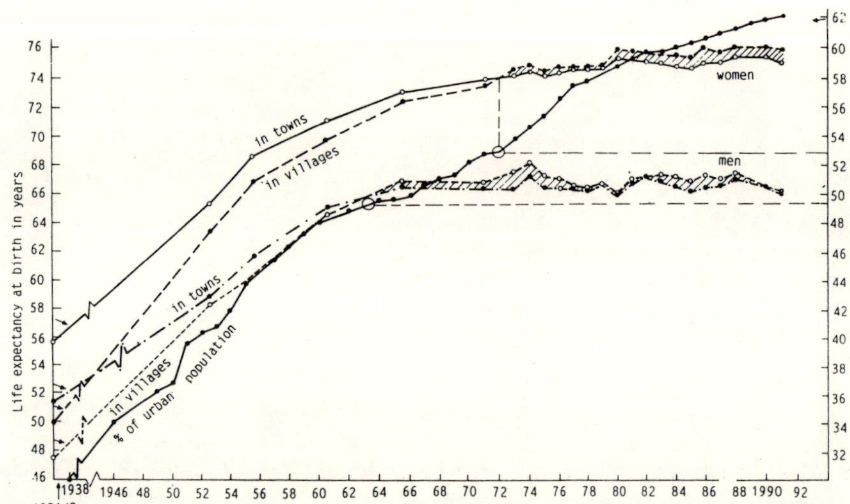

Fig. 20.8 : The expected life span at birth (in years) in men and women in Poland in 1931-91 in urban and rural areas, and percentage of population living in cities.

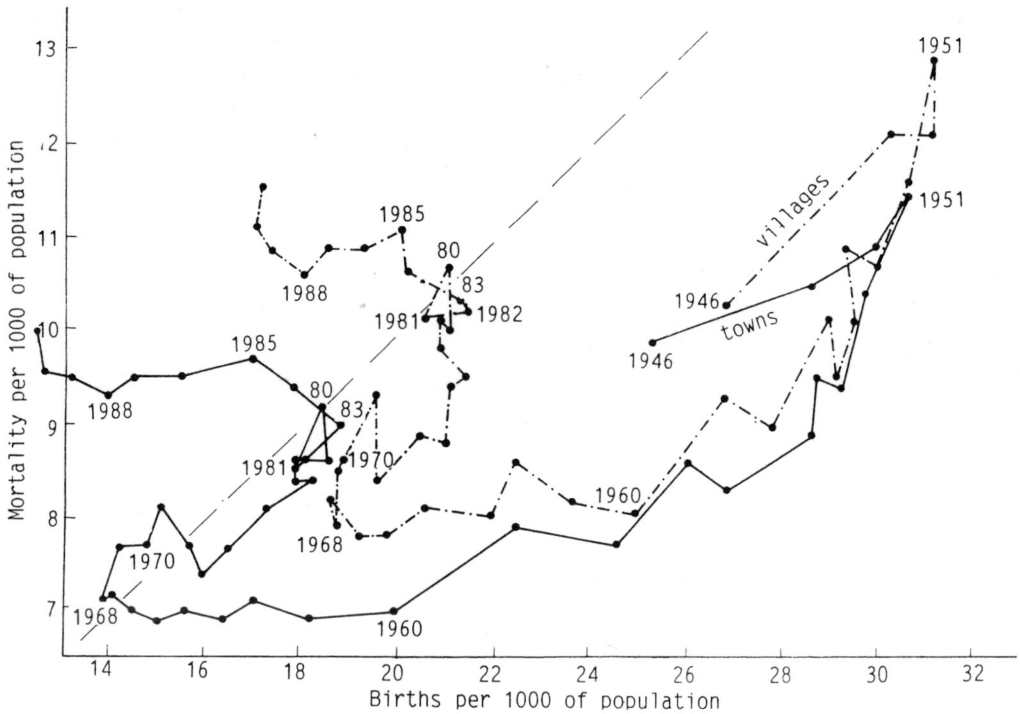

Fig. 20.9 : Changes in birth rate and death rate (per 1000 population) in Polish towns and villages in 1946-91.

References

Alexeeva T.I., 1986. *Adaptativnye processy w celoveceskion populacijach.* Izdat. Moskovskogo Universitieta, Moska.

Duda H., and Aleksandrowicz J., 1990. *Entity of Civilizational Diseases.* Unpublished manuscript.

Miklaszewski W., 1912. *Rozwoj cielesny proletariatu Warszawy w swietle pomiarow antropometrycznych.* Warszawa.

Roszkiewicz M., 1991. *Mechanisms of Demographic Behaviours.* Monografie i Opracowania, 334, SGPiS 19, Warszawa.

Spengler J.J., and Dunckan O.D., 1956. *Population, Theory and Policy.* Glencoe.

Toynbee A.J., 1934-54. *A Study of History.* London.

Wolanski N., 1989. *Human Life and Culture: Dynamic Components of Ecosystems.* Zygon 24 (4): 401-27.

——, 1991. Human Ecology and Problems of Demography. In *Collegium Antropologicum,* 15(1) 27-43.

——, Czarzasta T., Chung S., Tomonari K., and Tsushima S., 1992b. *Family Types and Offspring Growth in Various Countries.* II. *Stature of Offsprings in Various Family Types in Japan and Korea. Studies in Human Ecology,* in press.

——, Chung S., Czarzasta T., Dickinson T., Harada S., Liocheva V., Seiwa H., Tomonari K., and Tsushima S., 1992a. *Family Types and Offspring Growth in Various Countries.* I. *Frequency of Various Family Types in Bulgaria, Japan, Korea, Mexico and Poland. Studies in Human Ecology*, in press.

——, Chung S., Tsushima S., Tomonari K., and Czarzasta T., 1992c. *Family Types and Offspring Growth in Various Countries.* III. *Regression of Offspring's Stature in Relation to Parent's and Family's Factors in Japan and Korea. Studies in Human Ecology,* in press.

——, Henneberg M., 1991. Natural Selection in Recent Man: An Interpretative Problem. In *Studies in Human Ecology*, 9, 275-93.

List of Contributors

Gian Giuseppe Filippi	University of Venice S. Polo 2169-30125 Vanezia, Italy
Molly Kaushal	Janpada Sampada Indira Gandhi National Centre for the Arts New Delhi - 110 001
Madhu Khanna	Indira Gandhi National Centre for the Arts New Delhi - 110 001
Satish Kumar	Schumacher College The Old Postern Dartington, Totnes Devon TQ9 6EA, England
Natalia R. Lidova	Institute of World Literature Vorovskogo Street 25 A Moscow, Russia
S.C. Malik	5/90, Connaught Circus New Delhi - 110 001
John McKim Malville	Department of Astrophysical, Planetary and Atmospheric Sciences University of Colorado at Boulder Boulder, Colorado USA

Jayant V. Narlikar
Inter Univ. Centre for Astronomy & Astrophysics
Ganeshkhind
Pune - 411 007

Paul Nkwi Nchoji
Pan African Association of Anthropologists
BP 1862 Yaonde
Cameroon (Africa)

Triloki Nath Pandey
Crown College
University of California
Santa Cruz, California 95064
USA

A. Ranganathan
Locksley Hall
852, Poonamallee High Road
Kilpauk
Madras - 600 010

A.J.G.M. Sanders
507, Jack Hill
471, Andries Street
Pretoria 0002
South Africa

Baidyanath Saraswati
Janpada Sampada
Indira Gandhi National Centre for the Arts
New Delhi - 110 001

Haku Shah
16 Neminath Society
Narayan Nagar Road, Paldi
Ahmedabad - 380 007

John Mope Simo
Pan African Association of Anthropologists
BP 1862 Yaonde
Cameroon (Africa)

Yólotl González Torres	Museo de El Carmen Av. Revolucion 4-6, San Angel, C.P. 01000, Mexico DF Mexico
S.G. Tulpule	26, Sahwas Society Pune 411 052
M. Vannucci	A - 62, Sector 41 Noida 201 303, Uttar Pradesh
Kapila Vatsyayan	Indira Gandhi National Centre for the Arts New Delhi - 110 001
Napoleon Wolanski	International Union of Anthropological and Ethnological Sciences Deptt. of Human Ecology Polish Academy of Sciences 00-330 Warszawa, Nowy Swait 72 Poland
Ananda Wood	1A Ashoka, 3 Naylor Road Pune - 411 001
Anir H. Zekrgoo	No.14, Ground Floor Ist Street, Gandhi Area Tehran, Iran

Index

Absence of body :
  absence of *bhutas*, 118
Acaryopasanam, 125
Adam-Eve :
  story, 84
Advaita Vedanta, 92
Africa, 196
Agni, 209,230,232
Air, 97 :
  division of experience, 95-6
  numbered mole
    cules, 44
Ajnana, 125-6
Akasa, 120,123-5,127,226,229,231,238 :
  as origin of all things, 124
  concept, 127-8
  entry in mysterious world, 123
  importance, 124
  term meaning, 123 :
    Kabir, 127
    Ramdas, 125-6
Alpha canis majoris, 239
Amrta, 132,134, 136-7 :
  as water, 132
  Mahabharata concept, 134
Amrtamanthana, 131-2,134-8
  Hindu mythology, 131
  impact,
    post-Vedic culture, 137-8
  Rgveda concept, 132
  Vedic cult,
    soma, link with-, 135-6
Anal, 126
Anandamayakosa, 5,119
Annapurna, 103
Antahkarana, 96
Anumati, 103
Arbas or Jews, 219
Araqi, 238
Arbor mundi, 182
Art :
  a protest against,
    alienation, 215-6
  Irano-Islamic,
    modern view, 207
    traditional view, 208-9,212
Art and man's values :
  Irano-Islamic view, 212-3
Art-humanism :
  Irano-Islamic concept, 214-5
Astronomy theory, 48
Atharva Veda, 105-6,111,115,136,233,238
Atiratra, 235
Atma, 117,232
Ayurveda, 229

Baka :
  traditional knowledge, 201
Baka concept :
  forest ecology, 197-9
  man and nature, 196-7
  worship, 200
Baka food, 194-200
Beyond the duality, 63-4
Bhagavadgita, 123,125
Bhagiratha, 114
Bhuta suddhi, 150
Bhutas, 117-9,125-6,142,232
Biological systems, 15
Biology, 67 :
  chemical elements, 2-3
Biology and cosmology :
  relations, 15
Biosphere, 161-3
Birth :
  rituals,
    eastern slaves, 183-4

Blue coloured :
see
Visual impact, 44
Blue sky, 37
Bow priesthood :
Zuni culture, 161
Brahman, 3,126,128,136-8,232-4,321
Brahmasutra Bhasyas, 118
Brhadaranyaka Upanisad, 82,104,117
Bushman law :
constitutional law, 189
contract law, 190
cosmic nature, 187-93
family law, 189-90
property law, 190-1
settlement of disputes, 192-3
succession law, 191
Bushmen :
origin history, 118

Central intuitions, 5
Chandogya Upanisad, 117-8,124
Chemical elements :
nature, 18
origined, 18
Child birth :
Irano-Islamic art, 213-4
Colour phenomena, 45
Colours :
electromegnatic spectrum, 37
perception,
modern science, 46
Consciousness :
as Goddess, 104,107
conception of-, 83
definition, 80
expression, 84,86 :
nature, link with-, 91
human expression on, 90
nature, difference with-, 83
objective and subjective, 80-4
reflection and self-transcendence, 64-5
Cosmic equality :
Copernican concept, 13
Cosmic nature :
Bushman law, 187-93
Cosmogonic measurement :
India, 25
Creation spirituality :
Gaia concept, 222-3
Creativity :
tribal concept, 204
Cultural adaptation to environment :
modern concept, 245-52
Cultural maladjustment :
consequences, 250-2

Dadouchas :
functions for life, 241
Death :
conception of-, 18
rituals,
eastern slaves, 184
Devata, 230-1
Development :
consequences, 248-50
Dharatimata, 103
Dharma, 106,151
Distant dual God :
Mexica concept, 170
Divyavadana, 230
Dravya, 142
Dry stone :
as death,
eastern slaves concept, 183-4

Earth :
alternations science view of-, 1
and US, 111-2
as one organism, 219
as sacred women, 109-10
as supporter, 107
diver, 20-2
myths, 21
division of experience, 94-5
elements of-, 19-20
importance, 242
in the credle of *Rta*, 110-1
relationship, 108
Earth and sky :
Rgvedic concept, 232
Eastern slaves :
nature
concept of-, 179-85

Gods, 180
Ecological man, 149-50
Ecology, 67
Elementary particles :
theory of-, 49-50
Elements :
colour interaction of-, 49
divisions of experience, 93-7
Elements of nature :
fivefold order,
binding, 143
interlocking, 143-4
origination, 142-3
overlapping, 148
tribal cosmogony, 142
Encounter of man and nature, 243
Energy :
as Goddess, 104-7
Environment, 61-3
Ether :
division of experience, 96
Evolution and civilization, 246-8
Existence :
theory, 68
Expression :
living feculty, 85,
traditional form, 79
External world :
changing character, 90

Feminine principle :
conceptual understanding, 105
Fire :
as God,
Mexica cosmogony, 173-4
divisions of experience, 95
Fire and Sun :
link Mexica cosmogony, 172
Mesoamerican cosmovision, 169-85
Fire-water link :
Mexica cosmogony, 176-7
First human :
birth, 107
Five elements :
as Gods,
eastern slaves concept, 181-2
as origin of herbs, 118
Asian traditions, 228
Chinese tradition, 147
colour, link with-, 38
ecological view, 219
European concept, 229
fundamental axes, 6
human body, 118
Indian concept,
traditions, 227-8
original cultures,
link with-, 225-6
Five environmental elements, 226-7
Forest ecology :
Baka concept, 197-9
Four elements :
water offerings, 238

Gaia concept :
seven elements, 200-21
Gandhi, Mahatam, 53,221,223
Ganga, 103,113-4
Ganga *avatarana* :
in the light of ecology, 113-5
Garbha Upanisad, 142
Gell-Mann, 50-1
Geographical features :
presonifications of Goddesses, 103
Geometry :
form, 43
Ghatakasa, 123
Gitakasa, 123
Goddess :
as the waters life of-, 112-3
Gravitational masses, 14,49
Gunas, 94

Haoma, 131
Havis, 132
Havvah, 85
Herbs :
origin,
five elements, role of-, 118
Hiera, 240
Hiranyagarbha, 8
Homo sapiens, 61,247
Honar-mand, 212

Human beings :
  quantam theory, 56
Human biological month, 23
Human body :
  death,
    five elements, 119
    jiva, role of-, 118
  organic compounds, 118
Human creation :
  myth and science, 28
Human face :
  expression, 85
Human organism, 42
Hunting culture, 23

Indian circle :
  methods, 26
Individual experience :
  world, link with-, 88
Inorganic to organic :
  theory, 58-60
    integral biology, 4
Intellectual capacity, 56
Intelligence, 55
Interpretations :
  problems of-, 79
Islamic, *Frahang-e-Maaref-e*, 216

Jagaddhatri, 103
Jengi, 200
Jiva, 4,118-9
  as living personality, 84
  herbs,
    link with-, 4
  prana, difference with-, 4
Jyotisa, 150

Kabir, 126-8
Kah, 230 :
  Rgvedic humans, 22-3
Kalahari Bushman, 188
Kalahari desert, 189
Kalapurusa, 150
Kalila, 119
Kausitaki Upanisad, 85
Knowing self :
  mind, detachment with-, 82
Knowledge :
  branches, 43
  modern expression, 80
  traditional expression, 79
Komba, 200-1
Koyemshi, 161
Krokilos, 241

Lamas, 237
Latin *natus*, 80
Life :
  blood as fundamental element, 20
  elemental blocks, 18
  expression of consciousness, 84
  forms, 2
  jiva as word, 84
  modern physical biology, 88
  objective nature, 75
  problems,
    scientific thinking, 3
  rhythms of-, 23
  sciences, 87
  traditional concept, 84
    conception, 89
Living breath :
  conception of-, 84
Living personality :
  experience, 89
Living system :
  behaviour of-, 15

Mahabharata, 112,131,134,136,138
Mahabhutas, 123,125,128
Mahadakasa, 123
Maharaloka, 104
Making of person :
  natural order, 150-1
Man :
  culture,
    environment role of-, 8
  land, link with-,
    Zuni concept, 163-4
  place in universe, 2
Man and nature :
  Baka concept, 196-201

Man's orientation :
    Zuni concept, 163
Mandukah, 223
Manomayakosa, 5
Mantha, 133-4 :
    word meaning, 133
Mathematica, 1
Matter :
    traditional conception, 90
Mesoamerican cosmos, 19-20
Mexica :
    cosmogonic myths, 170
Mexica cosmogony :
    calender, 175
    distant dual God concept, 170-1
    fire-sun link,
        concept of-,172-3
    fire-water link with-, 176-7
    solar cycle, 171-2
    star forms, 173-4
Mexico :
    origin,
        archaeological fact, 169-70
Microwave radiation, 12
Mictlantecuhtli, 174
Mind :
    science, 57
Modern physical science :
    traditional conception,
        link with-, 92
Modern science :
    view of-, 1
Mongombo, 200
Moon :
    at stonehenge, 22-3
Mother earth, 109,112
Mrigavyadha, 239
Mundaka Upanisad, 84
Mundi, 180

Nama, 125
    word meaning, 231
Naqqash, 212
Natura naturata, 120
Natural order, 105
Natural order of culture :
    ecological man, 149-50
    making of persons, 150-1
Natural powers, 105
Nature :
    as God,
        eastern slaves, 101-2
    behaviour,
        defectiveness, 10
    concept of-, 80
    definition, 80
    eastern slaves, concept, 179-85
    European traditions, 94
    feminine conceptualization, 103
    objective and subjective, 80
    personal creation,
        as Goddess, 104
    Rgvedic hymns, 222-33
    theory,
        integral vision, 112-3
    traditional conception, 83
    transcendent order, 141
    value of-, 8
    Zuni view, 157-66
Nature deities :
    ecologistic passages, 106
Nature environment :
    celebrations,
        tribal concept, 204-5
Newton, Issac, 1
Nganga, 200
Nodiri brahmanatava, 127
Non-dualist position, 91-2
Nothingness :
    tribal cosmogony, 142
Nucleogeneses in the stars, 18-9

Objective and Subjective :
    approaches, 86
    description, 86
Opticks, 47
Organic evolution, 60-1
Organism, 61-3

Painting :
    theory, 49
Pancabhuta, 4,8,153 :
    interpretation, 4

Pancabhutas, 117
Pancagnividya, 118
Pancakosa, 4,8
Pancavati, 223
Pancikarana, 96
Patria, 241
People :
kinds,
Zuni concept, 163
Perfect cosmological principle (PCP), 10-2 :
deductive power, 11
observational challenge, 11
Persona, 89
Person's experience :
meaning, 83
Perun, 181
as purifier,
eastern slaves, 180
Philosophical stage, 63
Philosophy of life :
early traditions, 236
Physical
biology :
Upanisad concept, 4
phenomena :
description, 46
sciences :
mathematics role of-, 53
technological aspects, 87
world :
unity of-, 58
Physics :
revolutionary effect, 67
Physics and astronomy :
colour perception, 45
Pinda, 119
Planets :
as self-sacrificing stars, 18
Popular wisdom :
originality, 7
voice of-, 5-7
Potato eaters, 215
Prakrti, 1,7-8,68,80,105,203
Prana, 4,85,119
Prasna Upanisad, 118
Principia, 1
Prthivi, 103,107 :
earth mother, 107
Prthivi-sukta, 106
Puranas, 117,169
Purusa, 68,152 :
concept,
Indian culture, 15
use of-, 52

Rajas, 94
Raman, C.V., 38-9,43-6,49
Ramayana, 28
Rana cyanophlyctes, 234
Rana tigrina, 233
Rasayana, 238
Rgveda, 103,106,109,113,133-4,136-7,226, 238 :
hymns,
nature, 232-3
soma making, 132-5
Religion :
Zuni life, role in, 158
Ritan, 24
Rose, 179
Rta, 110-2

Sahib Honar, 210
Sakti, 104
nature, link with-, 104
Samkhya, 82-3,93,117
Samkhya philosophy, 91
Samvid, 128-9
Sangeeta Purusa, 152
Sanskrit, 85,90
Sarasvati, 103
Sattva, 94,96
Satyaloka, 104
Science :
nature of-, 65-7
Science and the modern world, 48
Scientist :
difinition, 55
Self :
identification, 82
Seven elements concept :
Gaia concept, 220
Shamanism, 235
Sirius :

Egypt concept, 239
Solar cycle :
Mexica cosmogony, 171
Soma, 131-3,135-7
rituals for making *Rgveda*, 132,135
Vedic concept,
epic myth, 136
wealth of difference, 134-5
Soma-moon-*amrta* concept, 136
Spacelessness concept, 5 :
timelessness,
mysteries, 128
Sraman, 236
Stars :
forms :
Mexica cosmogony, 173-4
nucleogeneses in, 18
Sun :
appearance-disappearance,
Mexica mythology, 174-5
at new-grange, 22
location, 14
outer layers, 18
Sun and moon creation :
Mexica cosmogony, 173-4
Sunya, 2
Sunyatva, 125
Surloka, 104
Surya, 209,230,232
Suryavamsa, 230
Susupti, 126
Svayambhu Manu, 107
Swadesi, 221
Synergy :
as Goddess, 104-7

Taiji, 24
Taittiriya Upanisad, 117-8
Tajjalana, 124
Tantras, 117
Tarrah, 212
Tattvas, 118,142
Tejas, 120,124
Telete, 241
Teotleco, 174
Theory of colour, 43
Theory of light, 43
Tona, 171 :
Mexica cosmogony, 171-2
Tonatiuh, 171
Traditional forms expression, 79 :
reinterpretation,
need of, 80
level, 93
Traditional knowledge, 79
Trees :
as God,
eastern slaves, 182-3
Tribal concept :
creativity, 204
nature-environment,
life lived, 205
Trilokagamini, 114
Tropical rain forest :
Baka culture, 197-8

Udgitha, 138
Unity of human knowledge, 46
Universe :
astronomical observations, 11
cosmological principle, 11
image, 104
man, place of-, 2
meaning, 88
oneness,
science, link with-, 53
unity of-, 58
world
concept of-, 66
Unmani, 126
Upanisad, 117
Uttar Pradesh, 113
Uttarayana, 232
Uwanami, 158

Vaisnava sources, 113
Vastupurusa, 152
Vasudhaivakutumbakam, 7,220
Vayu, 124,209,235
Vayu Purana, 25,113
Vedanta, 4,82-3
Vedanta philosophies, 93
Vedas, 103-4,106,111,113,131,169

Viraj, 110
Visnu, 113
Visnu Sahasranama Bhasya, 231

Water, 97
as God,
eastern slaves, 102
experience,
division of-, 96
Whirlpool, 105
Wholeness, 56-8
Worship :
Baka concept, 200
dynamic organising principle, 57
nature of-, 65-7
Rgveda concept, 230
Wuji, 24

Yajna, 223
Yamuna, 103
Yatokka tachu, 163
Yin and *yang* :
at Beijing, 23-4

Zaire, 196
Zuni :
appointment of officers,
now priests, role of-, 160
calendra,
sun, importance, 159-60
ceremonies, 158
cosmology, 161
nature,
concept of-, 157-66
oceans, importance, 162
people,
concept of-, 163
religion,
role of-, 158-60
rituals,
cosmic forces, 159